IMAGES of America

ELIZABETH CITY

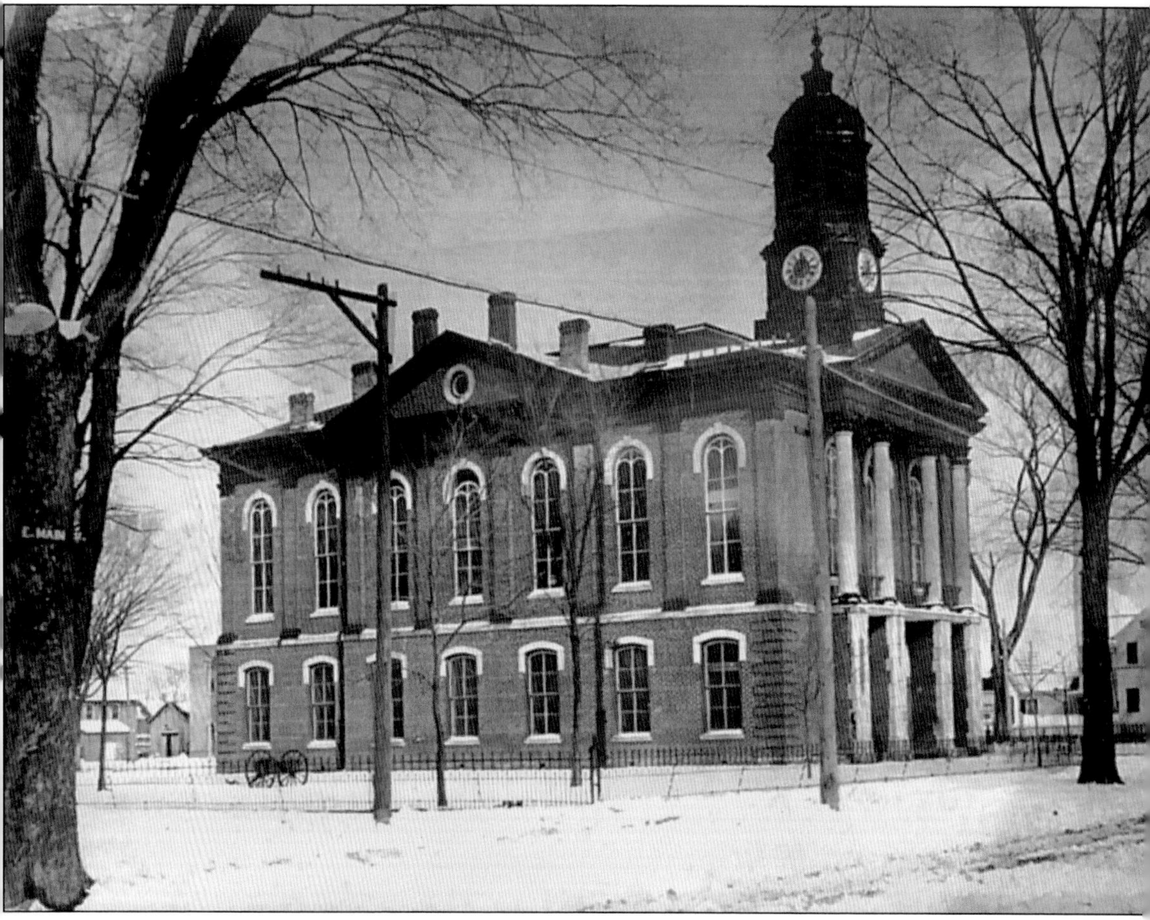

The courthouse was built in 1882 and the two wings were added in 1979–1980. It is located on East Main Street, on the same site where an earlier courthouse was burned by the residents of Elizabeth City; they wanted to prevent its capture by Union soldiers.

IMAGES
of America

ELIZABETH CITY

John C. Scott Jr. and the Elizabeth City
Historic Neighborhood Association

ARCADIA
PUBLISHING

ISBN 978-0-7385-1386-7

Published by Arcadia Publishing
Charleston, South Carolina

Printed in the United States of America

Library of Congress Catalog Card Number: 2001092151

For all general information contact Arcadia Publishing at:
Telephone 843-853-2070
Fax 843-853-0044
E-mail sales@arcadiapublishing.com
For customer service and orders:
Toll-Free 1-888-313-2665

Visit us on the Internet at www.arcadiapublishing.com

Contents

Acknowledgments

The Elizabeth City Historic Neighborhood Association would like to thank the many people who helped with this book. A special thanks goes to Hazel Pendleton Dixon who donated the first pictures and really helped to get the book started. Jean Baker presented the initial idea of doing the book and has given a lot of encouragement. Other people who have donated time and pictures are Jean Walston, Maxine Sweeney, Marilyn Madrin, Florence Stevens, Mr. and Mrs. William Small, Don Pendergraft with The Museum of the Albemarle, Ann Barker, Winifred Jones Wood, Patsy Houtz, Anita LaMothe, Frank Hollowell, Peggy McNaughton, Will Dunstan, and Frank Rabey with *The Virginian Pilot*. Many thanks go to Gary Hobbs for his help and support.

INTRODUCTION

The first people to settle in the Elizabeth City area were the Algonkian Indians. In the 1650s some of the settlers from Virginia began to inhabit the area that would later become known as Elizabeth City. In 1663 the governor of Virginia issued 28 land grants to settlers in the Albemarle area. One of the grants was for land that became Elizabeth City. Pasquotank County was established in 1738. During this time there was a group of Quakers that settled the region; they had the largest religious group in the area.

The first national census showed that Pasquotank County had a population of 5,497. In 1790 plans were being made to dig the Dismal Swamp Canal. The beginning was to be Norfolk and the need for a southern ending was to be made by the establishment of Elizabeth City.

The town was called Redding in the beginning. Fifty acres were bought from Adam and Elizabeth Tooley. This land was divided into lots and a drawing was held to see who would get which lots. In 1794 the General Assembly changed the name to Elizabeth (Elizabethtown). In 1801 the name was changed again to Elizabeth City to eliminate confusion because there was another Elizabethtown in Tyrrell County.

Elizabeth City became the county seat of Pasquotank County in 1800. Many people migrated to the community because they saw a good opportunity to start businesses. A courthouse was built along with a jail. As the Civil War started in 1861, Elizabeth City tried to prepare for its own protection. As the Union forces came closer, the prideful citizens decided to burn the courthouse so the soldiers could not capture it. The town had prospered greatly before the war and many stores, warehouses, and elegant homes had been built. One of the biggest problems at this time was the outbreak of many devastating fires.

In 1881 the first railroad was completed to Elizabeth City—the Elizabeth City and Norfolk Railroad. Later other lines came to the town. As a result of the railroads, many new mills and other businesses were established, including Elizabeth City Cotton Mills (1897), Pasquotank Hosiery Company (1914), Pailin-Elizabeth City Coca-Cola Bottling Company (1917), and Crystal Ice Company (1890s). Elizabeth City continued to prosper and grow in land area and population. The Wright brothers spent some time here in their attempt to get to the Outer Banks to build the first successful powered airplane.

Today Elizabeth City continues to grow and prosper, with more than 17,000 people calling it home. Many new industries are locating here. The United States Coast Guard Base bolsters the town's economy. Also, the community is home to College of the Albemarle, Elizabeth City State University, accounting firms, a regional airport, building suppliers, Hockmeyer Equipment Company, Pell Paper Box Company, and J.W. Jones Lumber Company.

There are still those who settle in Elizabeth City simply because they like the town's charm and character. People who enjoy small-town life are moving here. Many Elizabeth City residents have taken on a zeal for preserving the town's character and their pride is being manifested in the careful restoration of many homes and businesses.

One

Downtown

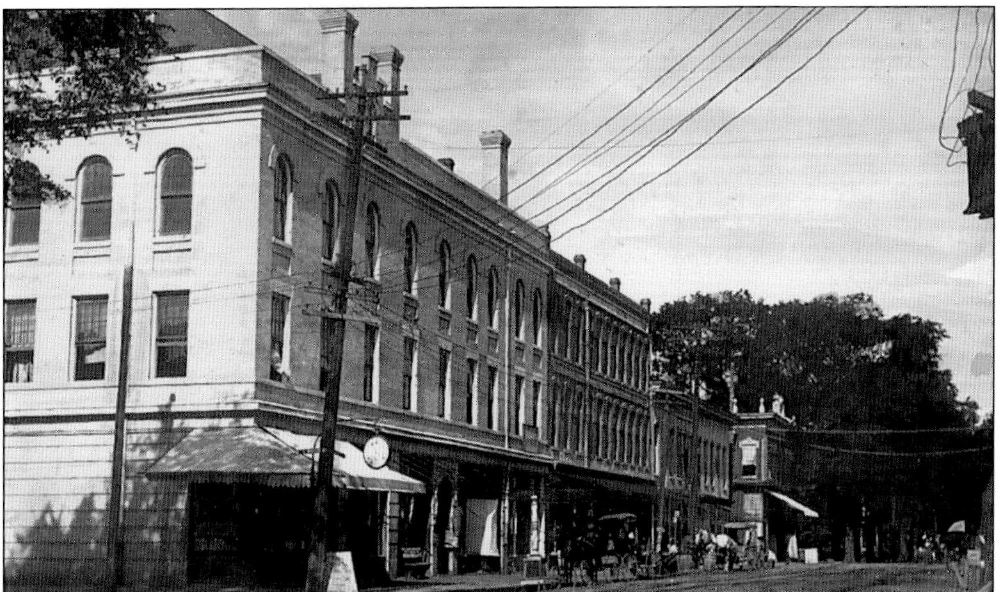

Elizabeth City's downtown area was the center of activity in the town at the turn of the century. This view was taken at the corner of Main and Water Streets.

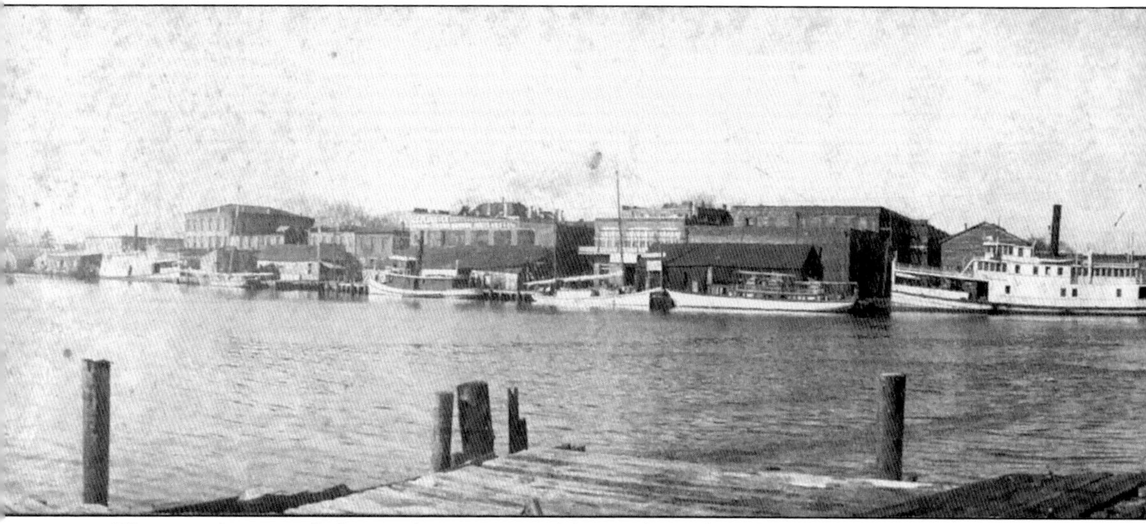

This is a photograph depicts businesses and boats along the Elizabeth City harbor. It was taken

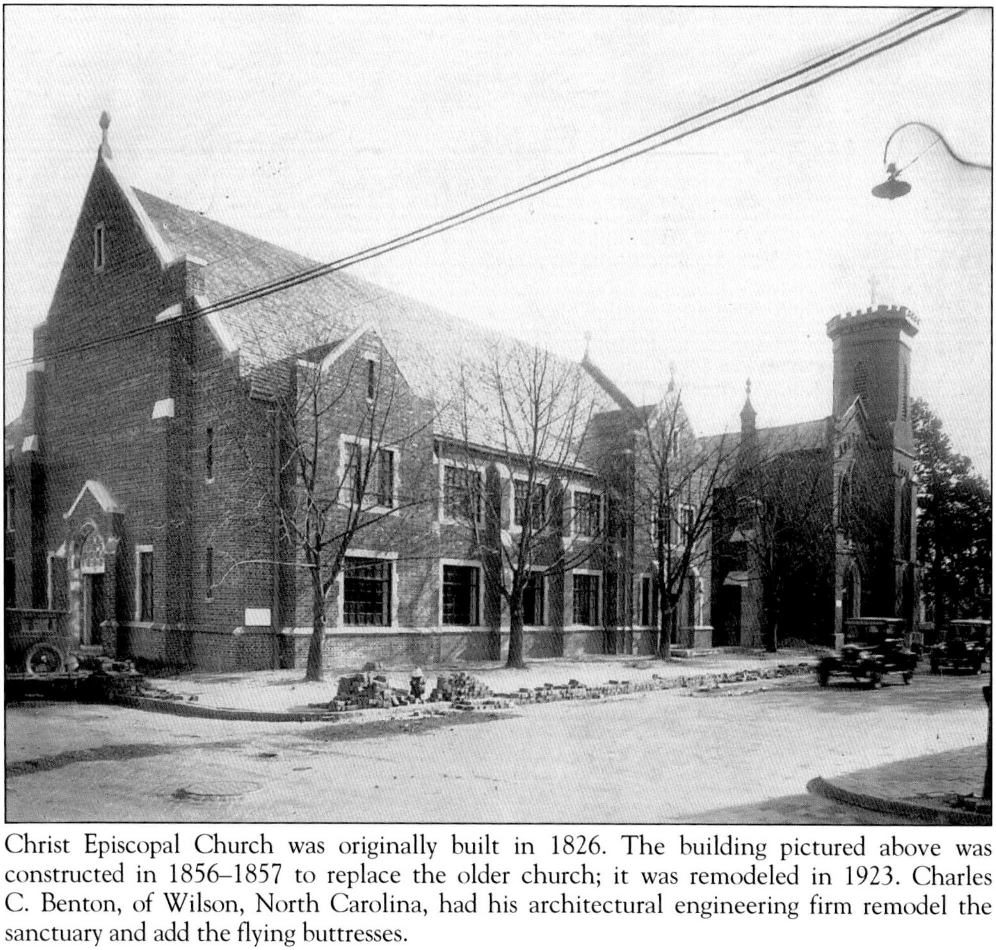

Christ Episcopal Church was originally built in 1826. The building pictured above was constructed in 1856–1857 to replace the older church; it was remodeled in 1923. Charles C. Benton, of Wilson, North Carolina, had his architectural engineering firm remodel the sanctuary and add the flying buttresses.

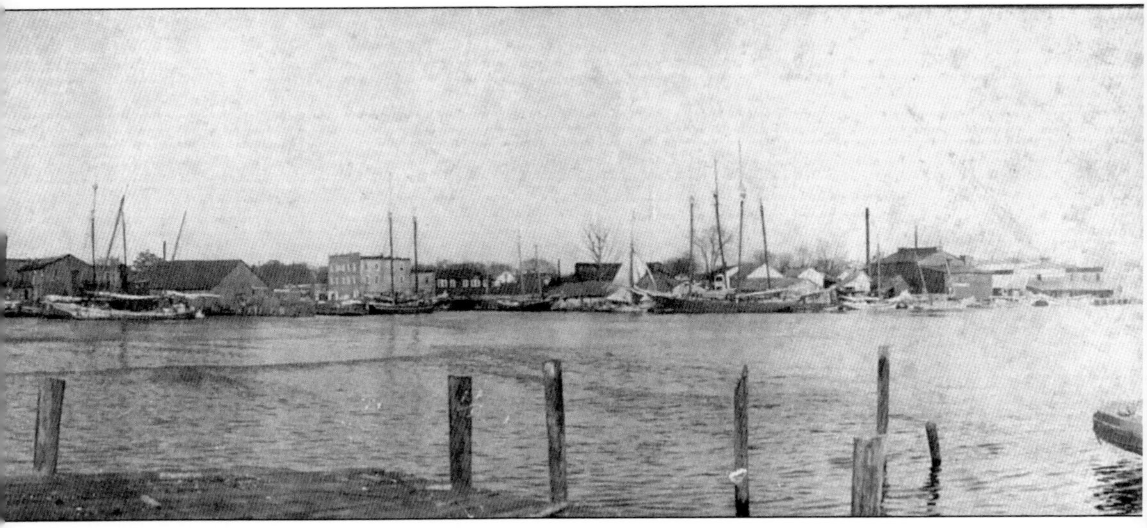

from the Camden side of the Pasquotank River.

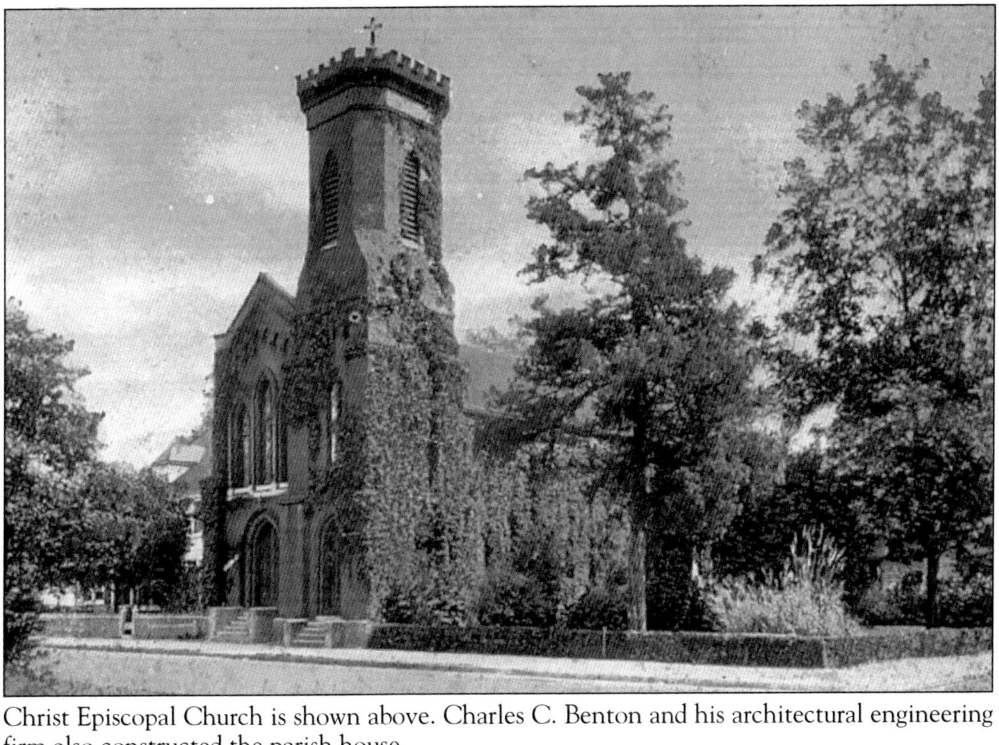

Christ Episcopal Church is shown above. Charles C. Benton and his architectural engineering firm also constructed the parish house.

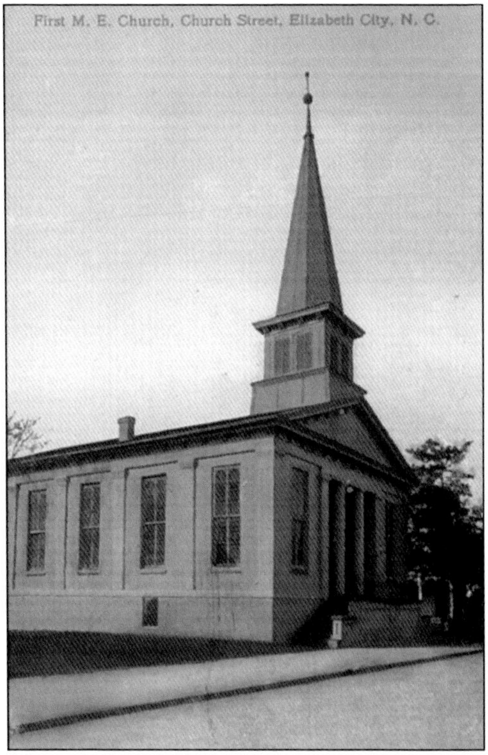

The First Methodist Church was built on West Church Street. It was later sold and converted to a three-story apartment building called the Perry Apartments.

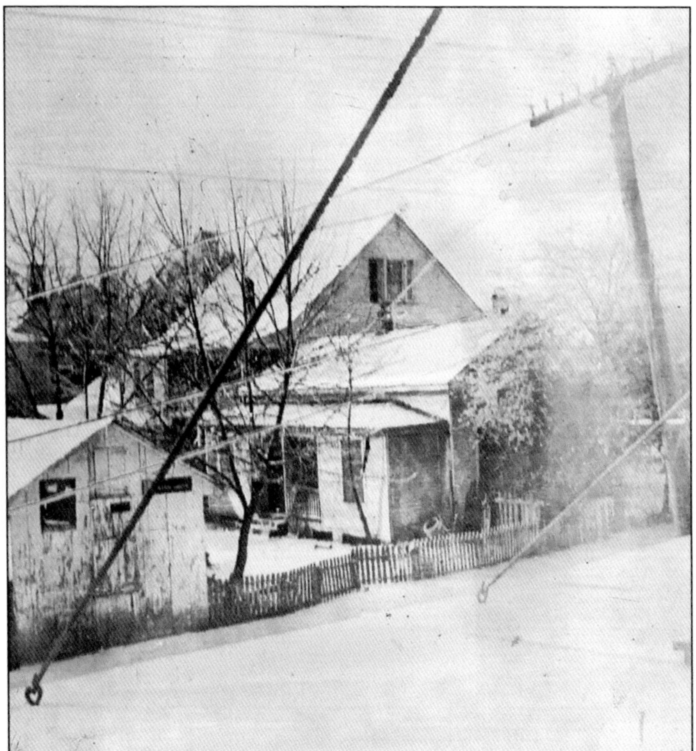

The old Fearing house is on the corner of Road and Fearing Streets. This is a back view taken during a snowstorm.

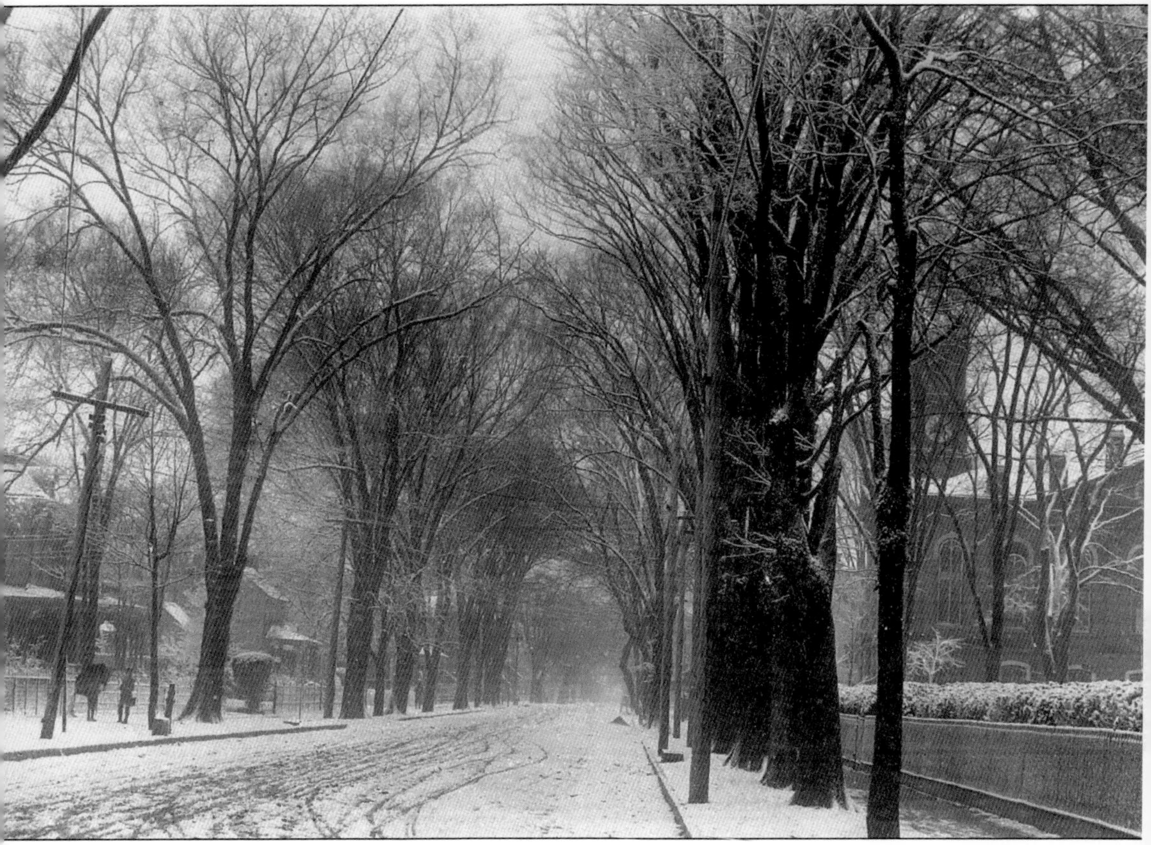

East Main Street was originally a dirt street but it was later paved with bricks. In this view, the courthouse is to the right.

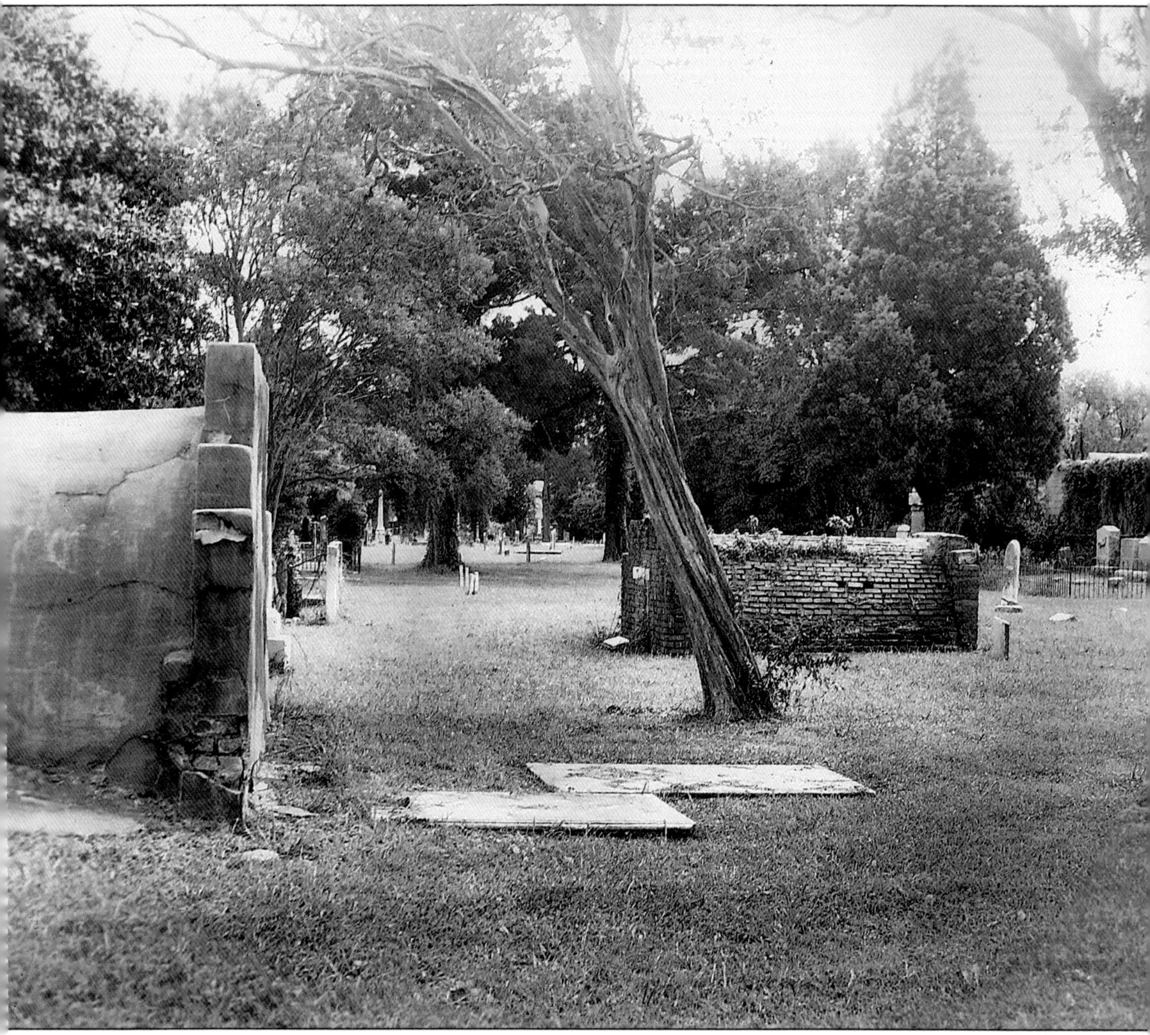

The Episcopal Cemetery was started *c.* 1828. It is located on Ehringhaus Street and Gov. John Christopher Blucher Ehringhaus is buried there. Born in 1882, Ehringhaus served as governor from 1933 to 1937. He died in 1949.

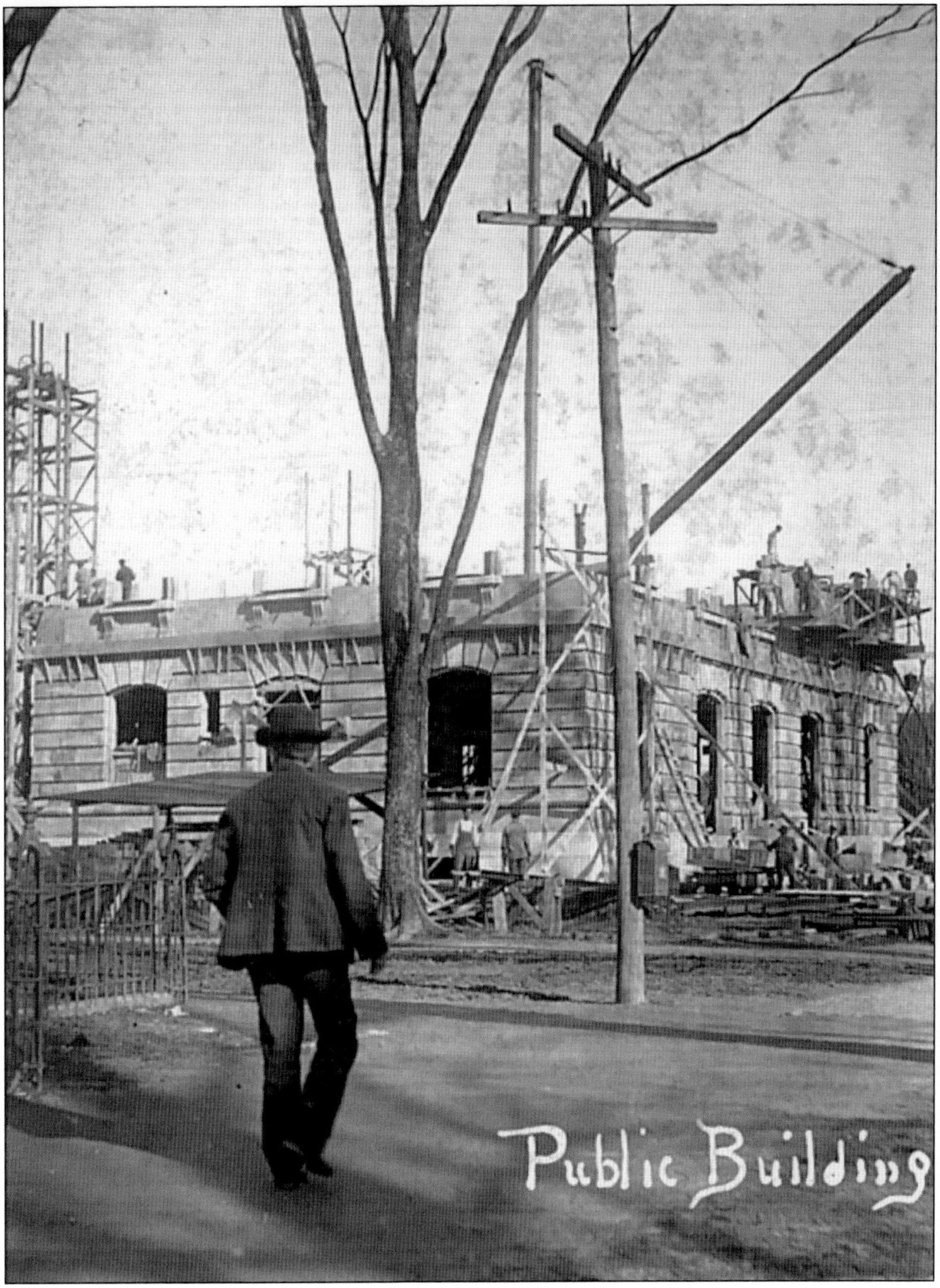

This *c.* 1905 photo shows the post office and courthouse under construction.

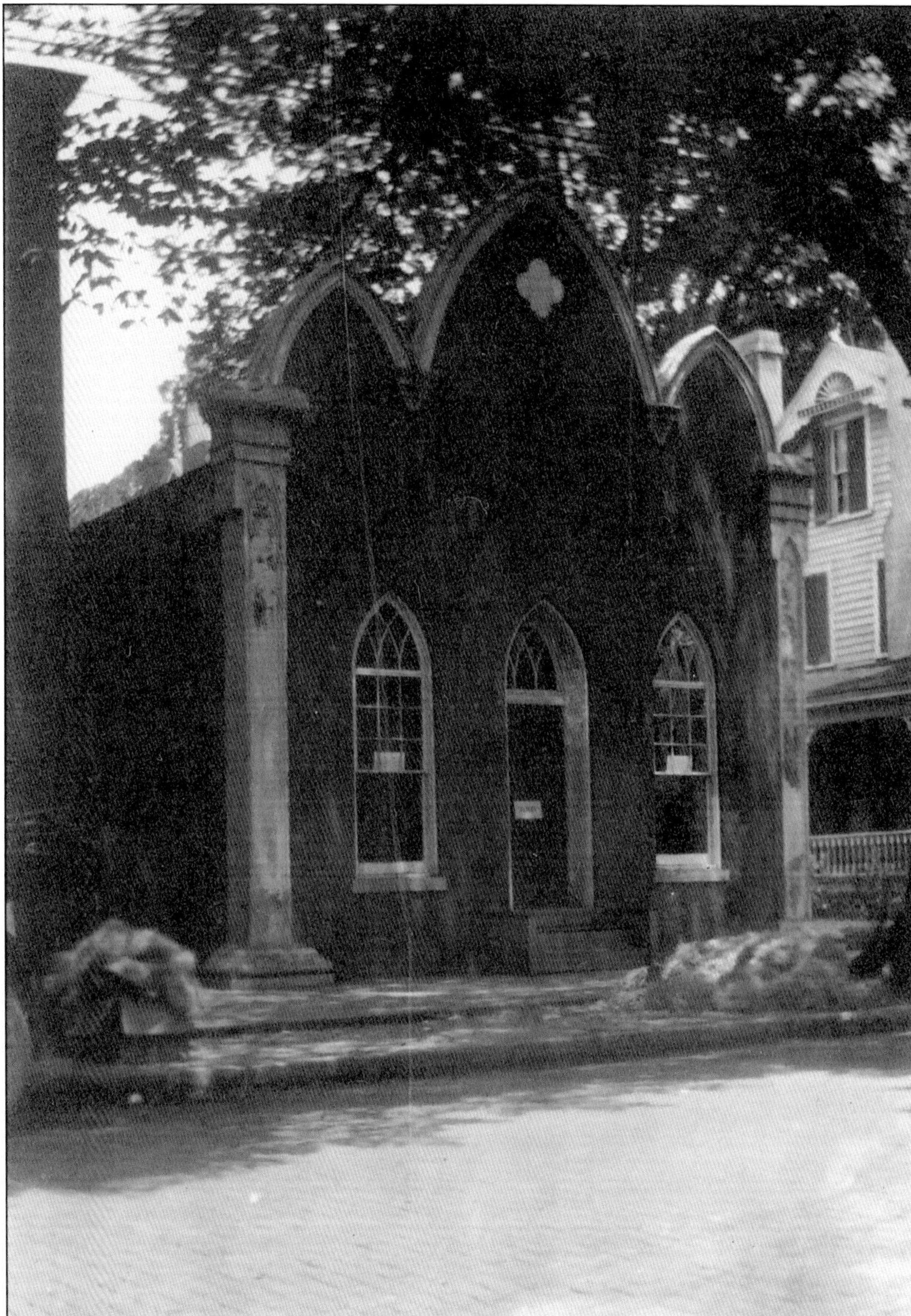

The old Cobb and Guirkin Bank (Old Farmers Bank) located at 108 East Main Street was used during the war as a tearoom. The bank is a rare example of the Gothic Revival style of architecture. The law office of Van H. Johnson now occupies the building. (Notice the brick street.)

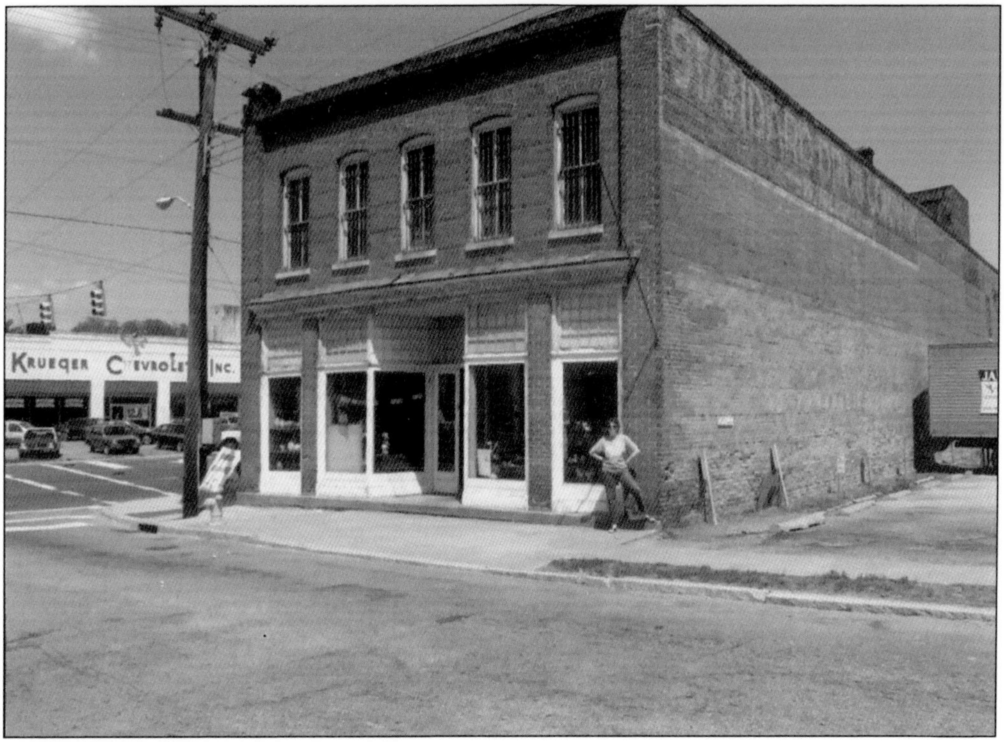

These pictures show Standard Drug Company in 1982. Dr. A.L. Pendleton owned it. The front of the pharmacy resided on Martin Street.

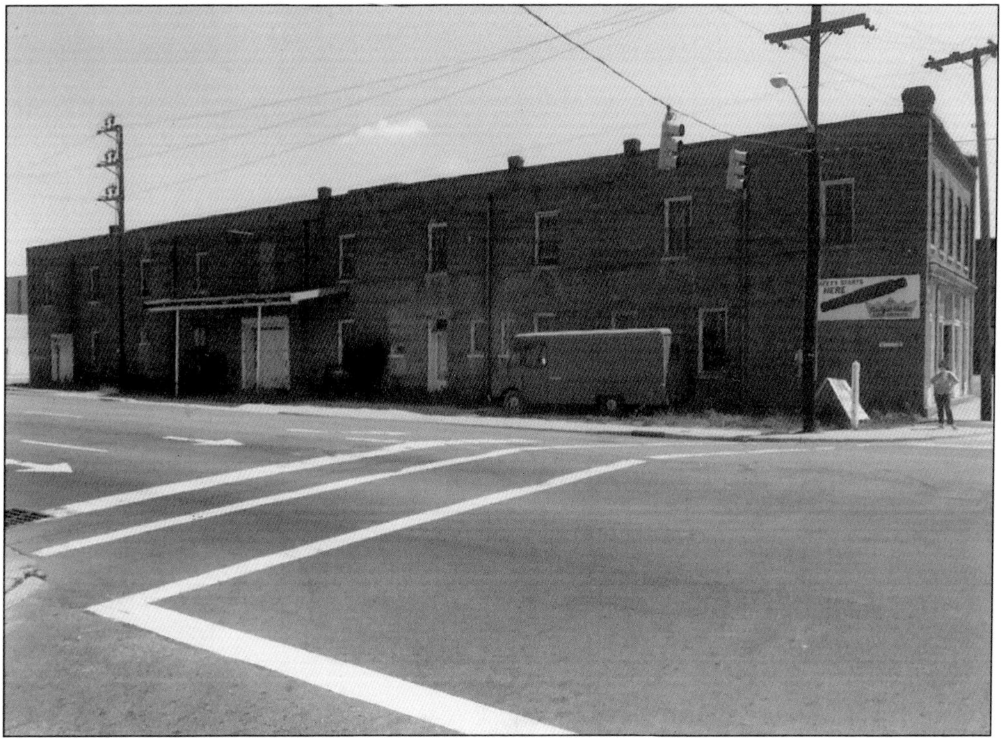

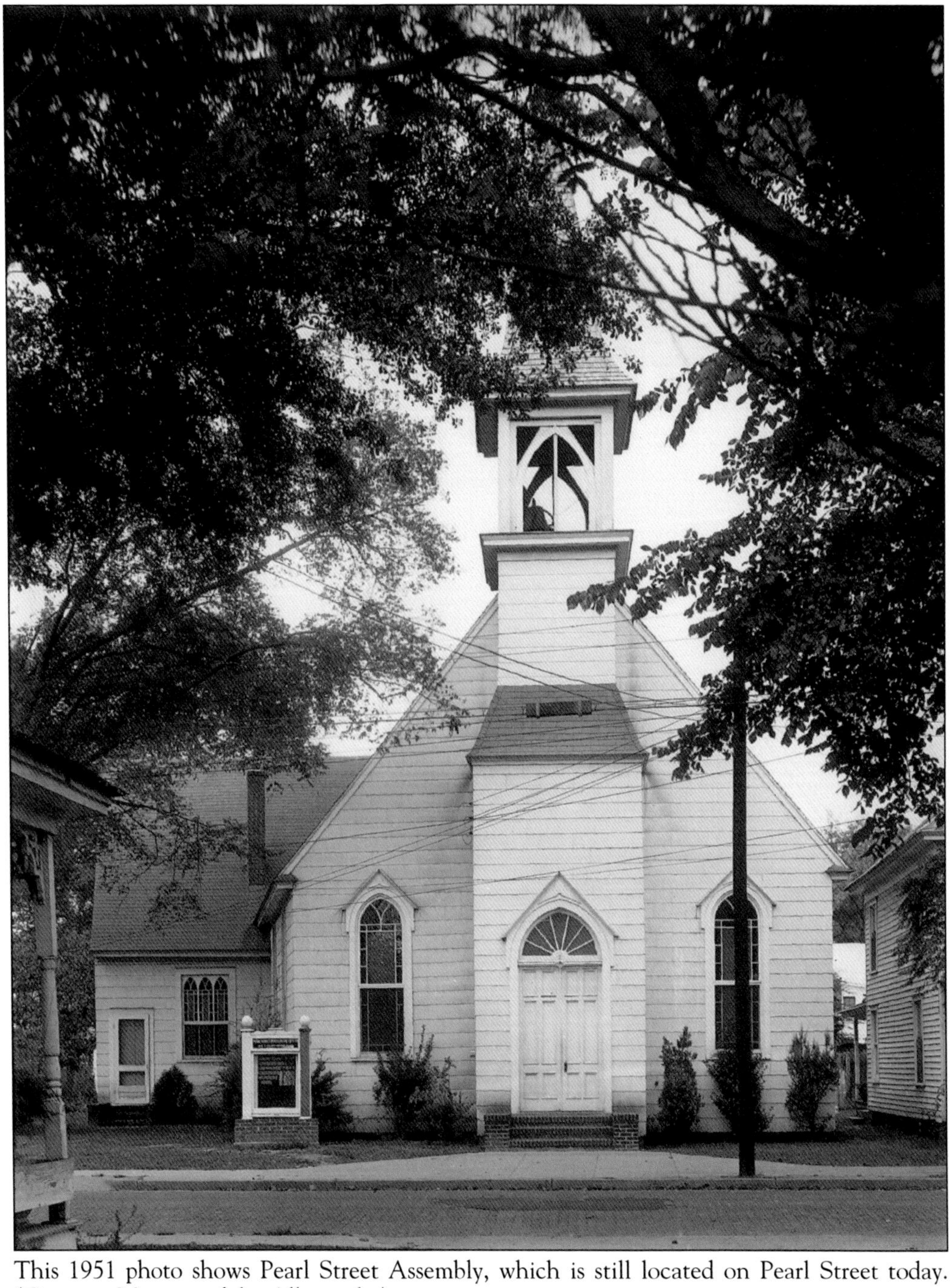

This 1951 photo shows Pearl Street Assembly, which is still located on Pearl Street today. (Courtesy Museum of the Albemarle.)

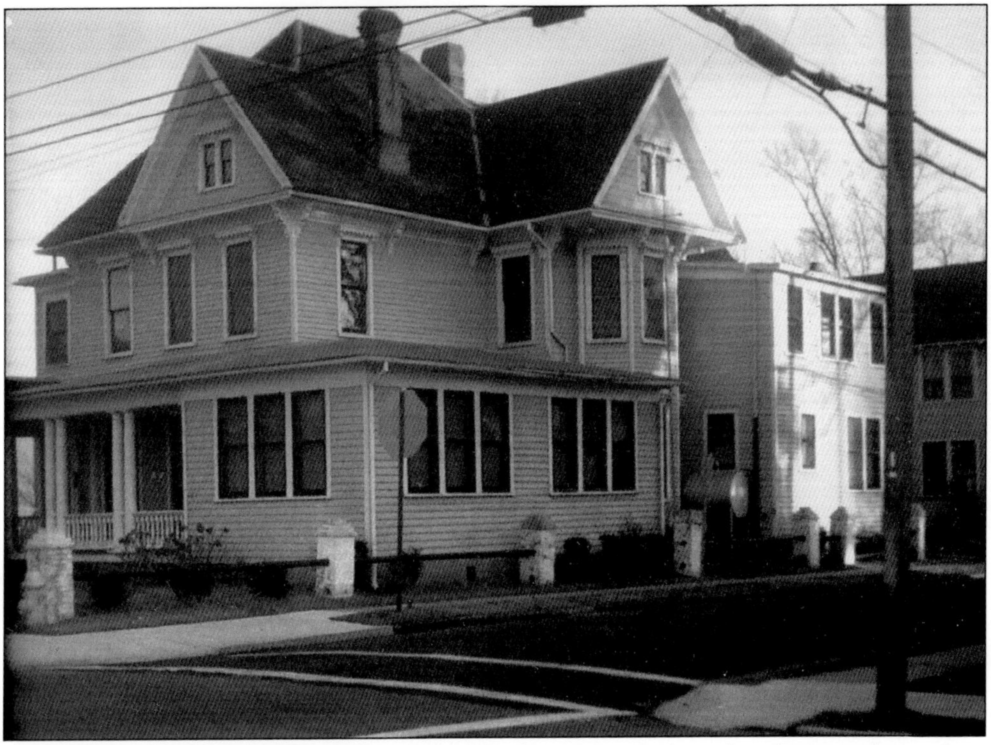

Many houses were torn down in the 1980s. The house pictured on this photograph stood on Church Street and was demolished in 1987.

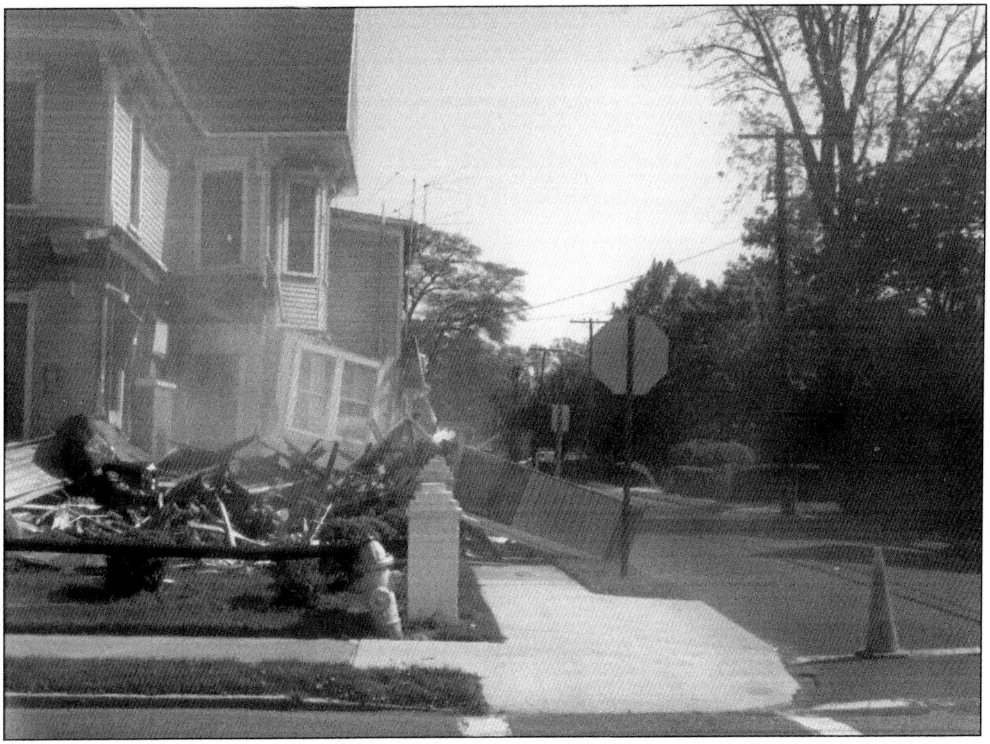

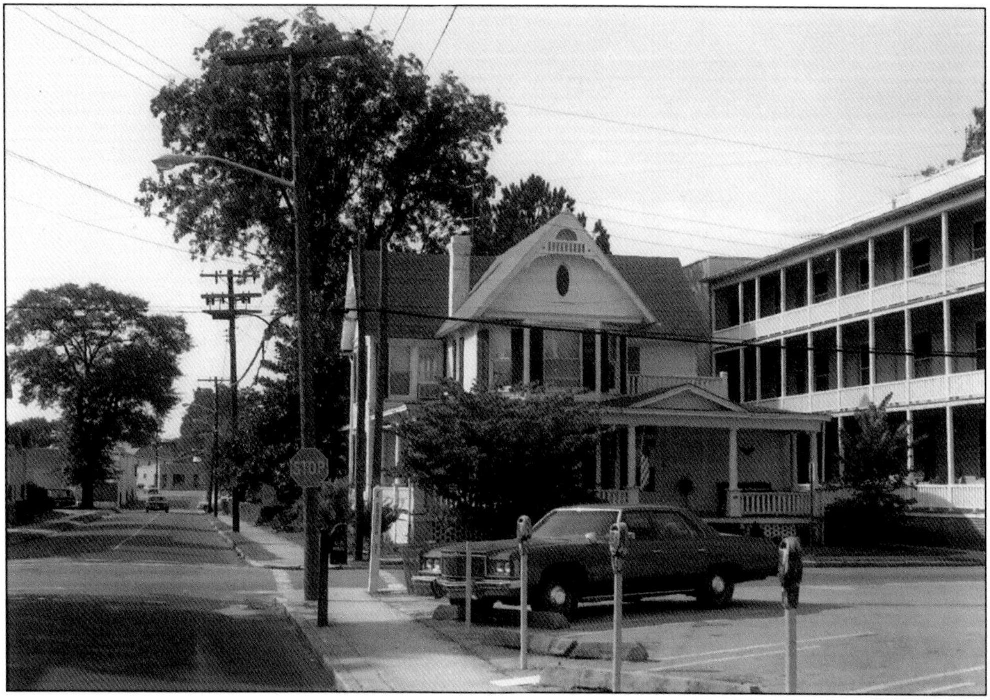

Potter and Hazel Dixon resided in the house above. The home is currently used as a law office. The building to the right of the house is the Perry Apartments. Notice the porches that wrapped around the sides and front of the building.

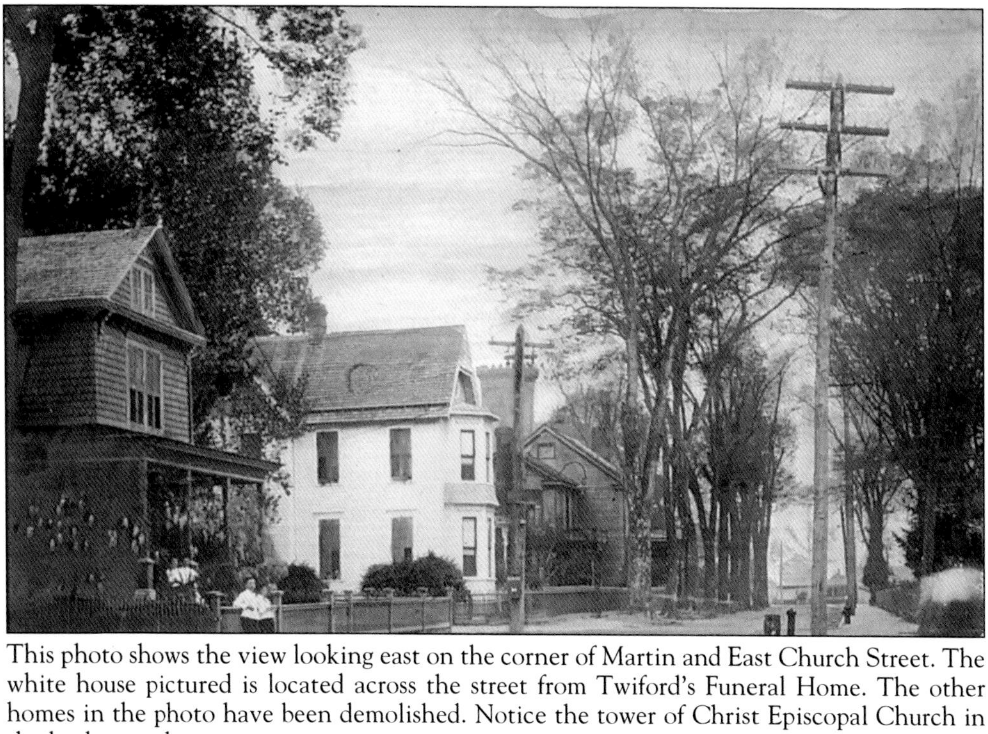

This photo shows the view looking east on the corner of Martin and East Church Street. The white house pictured is located across the street from Twiford's Funeral Home. The other homes in the photo have been demolished. Notice the tower of Christ Episcopal Church in the background.

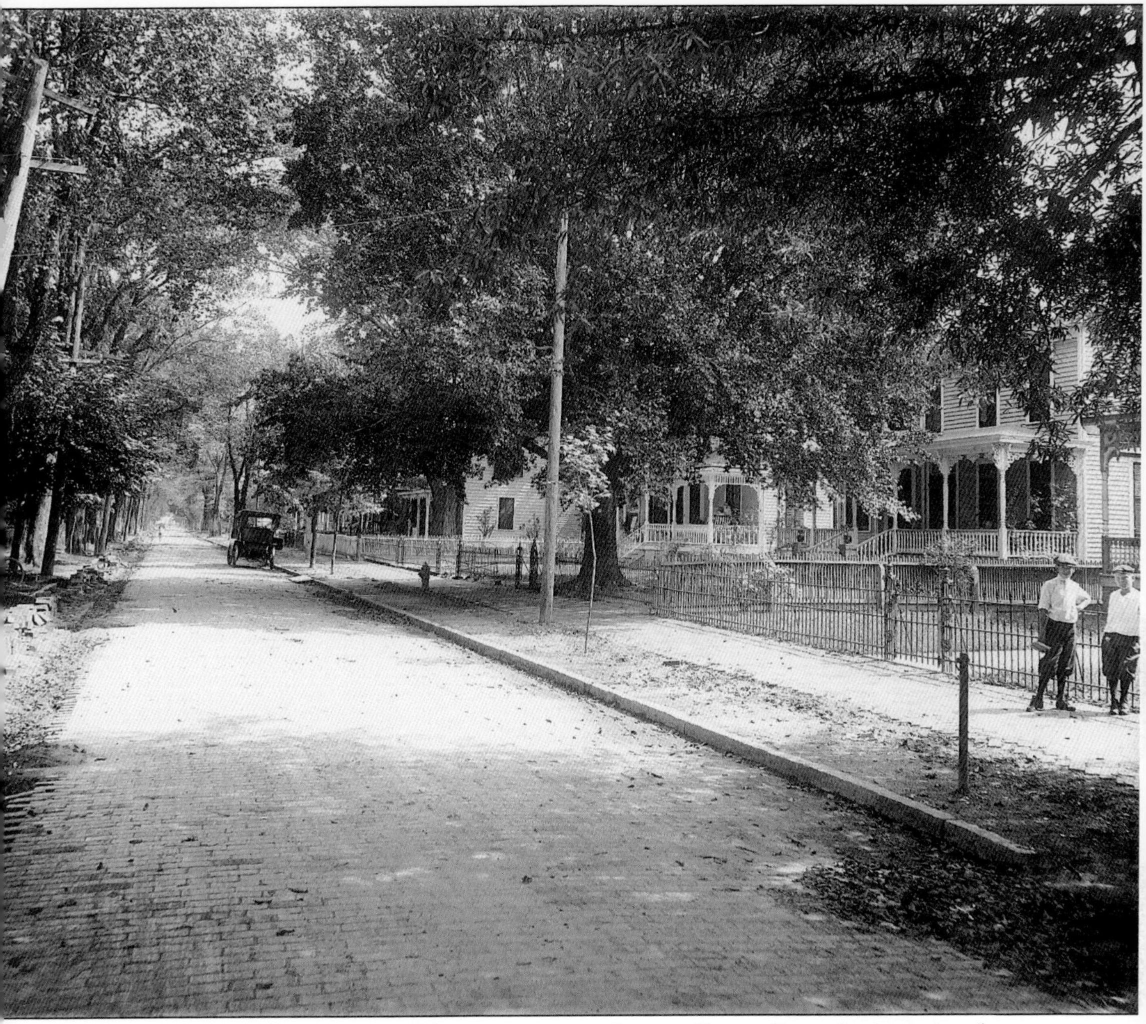

Main Street is shown here *c.* 1911. This picture was taken on Persse Street looking east down Main Street.

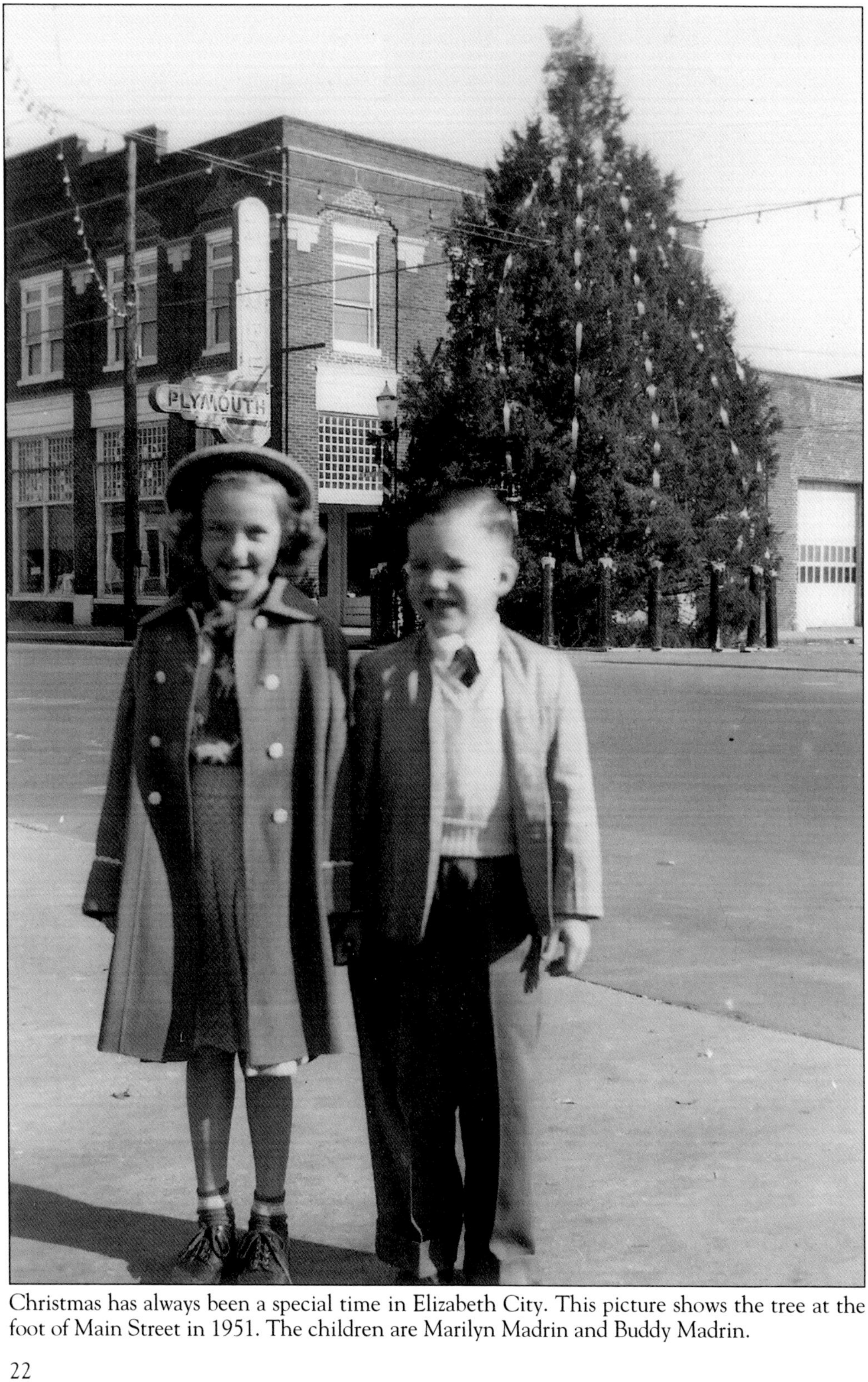

Christmas has always been a special time in Elizabeth City. This picture shows the tree at the foot of Main Street in 1951. The children are Marilyn Madrin and Buddy Madrin.

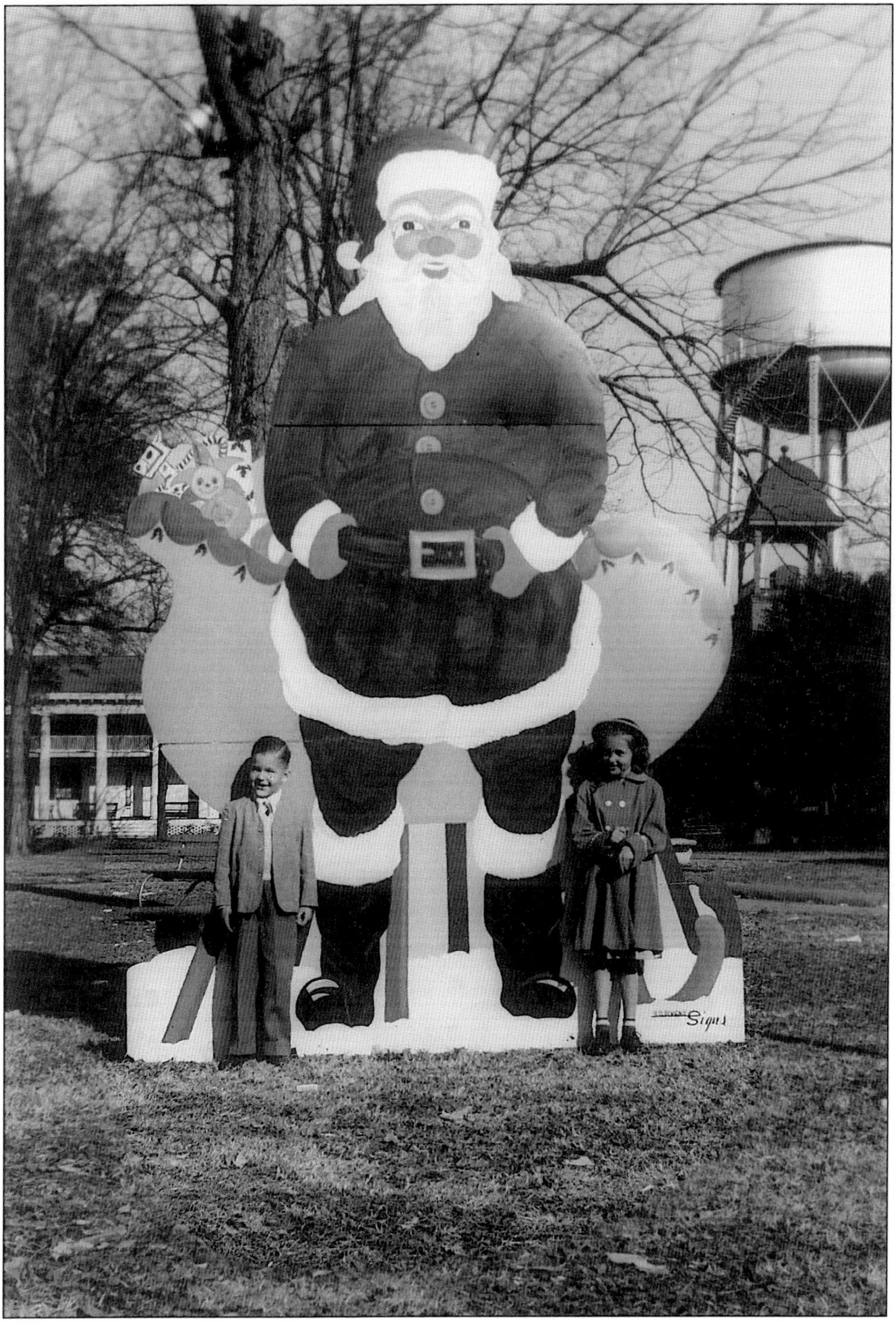

Marilyn Madrin and Buddy Madrin are pictured with a large Santa on the lawn of the courthouse. The house in the background is the Pool-Greenleaf-Small home and has since been demolished.

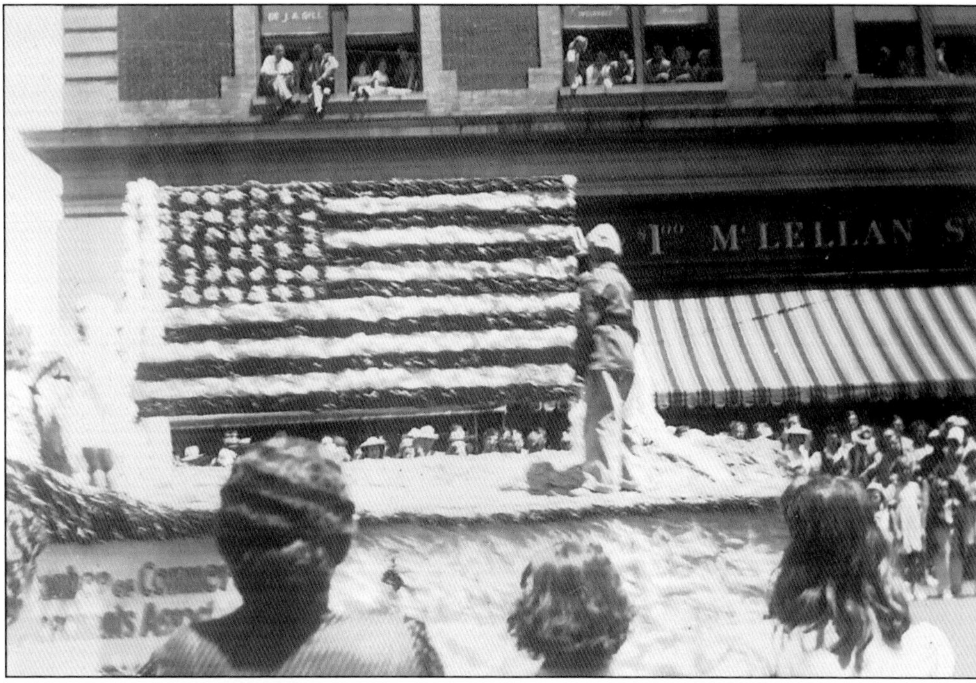

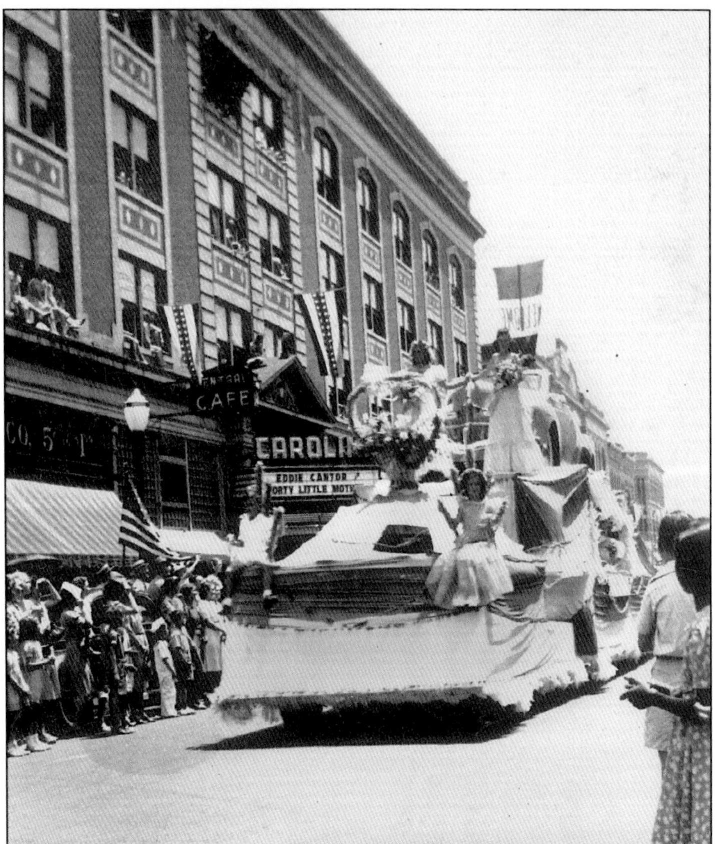

In 1940, the Potato Festival was held in Elizabeth City. There was a parade and prizes awarded to the best floats. The Potato Festival was renewed again in 2001 with a dance, parade, potato-peeling contest, and many other events.

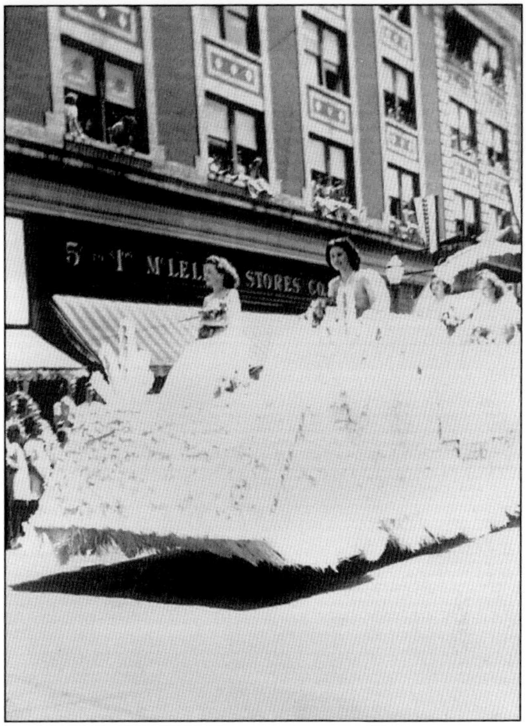

The Potato Festival also included many beauty queens and local high school bands.

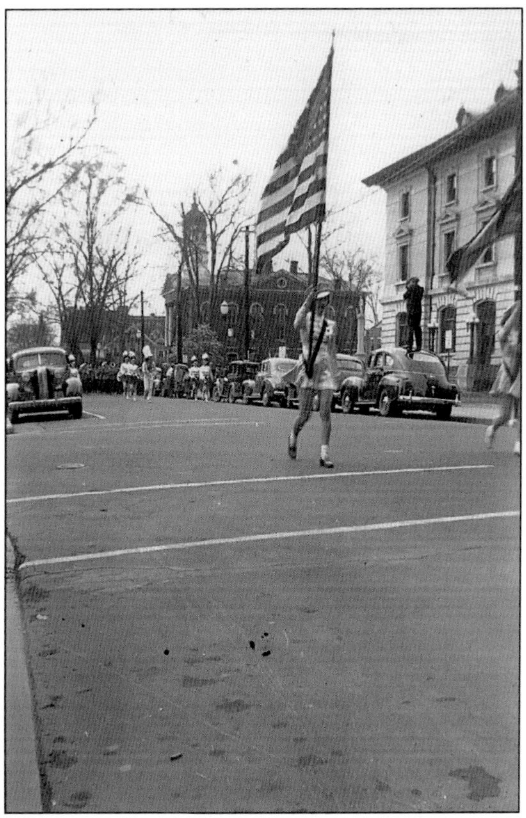

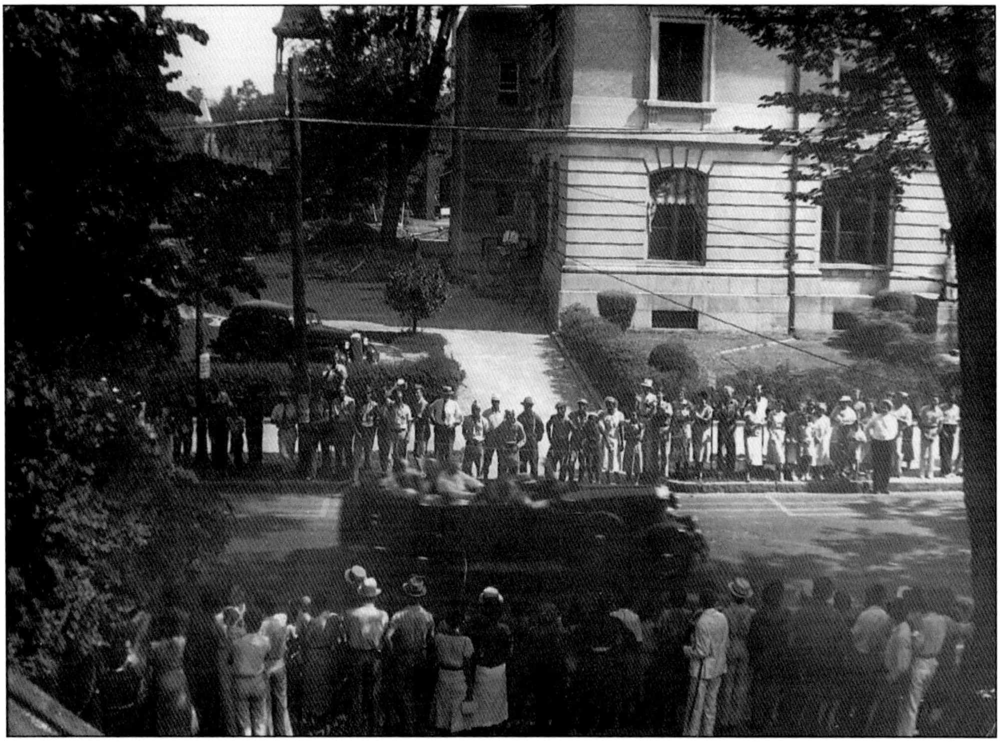

President Franklin D. Roosevelt visited Elizabeth City on August 18, 1937. It was part of the 350th Anniversary of the Birth of Virginia Dare on Roanoke Island. Virginia Dare was the first English child born in the New World. She was a part of the "Lost Colony" which was never found.

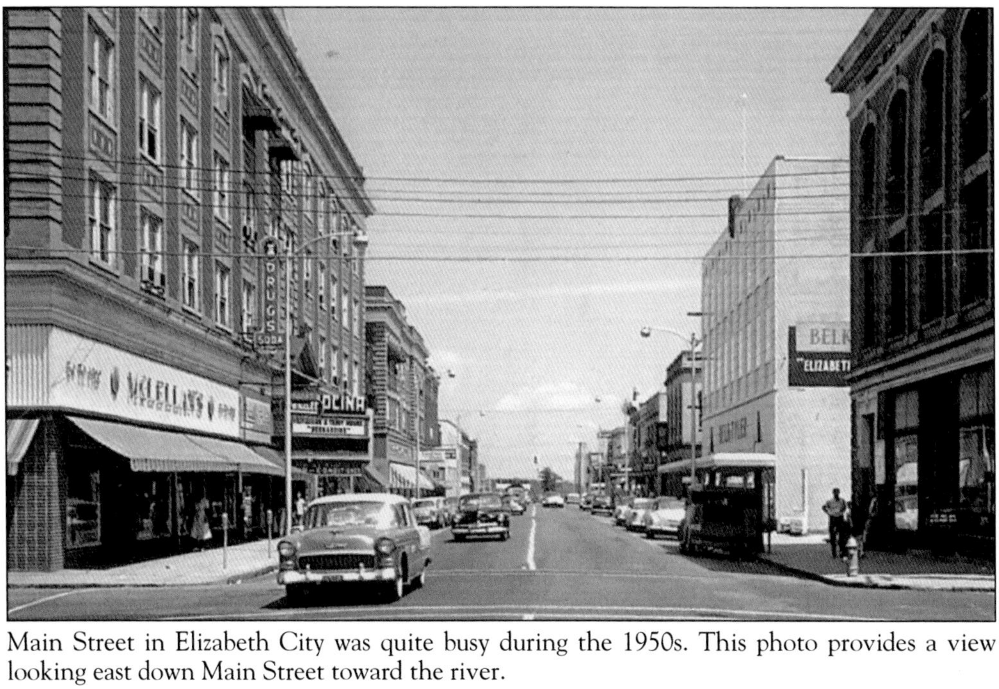

Main Street in Elizabeth City was quite busy during the 1950s. This photo provides a view looking east down Main Street toward the river.

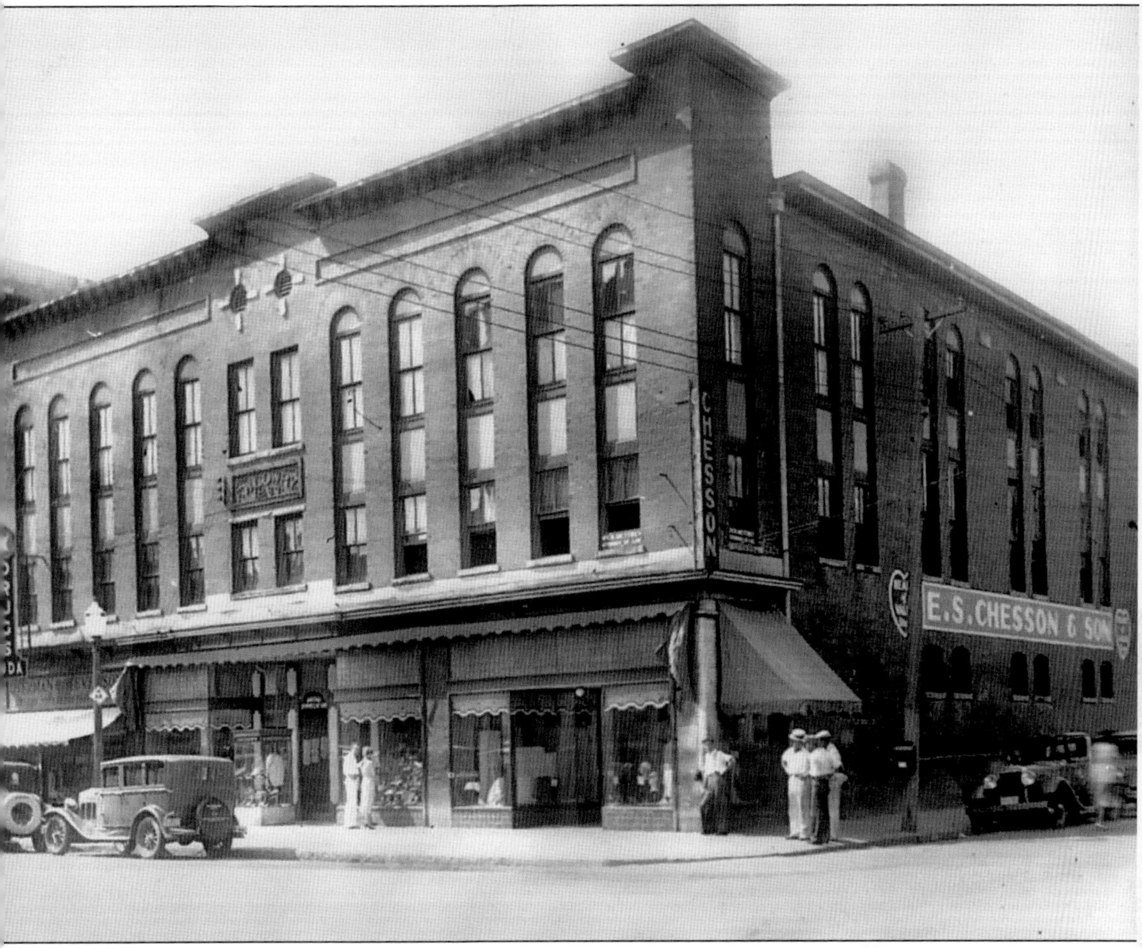

Chessons Department Store was located on the corner of Main and Poindexter Streets. The Opera House is located on the second and third floors. Collapsed beams led to the store closing in 1999. The Elizabeth City Historic Neighborhood Association (ECHNA) rescued the building and has completed the stabilization phase of the project. The drug store on the left is Overman and Stevenson. (Courtesy of Museum of the Albemarle.)

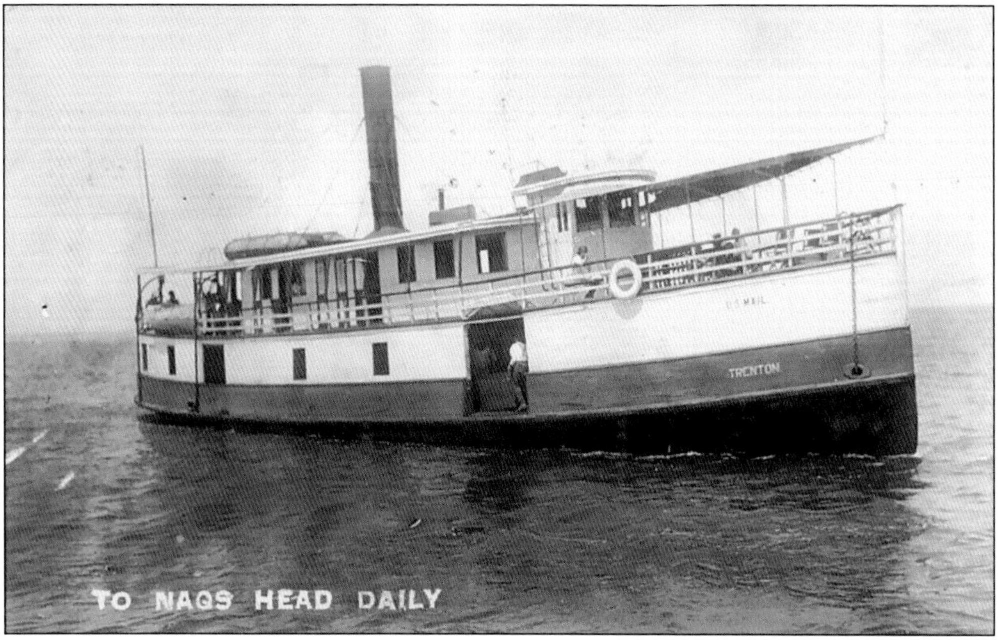

The Trenton took people to Nags Head from Elizabeth City. There were no bridges to the beach, so boat travel was the only means of transportation.

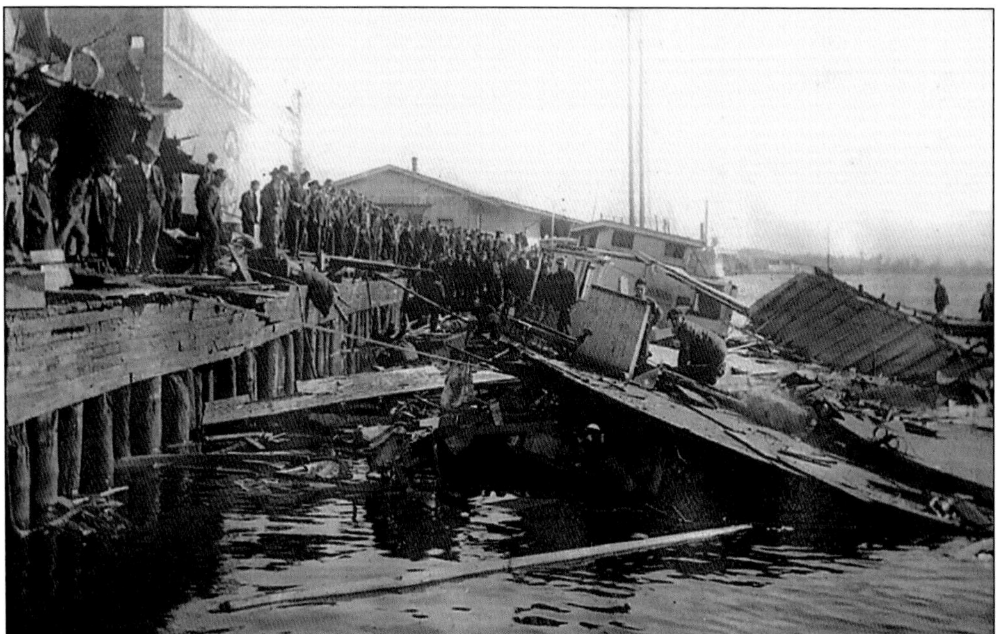

On April 12, 1918, the ship *Annie* exploded in the Elizabeth City harbor. Officers of the ill-fated *Annie* were Capt. J.D. Johnson, Assistant Engineer John Dowdy, and First Mate Manus Kinsey. Kinsey had served on the *Hattie Creef* at one time, which carried the Wright Brothers to Kitty Hawk.

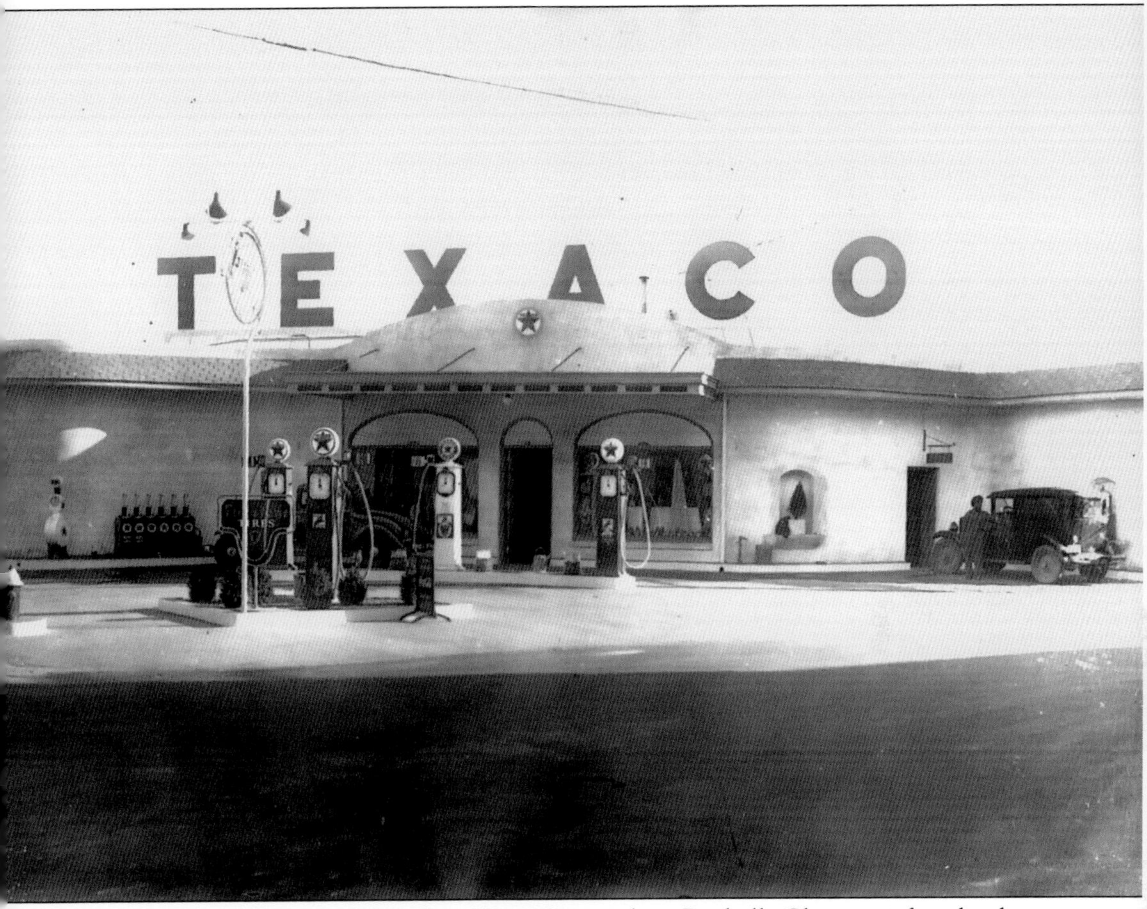

The Texaco Gas Station was located on Water Street where Rochelle Cleaners is found today. (Courtesy of Museum of the Albemarle.)

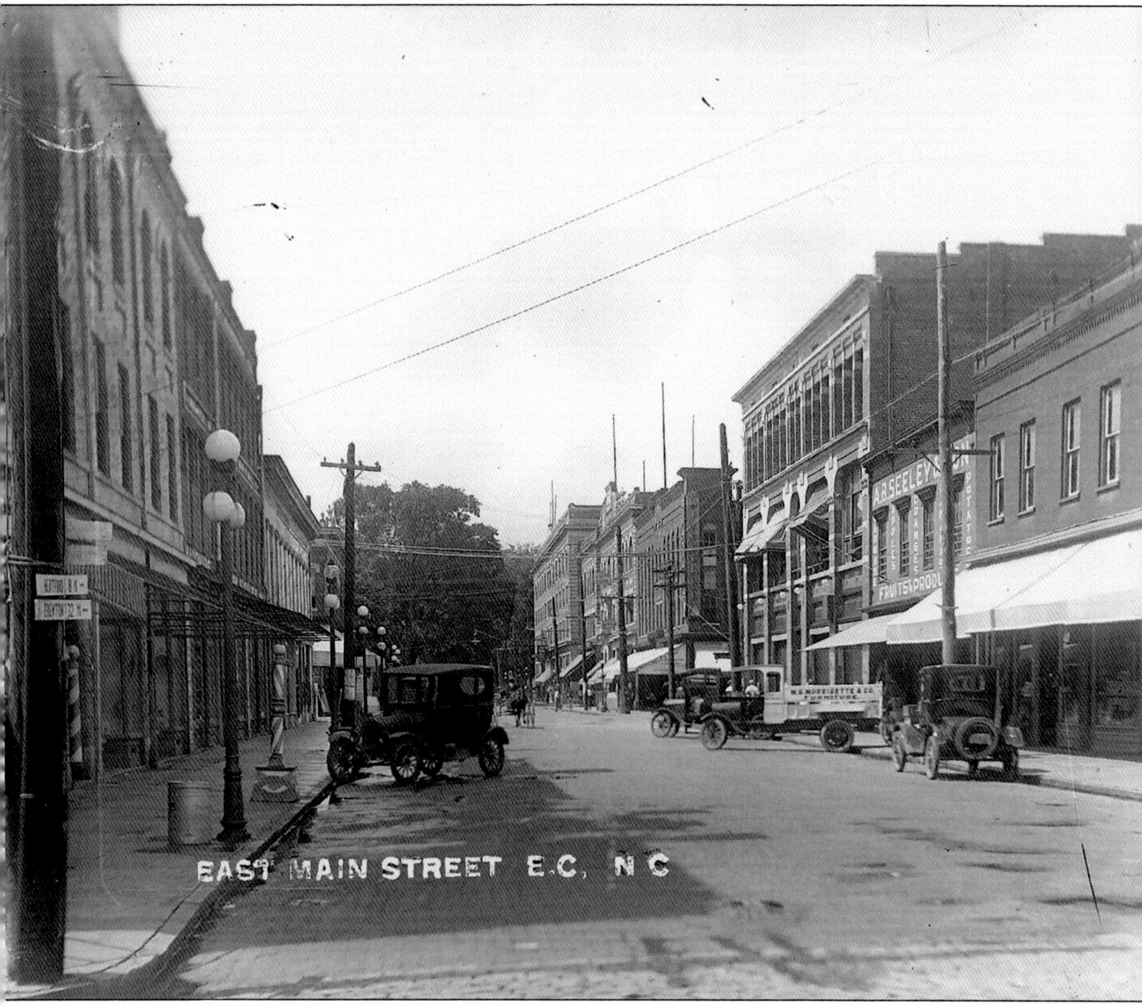

Pictured above is the corner of East Main and Martin Streets in the downtown area. (Courtesy of Museum of the Albemarle.)

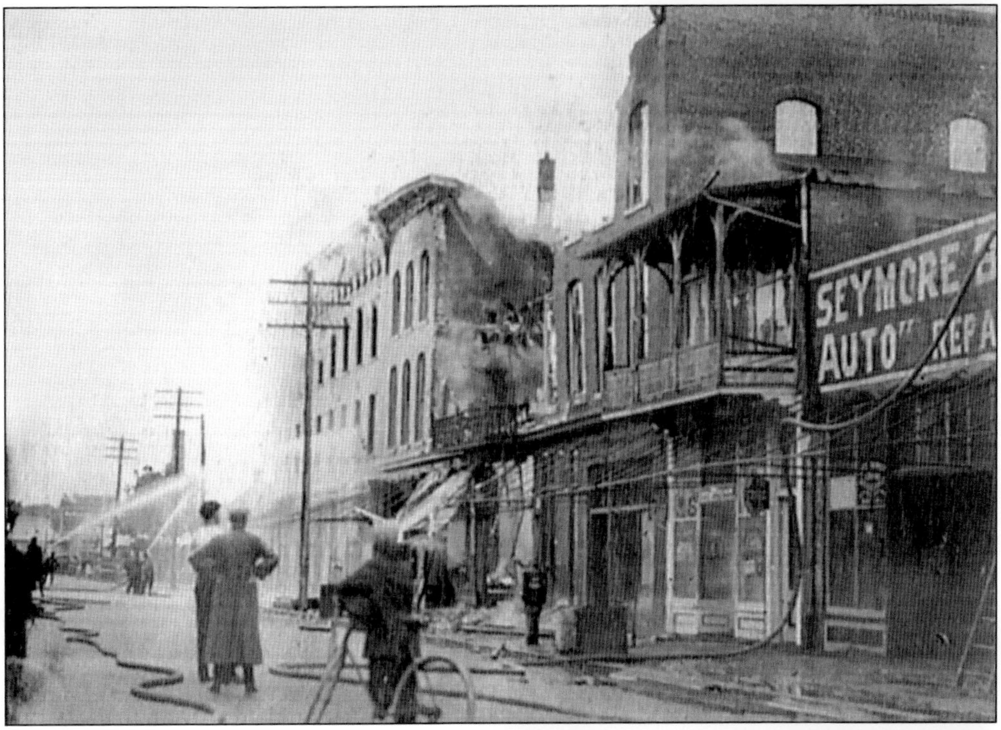

An immense fire destroyed several buildings on Main Street.

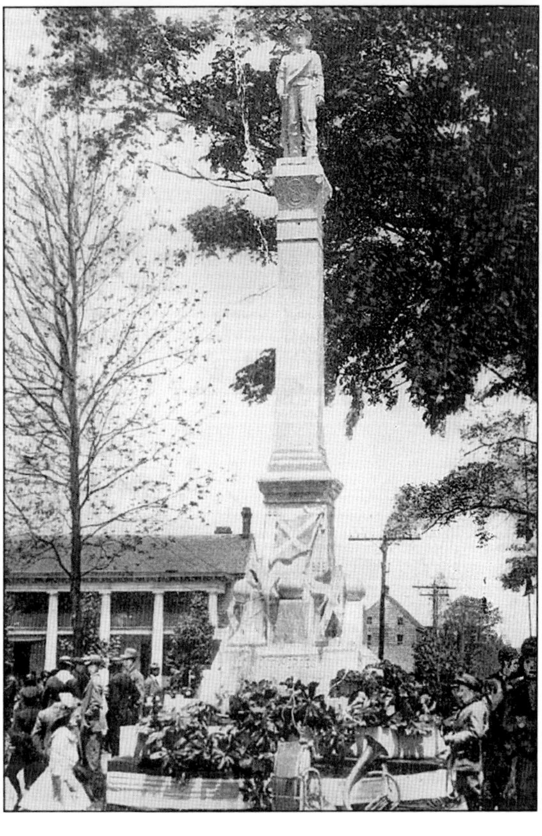

In 1911 the Civil War monument was dedicated on Main Street. (Courtesy Museum of the Albemarle.)

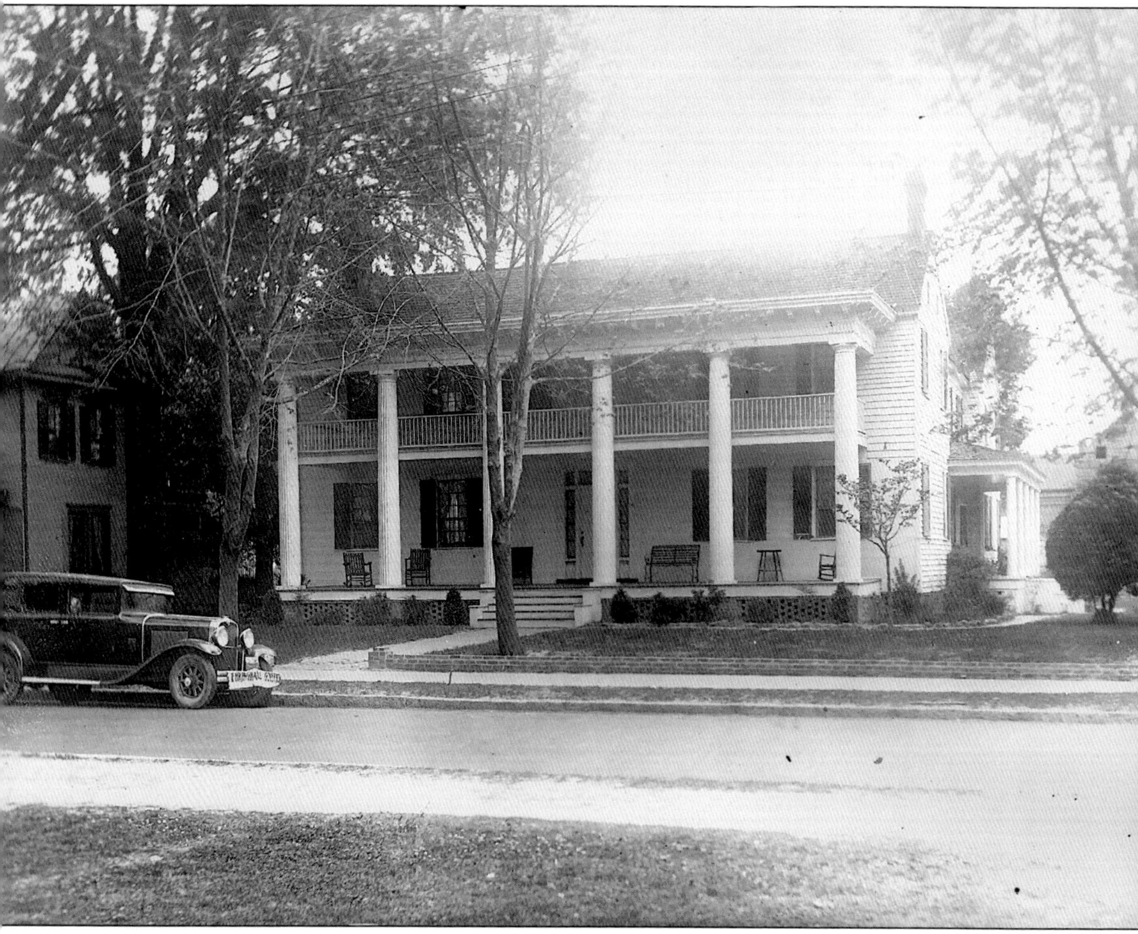

The Pool-Greenleaf-Small home was located on the 200 block of East Colonial Avenue. Built by Jethron Goodman, it originally stood where the federal building (post office) stands today. In 1903 the house was moved to the corner of Colonial Avenue and Pool Street. It was a boarding house run by the Greenleaf family and later Mrs. Arthur S. Mann. It was then purchased by Judge Walter Small who owned the house until it was demolished. The property is now used as a parking lot. The Melick home is located on the left side. (Courtesy of Museum of the Albemarle.)

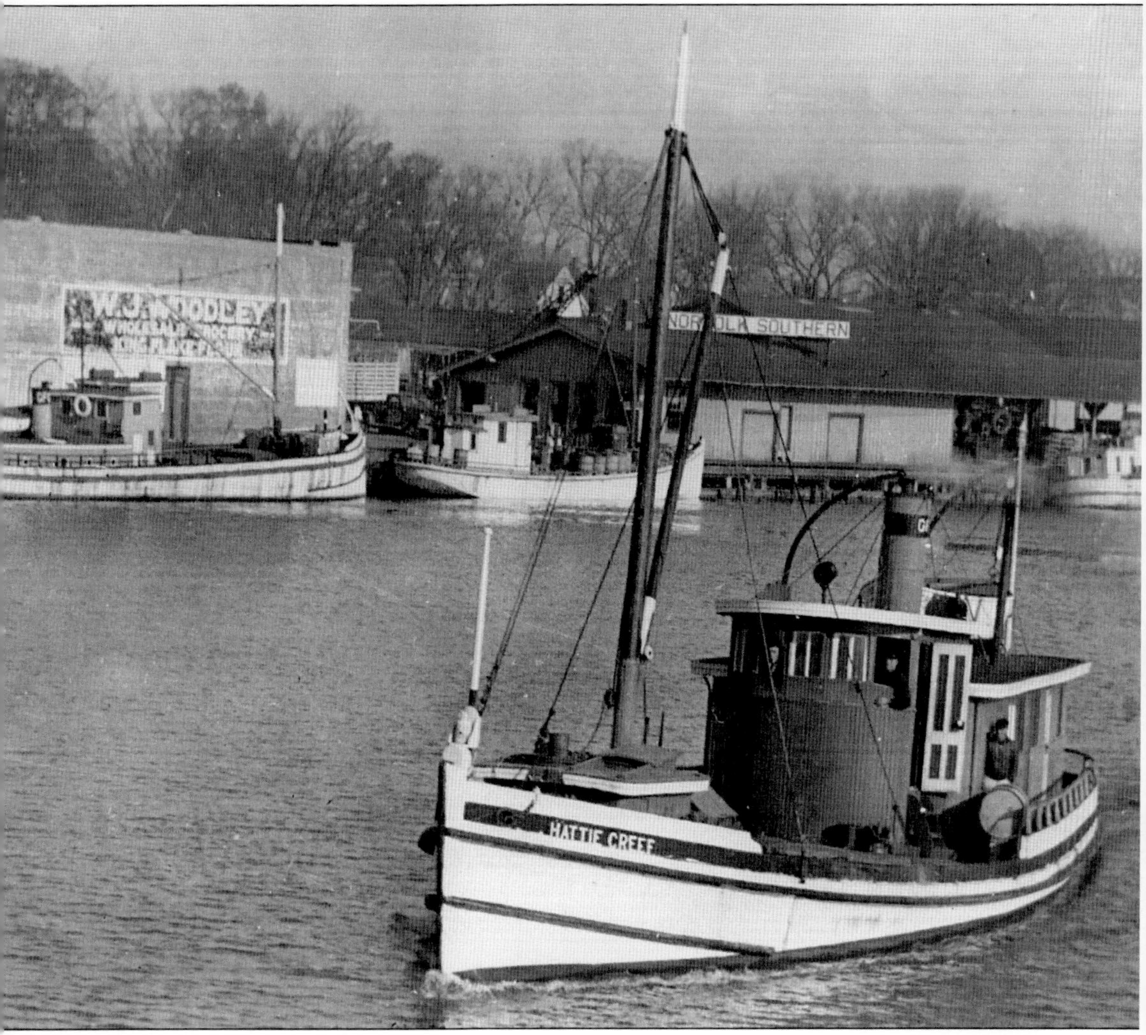

The Hattie Creef is just one of the boats that ferried people from Elizabeth City to Nags Head. The Wright Brothers rode on this boat many times. (Courtesy of Museum of the Albemarle.)

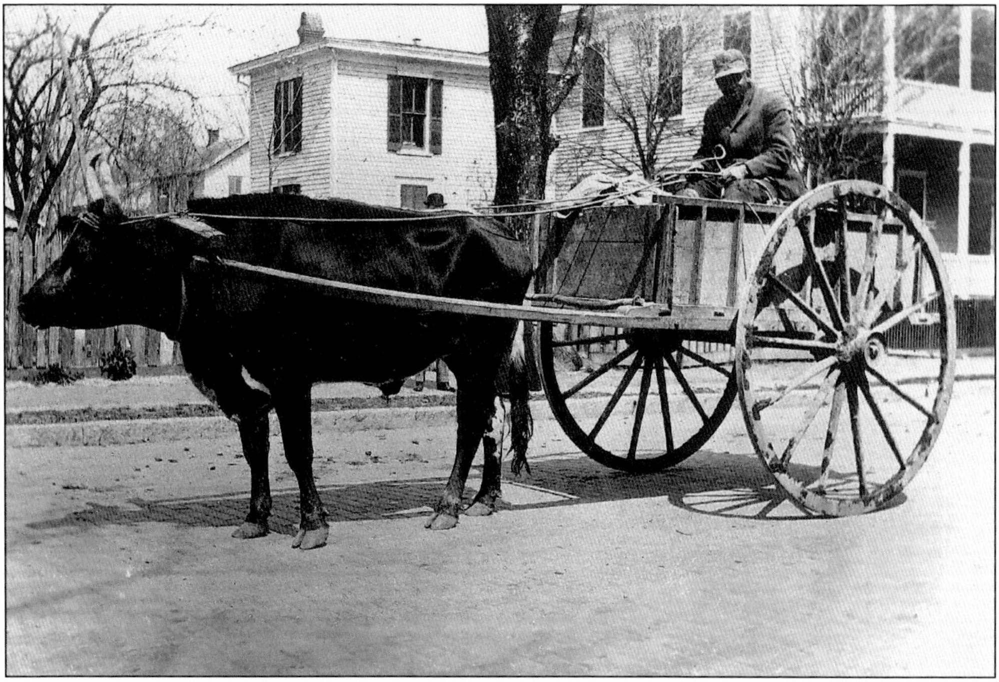

Charles McDonald is shown driving an ox cart on West Church Street. The house in the background is the Tillett-Nixon house at 400 West Church Street. Notice the double-tiered porches that have since been removed. (Courtesy of Museum of the Albemarle.)

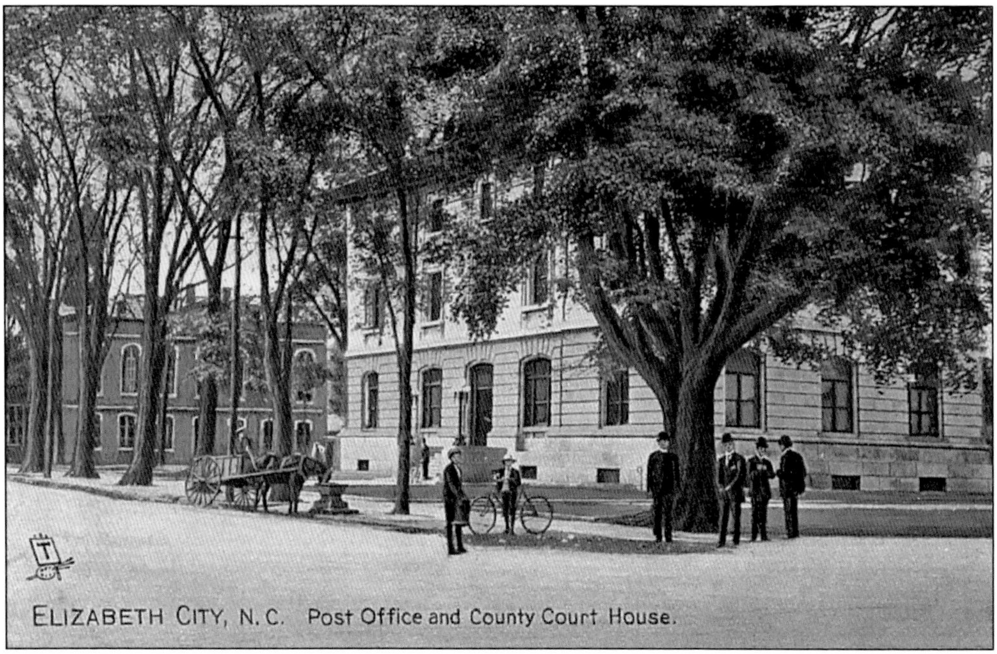

This postcard shows of the post office that remains today on East Main Street. To the left is the Pasquotank County Courthouse.

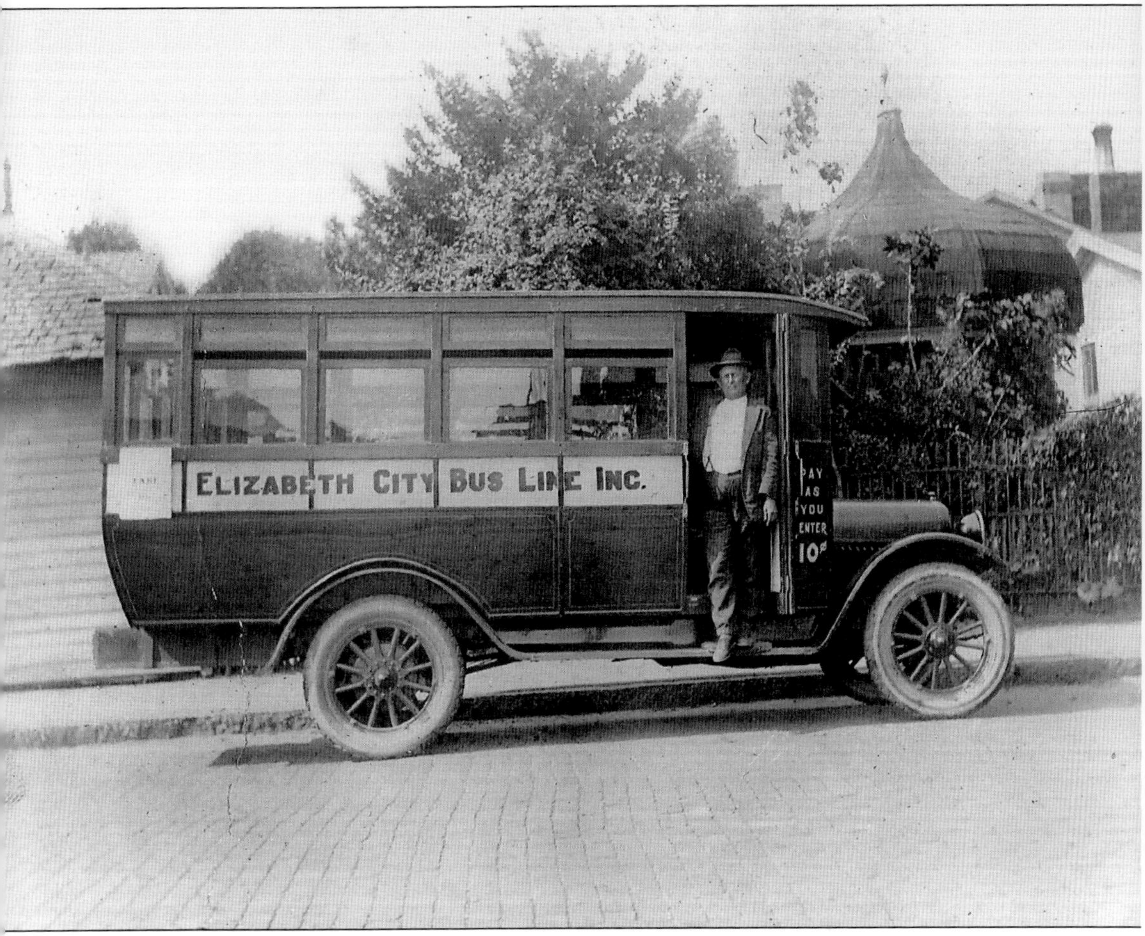

W.H. Whitehurst drove this bus for Elizabeth City's Chamber of Commerce bus line. The bus ran from the Norfolk & Southern Depot to Bradshaws Jewelers. Mr. Whitehurst lived at 301 West Fearing Street. (Courtesy of Museum of the Albemarle.)

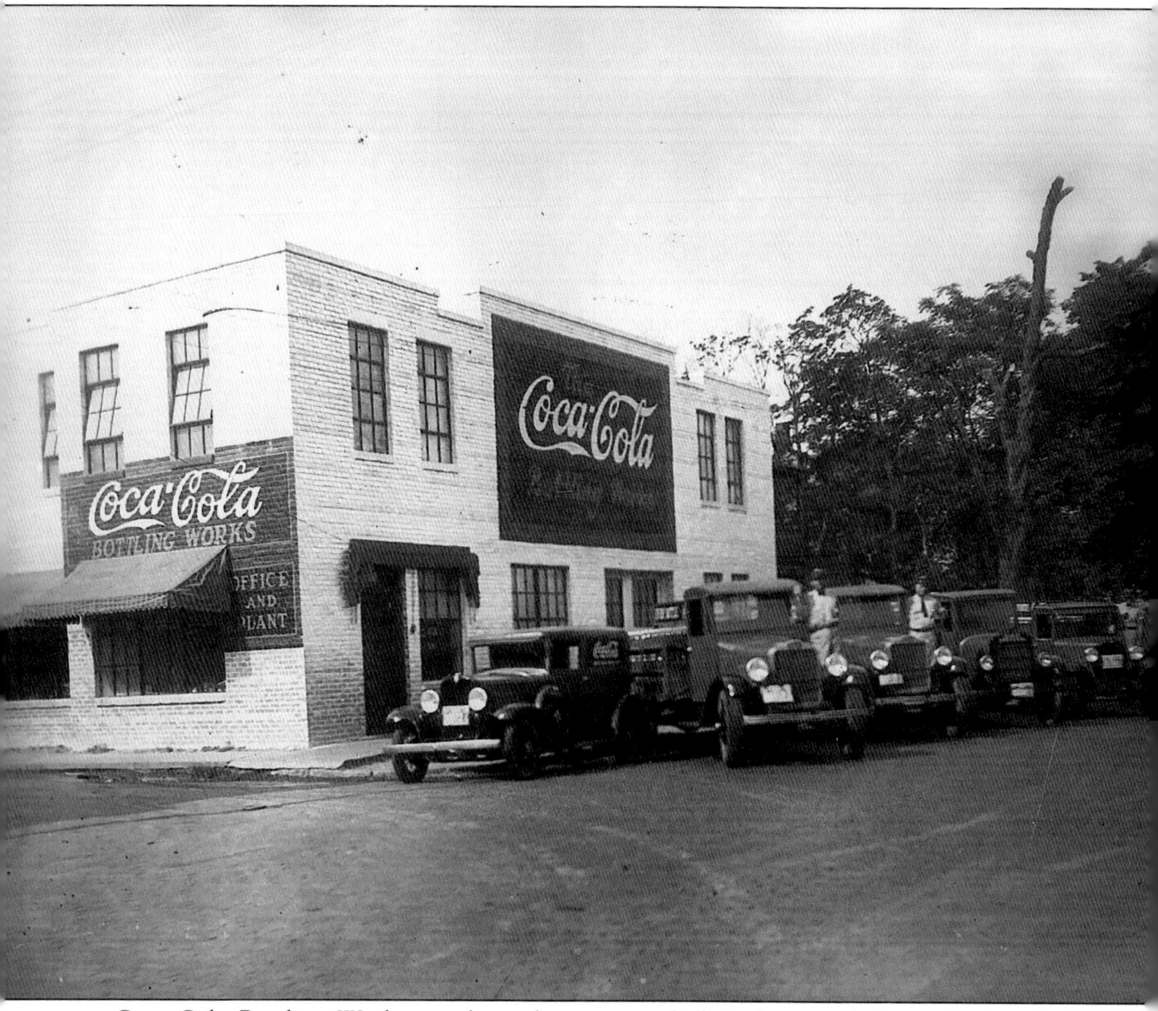

Coca-Cola Bottling Works stood on the corner of Ehringhaus and Green Streets. It was located on the present site of the new Museum of the Albemarle. (Courtesy of Museum of the Albemarle.)

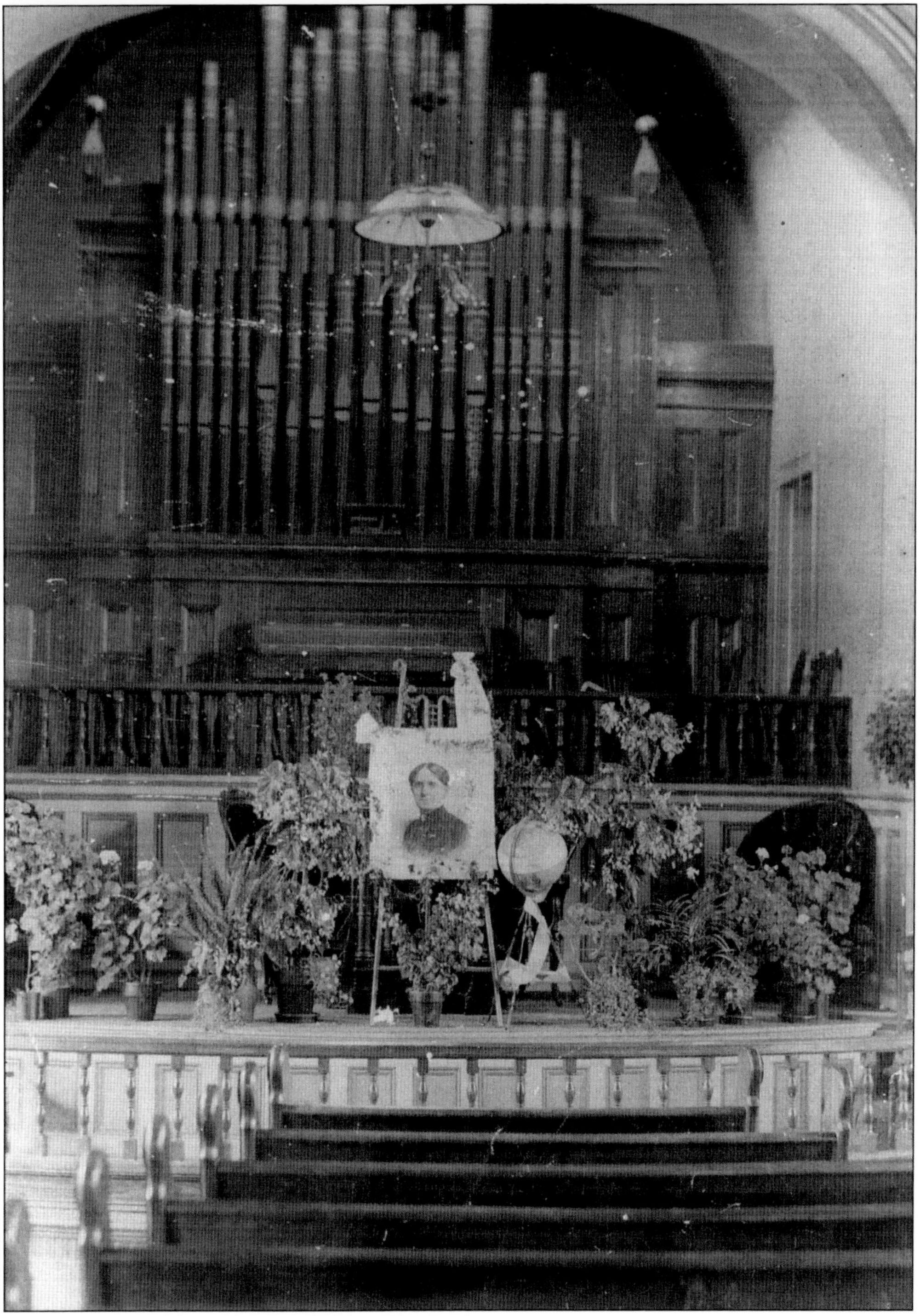

This is the interior of the First Methodist Episcopal Church that was located on East Church Street. It was later converted to the present-day Perry Apartments at 305 East Church Street. Francis Willard, a missionary to Africa, is shown in this 1898 portrait. (Courtesy of Museum of the Albemarle.)

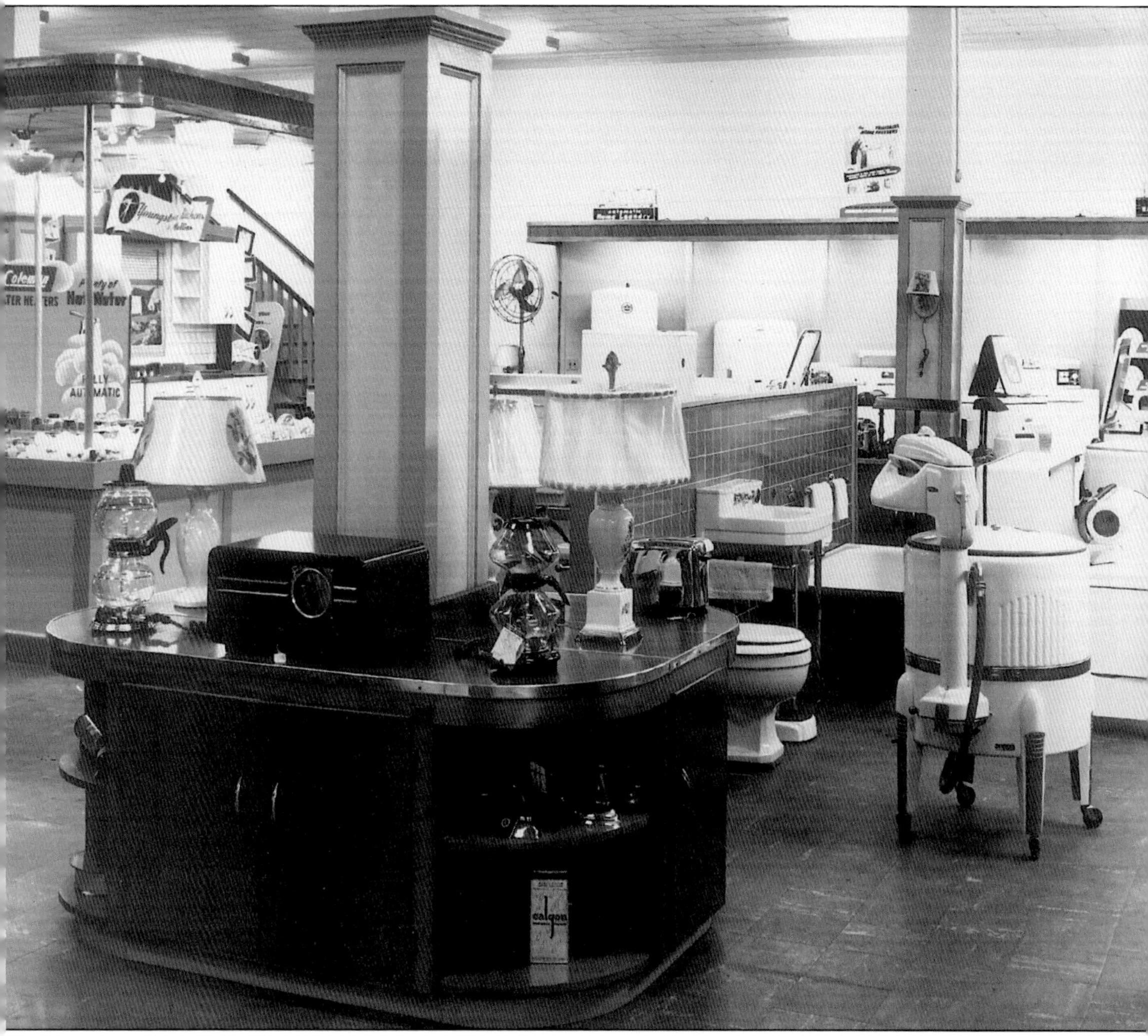

R.S. Jordan and Company provided home appliances such as brand-new washing machines complete with wringers in 1950. The store was located in the downtown area. (Courtesy of Museum of the Albemarle.)

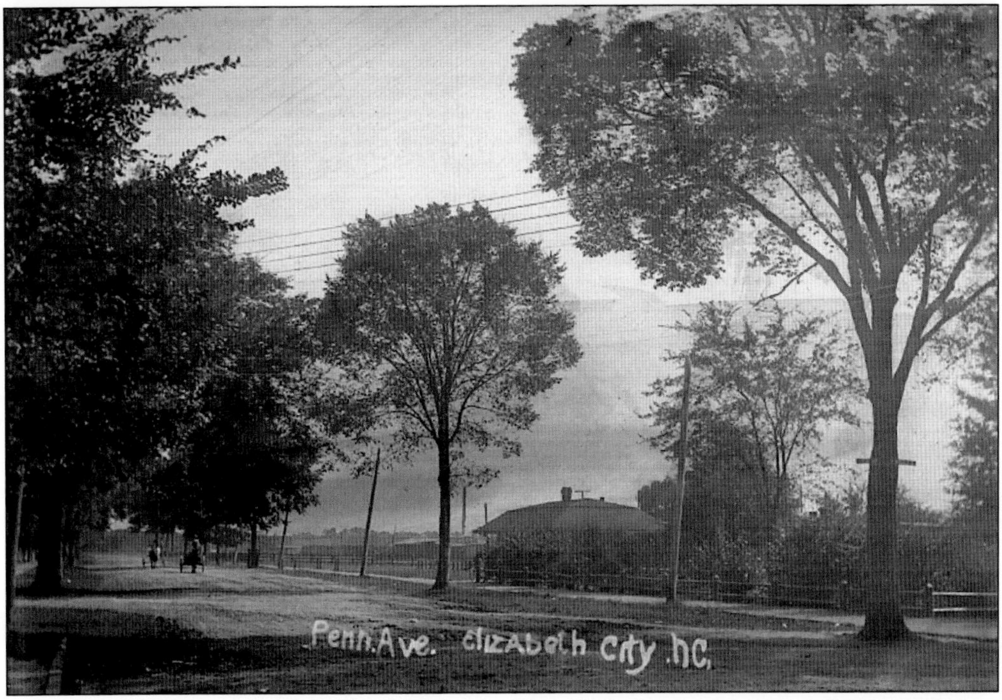

Pennsylvania Avenue (present-day Poindexter Street), shown in these two photos, was once the location for the town's train station.

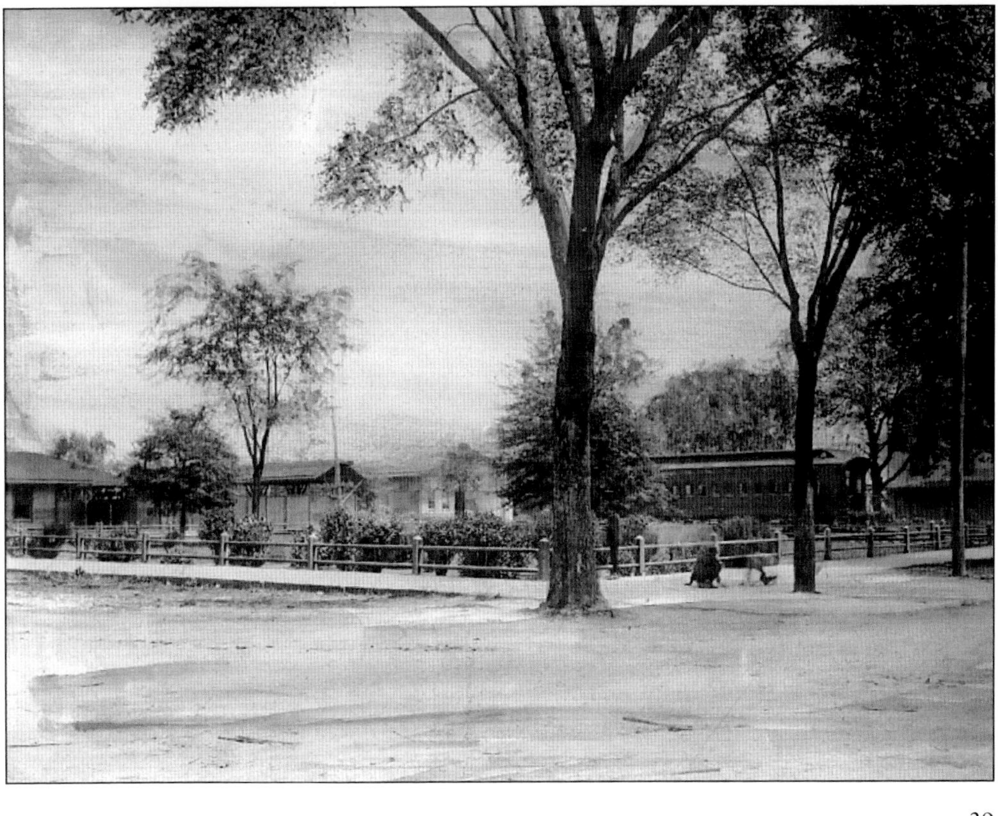

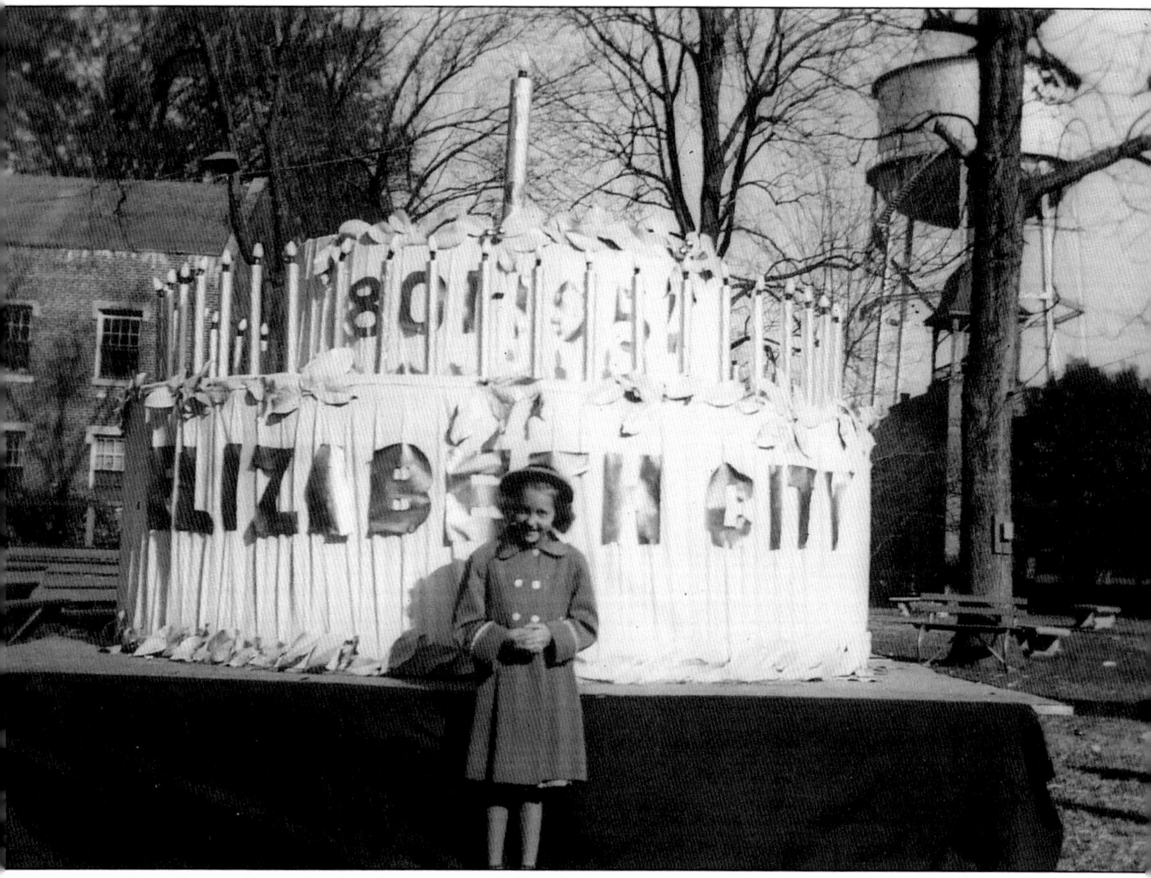

The photo above highlights some of the festivities during Elizabeth City's 150th anniversary celebration in 1951. Marilyn Madrin, age eight, stood in front of a big cake with pink magnolia leaves and pink candles. This year, 2001, is the 200th anniversary of Elizabeth City.

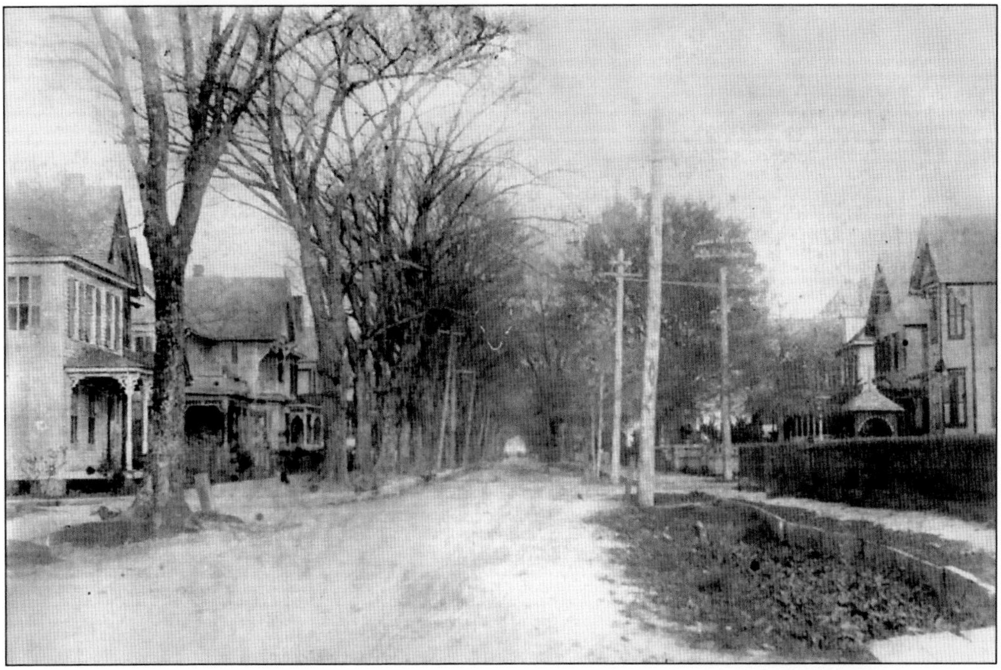

The photo provides a scene of East Burgess Street, a residential area. (Courtesy of Museum of the Albemarle.)

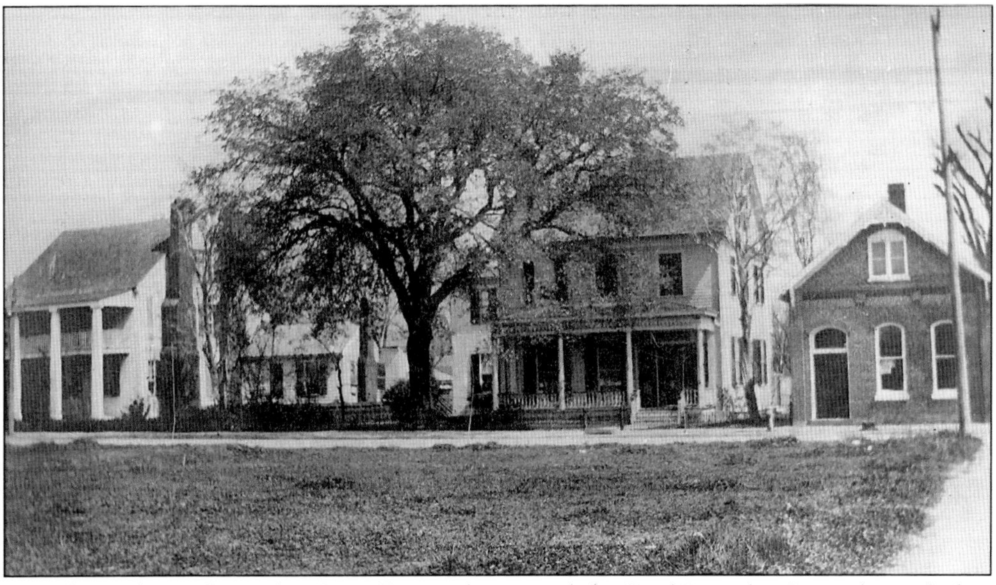

The photo above shows the Grice-Fearing house and the Pool-Lumsden-Peters house before the Methodist Church was built on the corner of Road and Church Streets. Dr. Peter's office is on the corner. Notice the porch on the Pool-Lumsden-Peters house that was added during the Victorian period. (Courtesy of Museum of the Albemarle.)

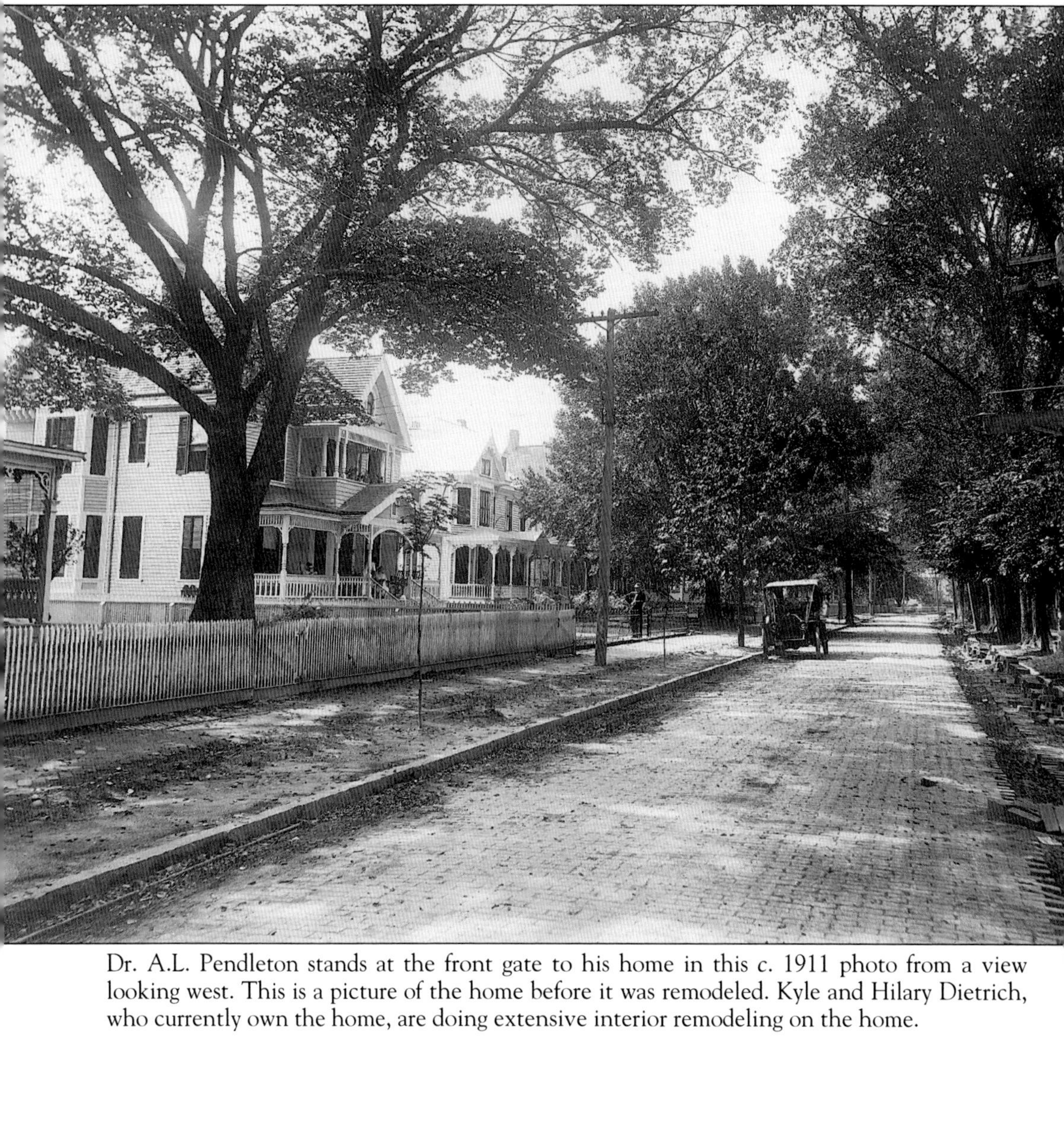

Dr. A.L. Pendleton stands at the front gate to his home in this *c.* 1911 photo from a view looking west. This is a picture of the home before it was remodeled. Kyle and Hilary Dietrich, who currently own the home, are doing extensive interior remodeling on the home.

Two

PEOPLE

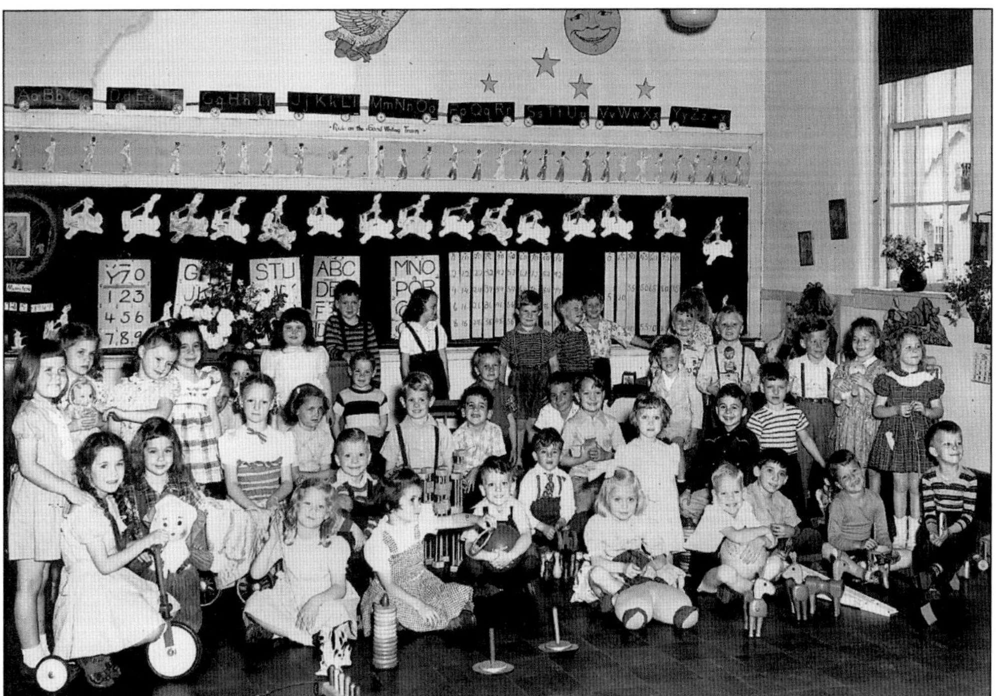

This 1949 photo shows the four- and five-year-old children that were in Sister Mary Martin's kindergarten class at the Catholic school on Main Street.

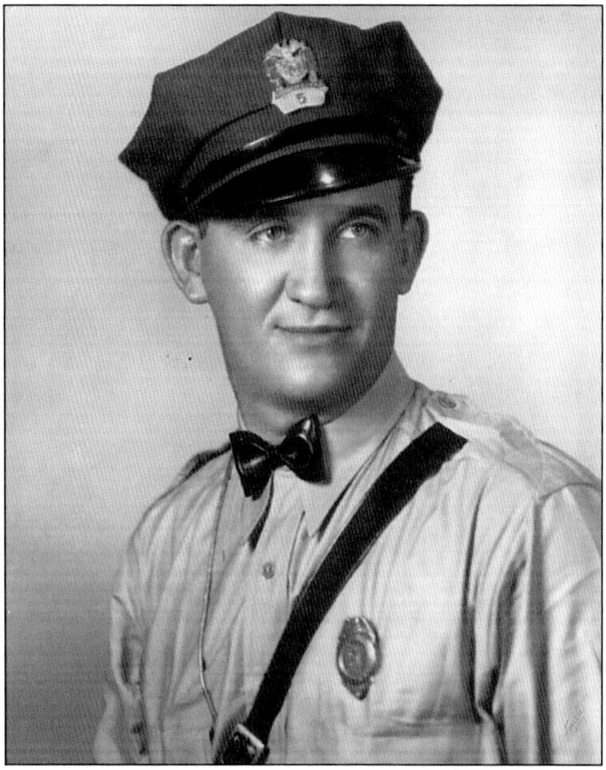

R.C. Madrin served as the chief of police in Elizabeth City in the 1940s.

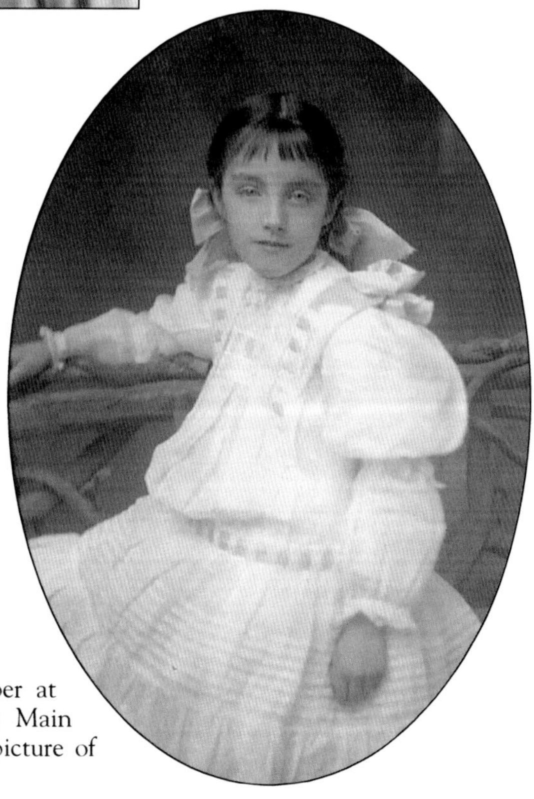

Evelyn "Skinny" Jones was the bookkeeper at Overman and Stevenson Drug Store on Main Street. She was born in 1896. This is a picture of Skinny at age 9 or 10.

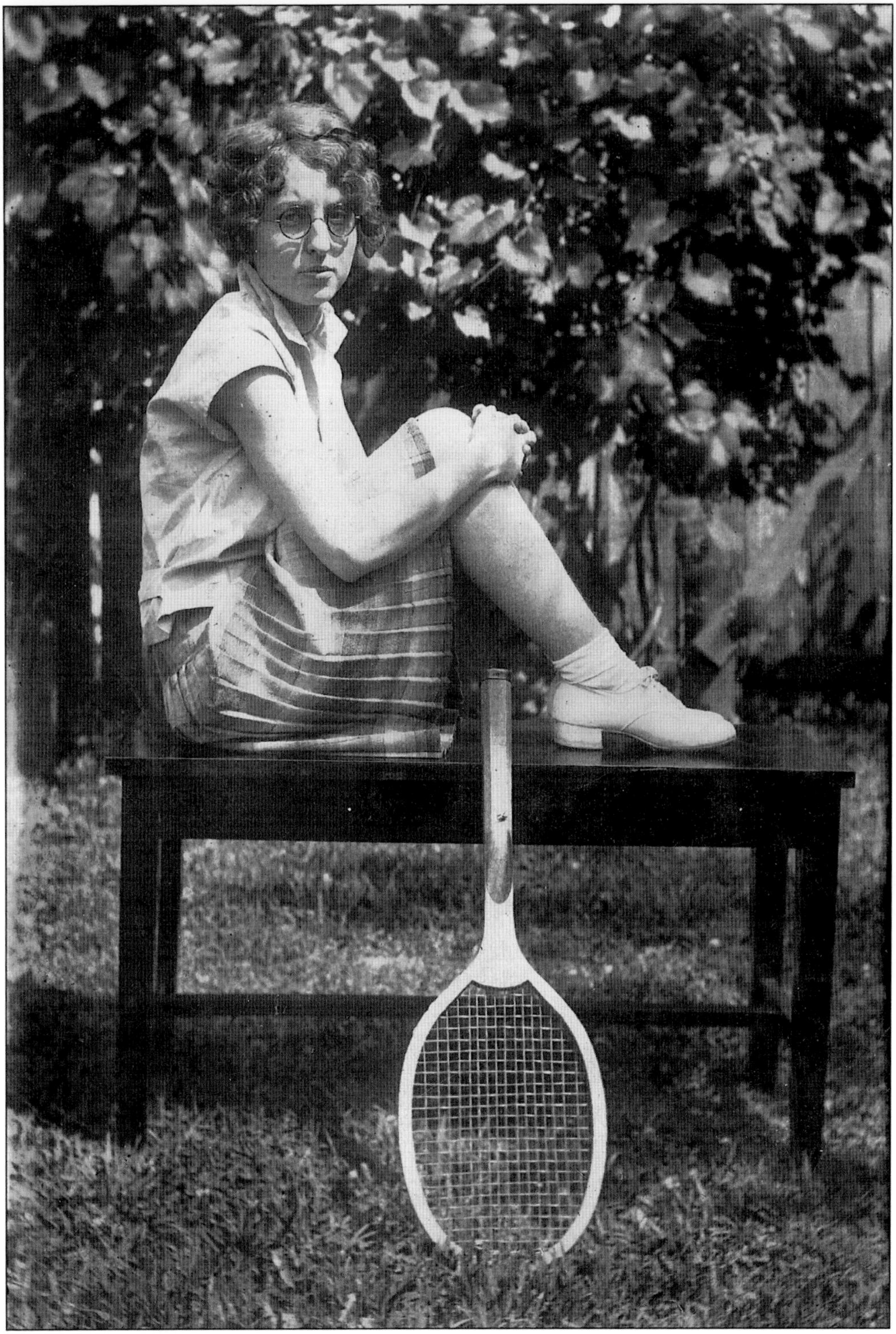

Hazel Jennings (Bunch, Hartzog) enjoyed playing tennis during the summer of 1928. She was the mother of Patsy Houtz.

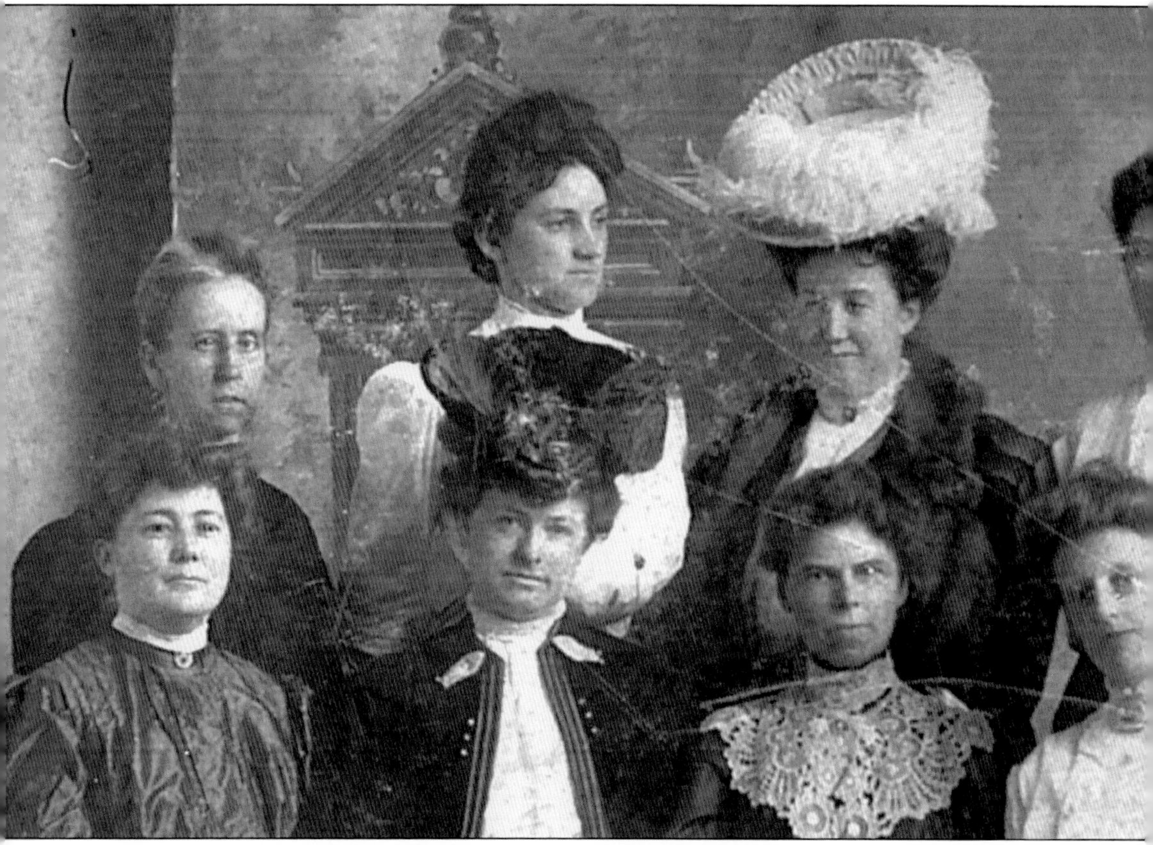

The members of the Fortnightly Club, a women's group in Elizabeth City, are pictured in elegant

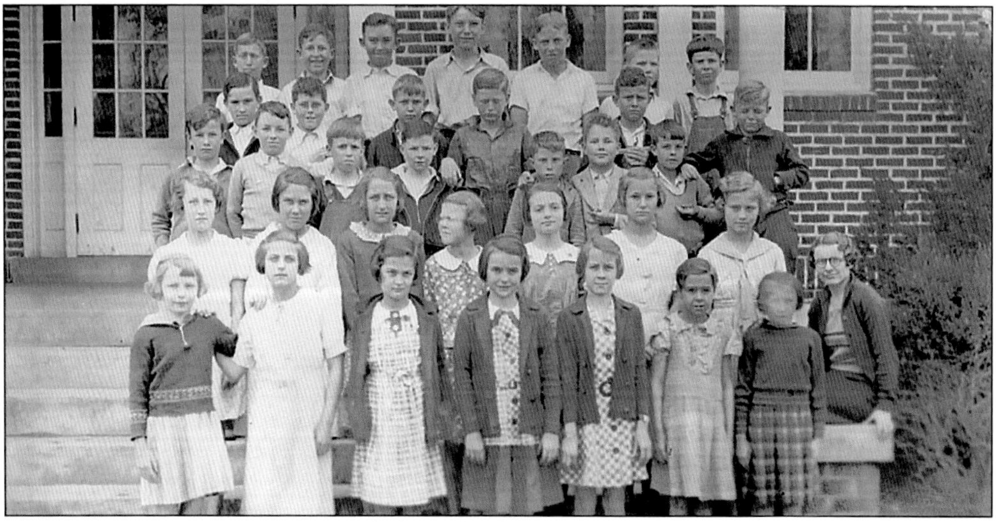

This photo shows the 1934–1935 fifth-grade class at Central School. It was built in 1926 as a consolidated school and was later demolished. Central Elementary School was built on the site along US 17 South. Students on the front row, from left to right, are Pauline Davis, Grace Brothers, Anne Pritchard, Janice Pritchard, unidentified, Virginia Pritchard, Bernice Sample, and teacher Eva Sawyer.

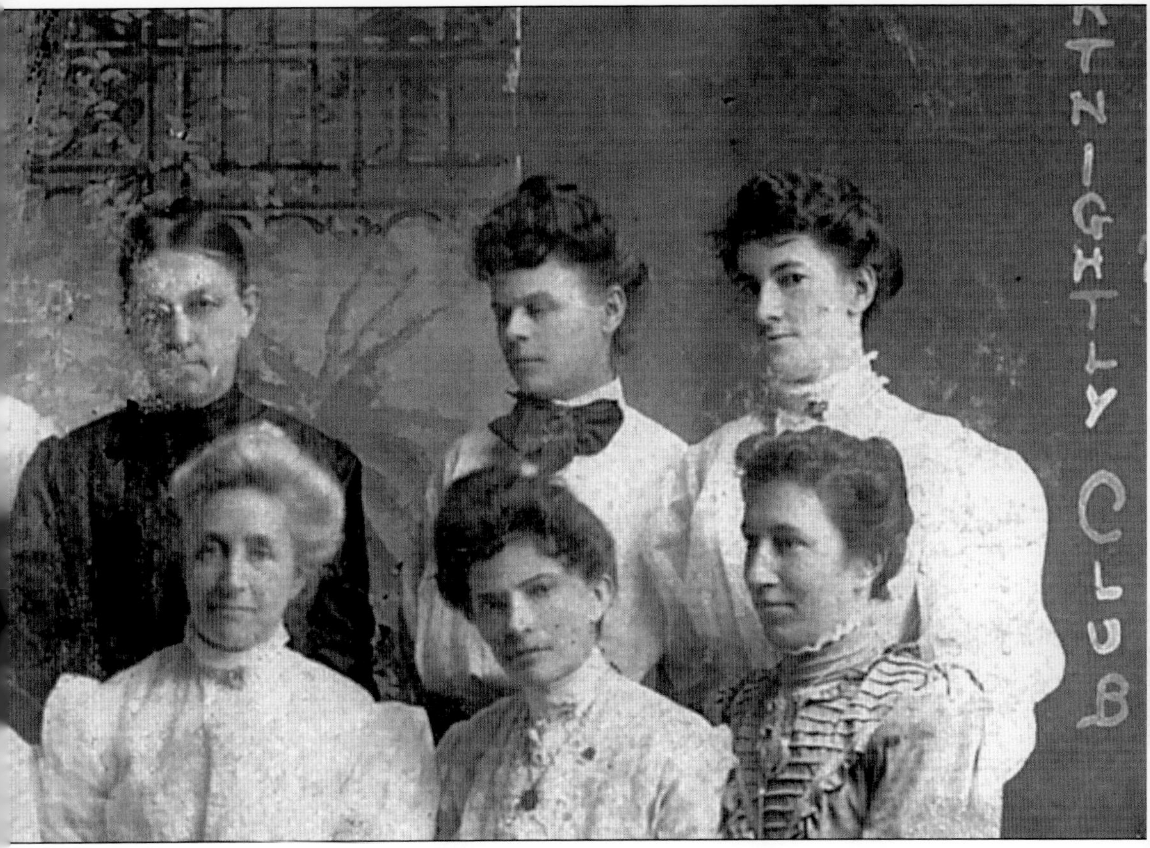

attire in a photo taken on April 20, 1906.

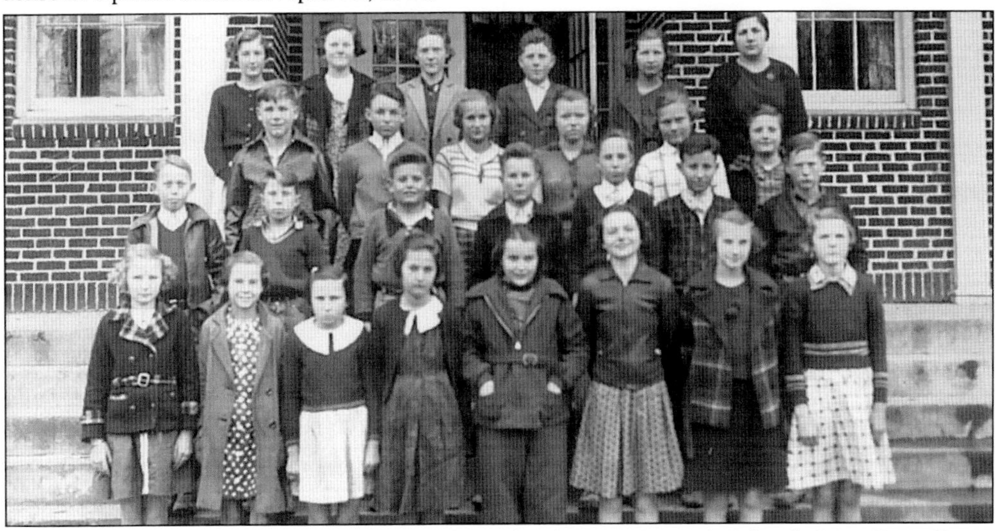

This photo shows the 1936–1937 seventh-grade class at Central School. Mrs. Perri Davis was the teacher. On the front row, from left to right, are Pauline Davis, Virginia Pritchard, Bernice Sample, Anne Pritchard, Janice Pritchard, Jean Walston, Edith Jennings, and Mary Louise Onley. The second row includes Melvin Sanders, Ducky Morgan, Dickie Poulos, Calvin Chapel, and Wesley Culipher.

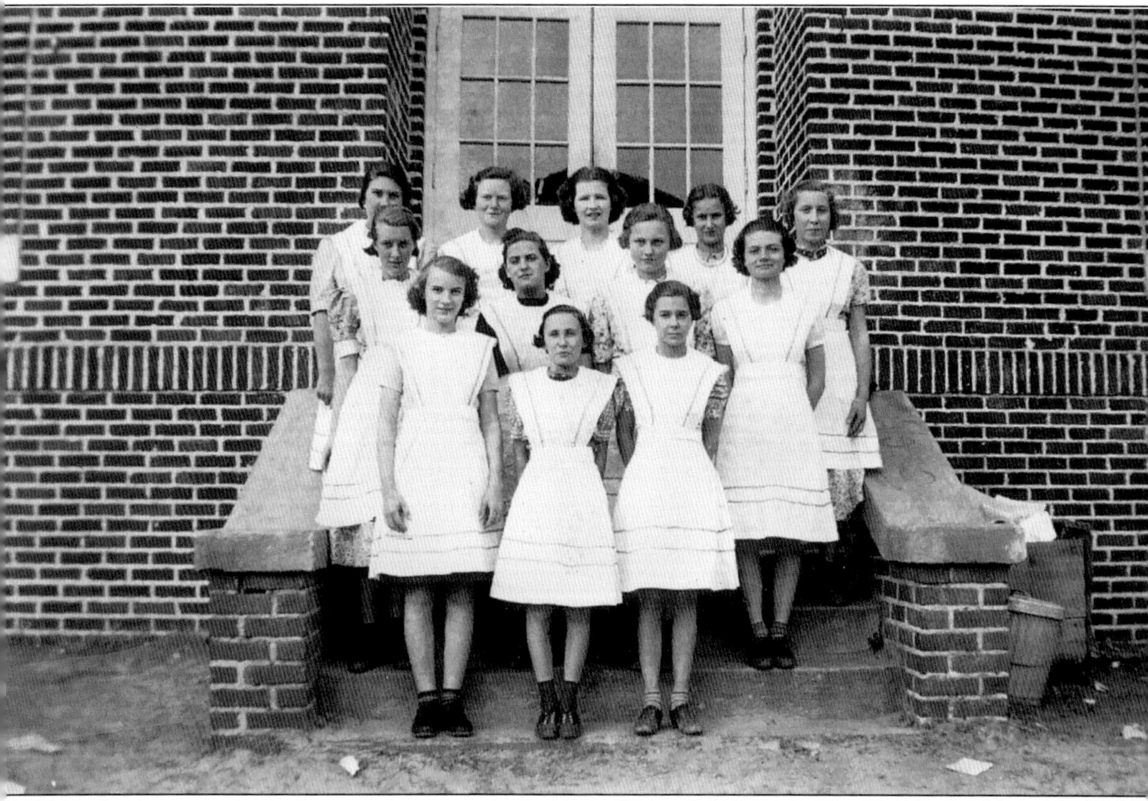

This picture was taken during 1937–1938 school year at Central High School. From left to right are (front row) Edith Jennings, Bernice Sample, and Virginia Pritchard; (middle row) Evangeline Pettijohn, Grace Brothers, Inez White, and Jean Walston; (back row) Bessie Mae Pike, Maude Pritchard, Margaret Pearl Smithson, Dorothy Williams, and Margaret Key.

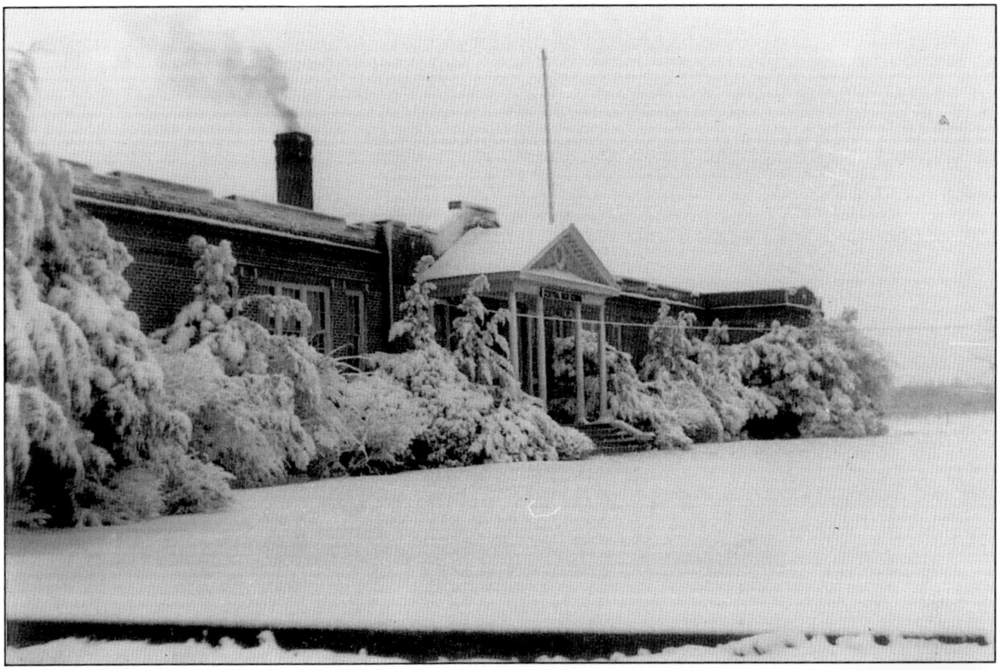

A snowstorm hit Elizabeth City on February 28, 1941. The photo shows how the storm affected Central High School.

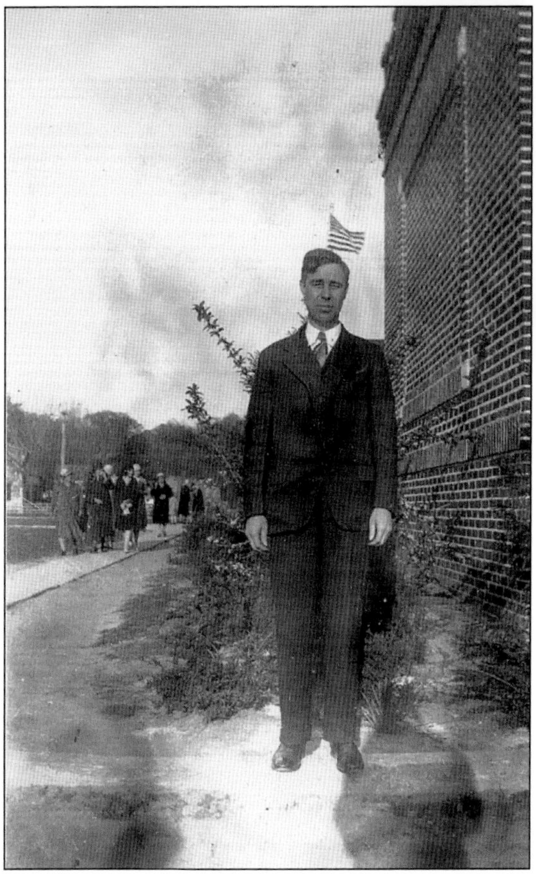

Mr. Ralph Holmes was the principal of Central High School from its opening in the 1920s to the late 1940s. He was a much-beloved man. He started his career as a teacher at Elizabeth City High School.

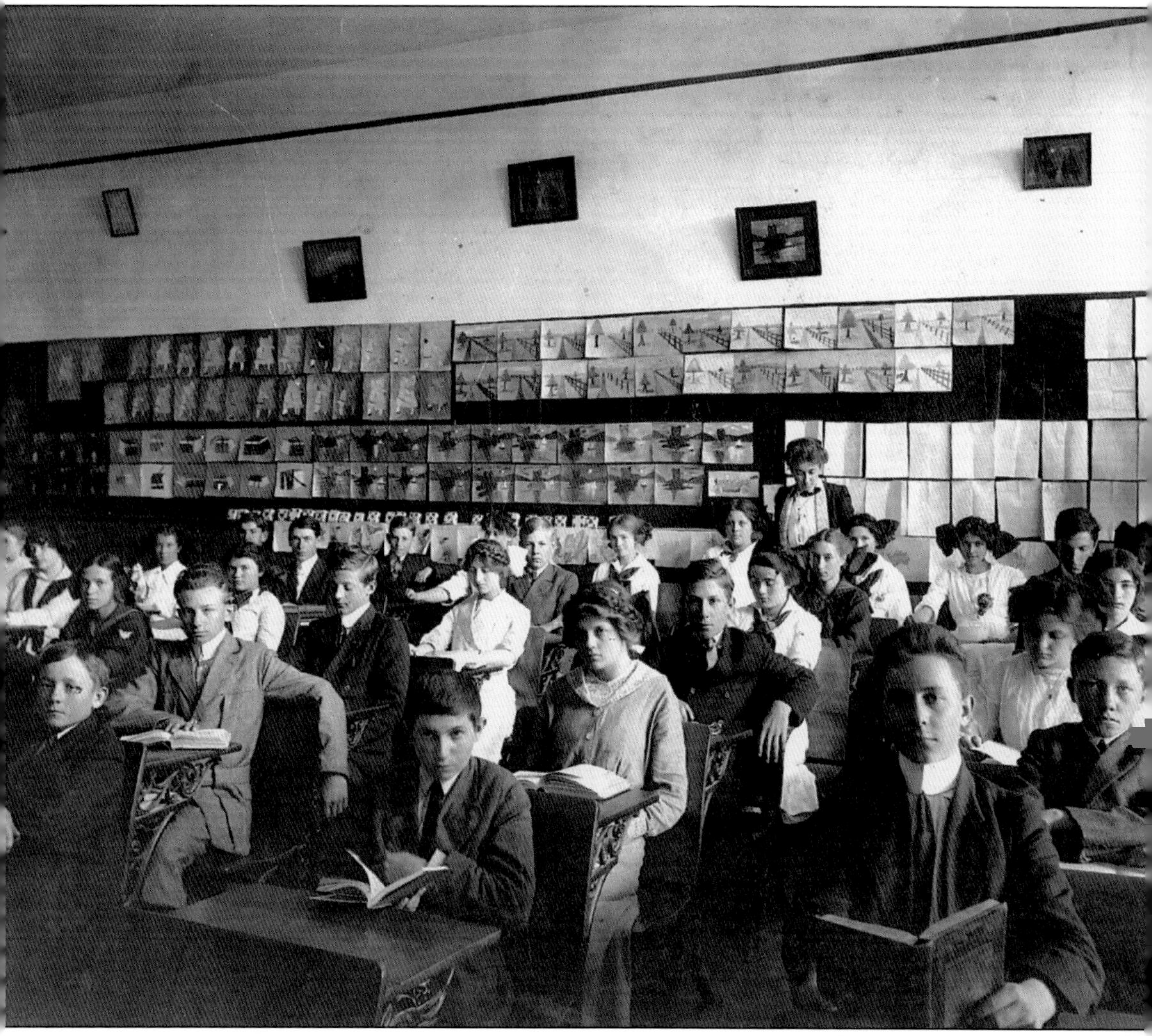

Ms. Celia Winslow taught seventh grade during the 1912–1913 school term at S.L. Sheep School. The fourth student from the left in the second row is Winnie Marie Wood. The third student from the left in the fourth row is Mattie Brite. Samuel Lloyd Sheep School operated from 1856 to 1928.

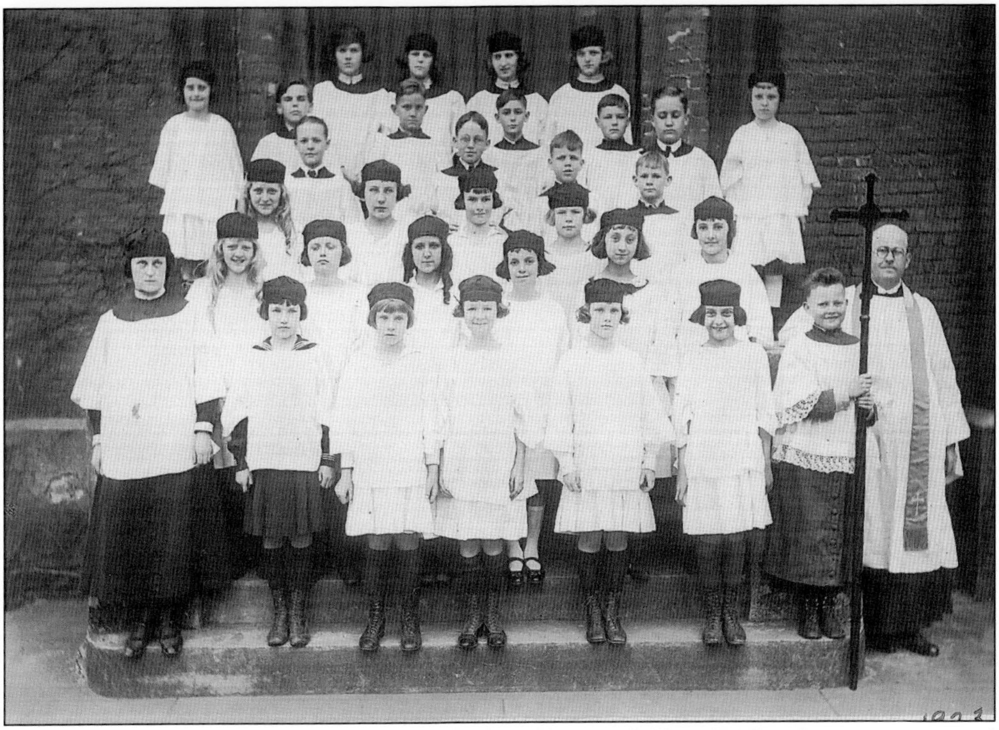

These pictures showcase the junior choir of Christ Episcopal Church. The choir was composed of the church members' children. The top photo shows the choir in 1923; the bottom shows the choir in 1925.

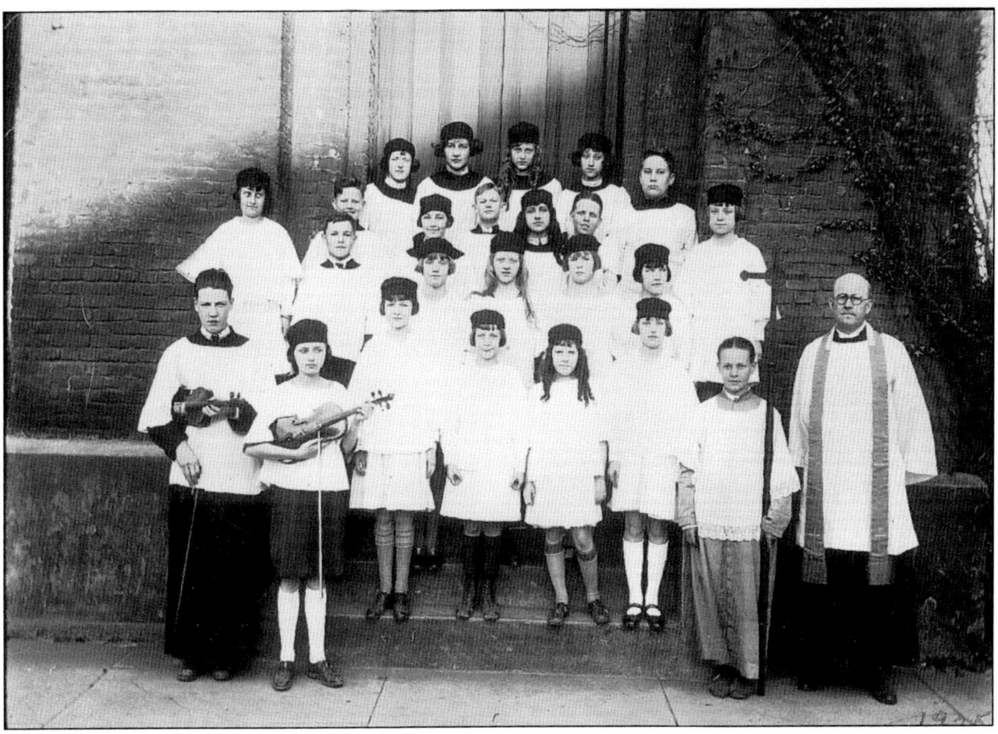

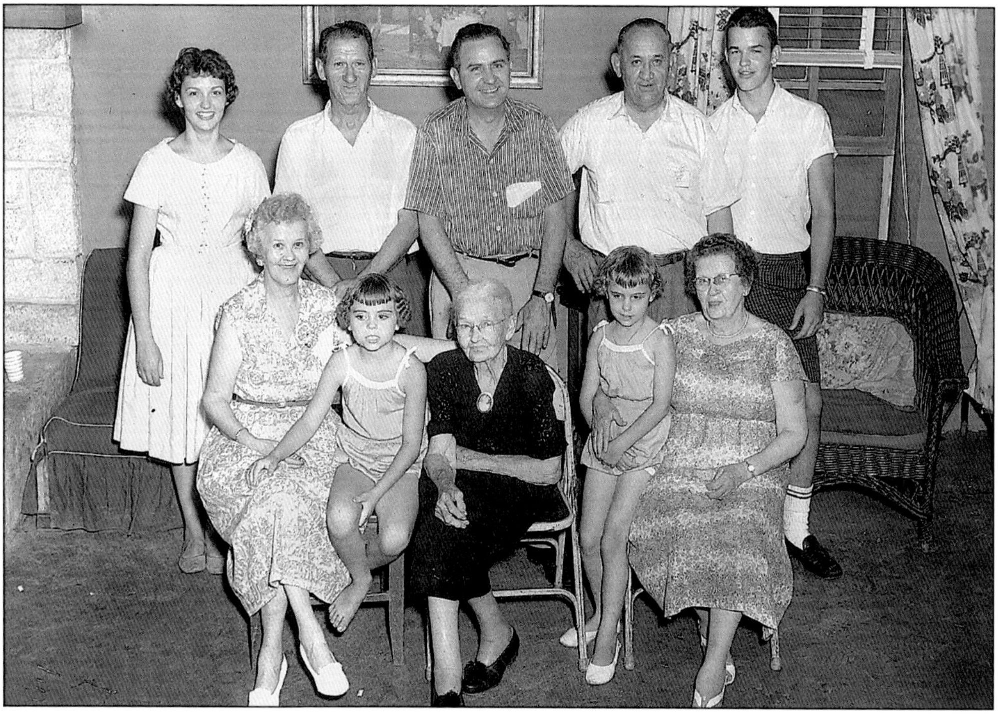

In 1961, the Madrin Family held a reunion. From left to right are the following: (front row) Francis Madrin Gardener, unidentified, Alice Bailey Madrin, unidentified, and Naomi Madrin Bush; (back row) Marilyn Madrin, Lawrence Madrin, Bobby Madrin, R.C. Madrin, and R.C. Madrin Jr.

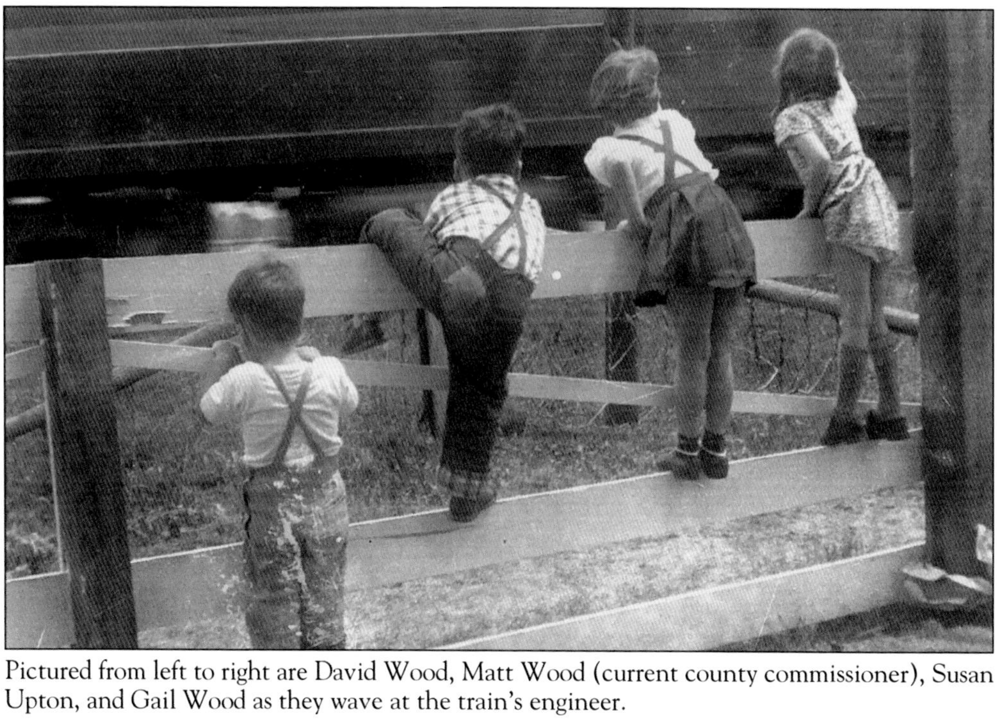

Pictured from left to right are David Wood, Matt Wood (current county commissioner), Susan Upton, and Gail Wood as they wave at the train's engineer.

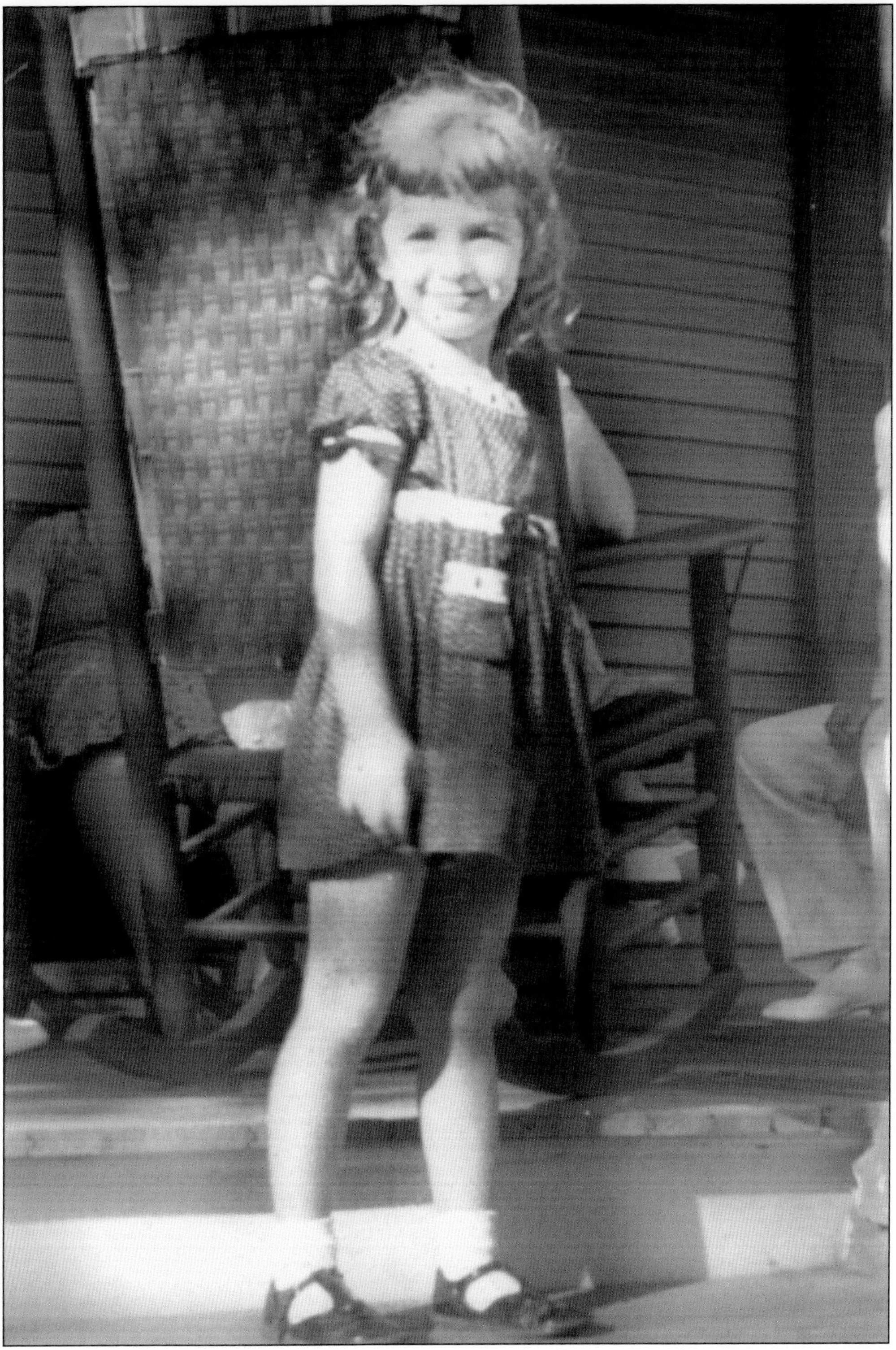
Patsy Bunch Houtz poses for a picture on the back porch of her parents' home in 1940.

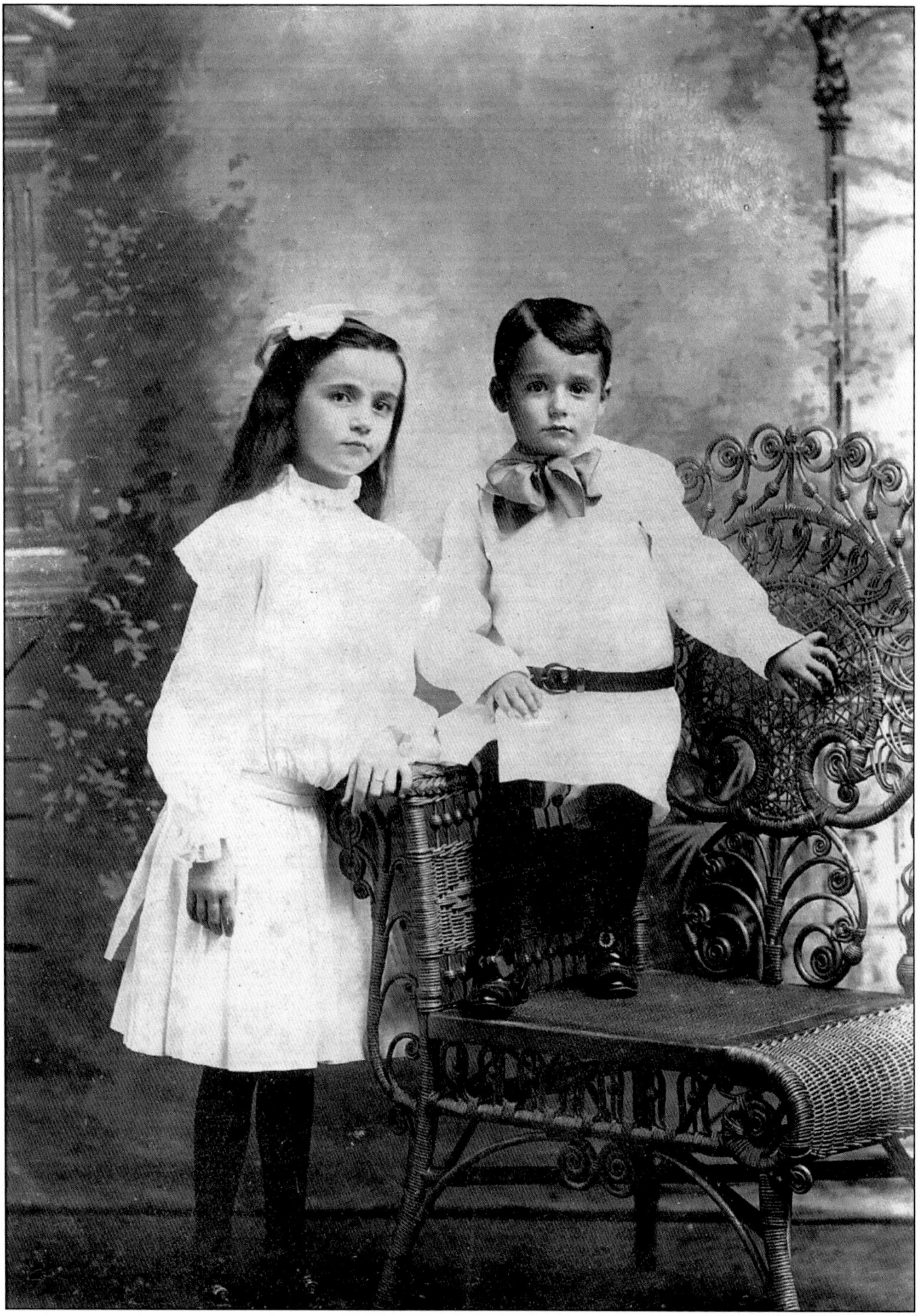

William Zoeller took this photo of Winnie Wood (Walston), who was born October 4, 1896, and Guy Wood, who was born October 8, 1900. They were the children of Margaret Ann and Henry Clay Wood. Zoeller was a well-known Elizabeth City photographer and lived at 303 West Church Street.

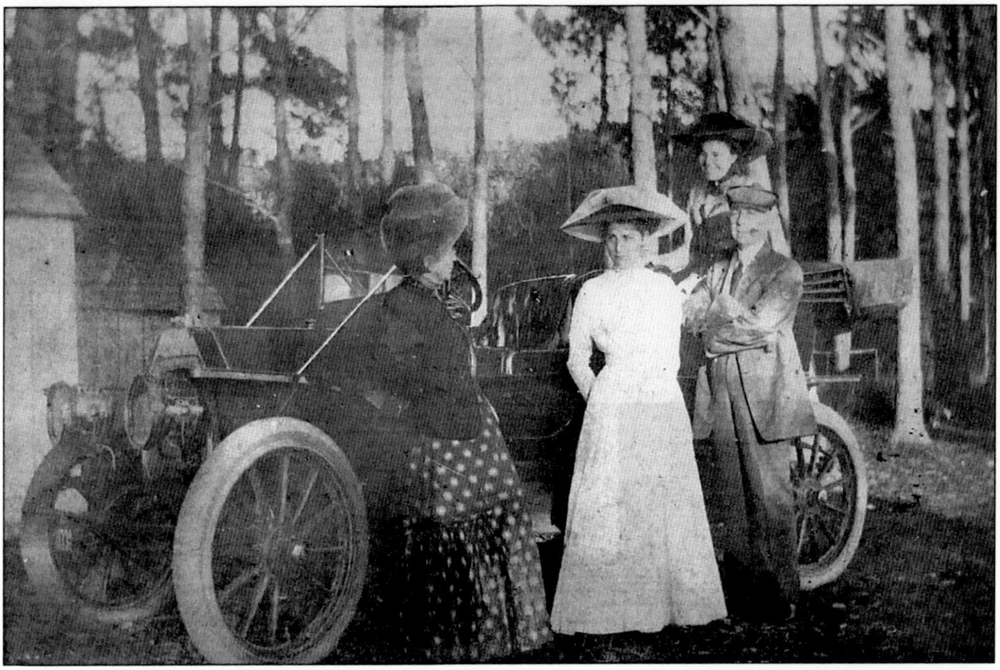

Dr. A.L. Pendleton owned the first car in Elizabeth City. In this 1910 photo from left to right are Mrs. Mollie Fearing Evans, Hazel Evans (Mrs. A. L. Pendleton), Gertrude Evans (Mrs. E.P. Fearing), and Dr. A.L. Pendleton.

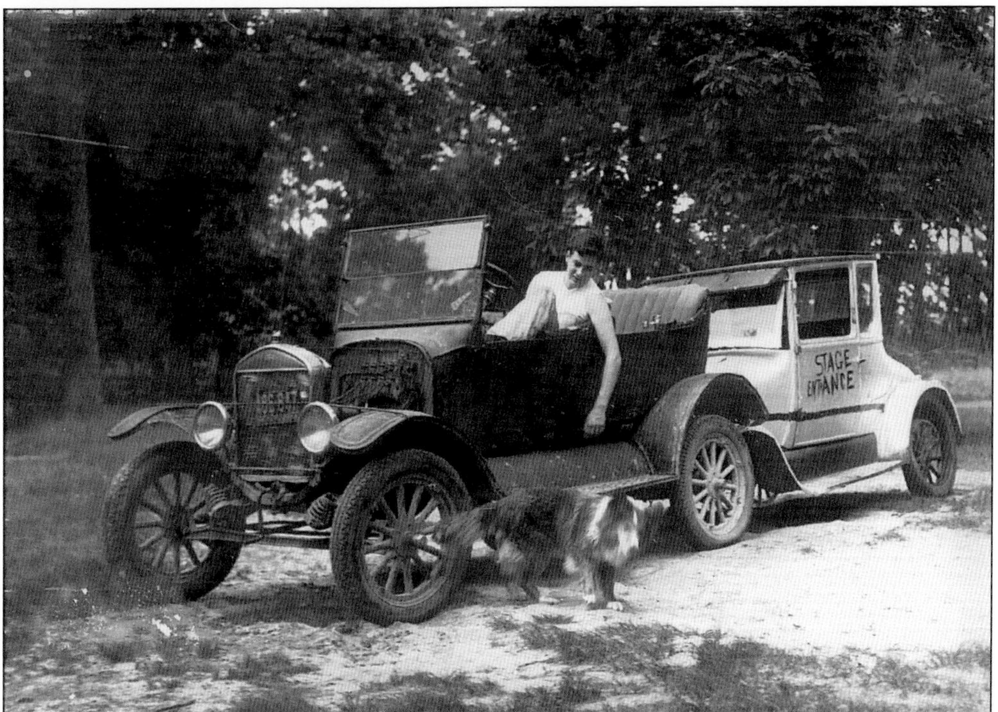

Frank Hollowell is shown here with his dog Sandy and the car he purchased for a mere $5. After he bought many parts for the car, it was not long before he had it running.

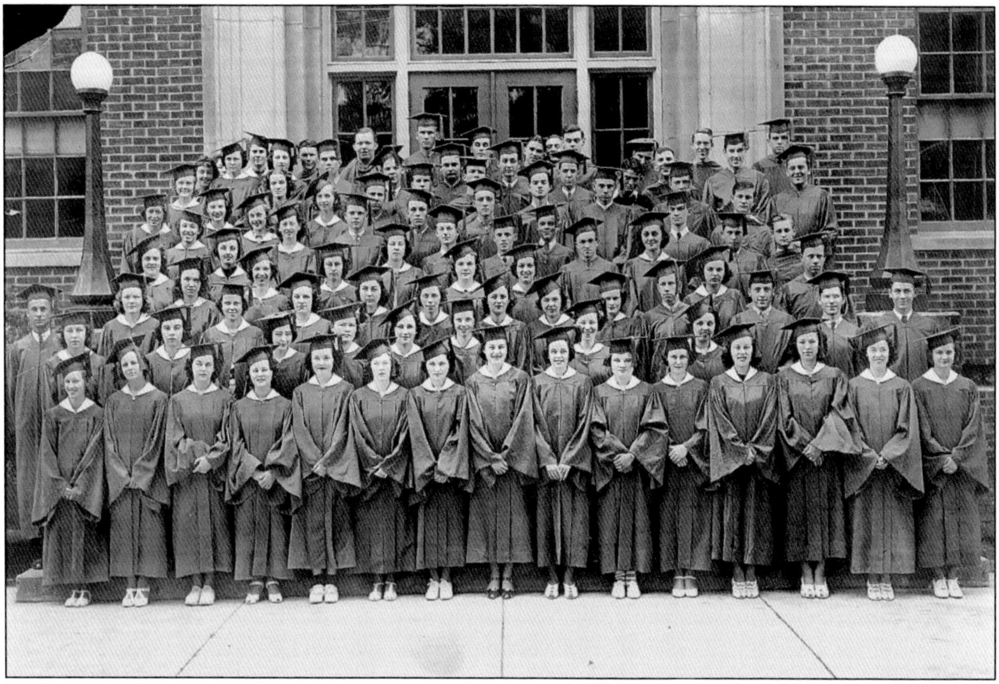

This 1938 picture showcases the graduating class of Elizabeth City High School, which is now Elizabeth City Middle School. Frisby's Studio of Elizabeth City captured the moment.

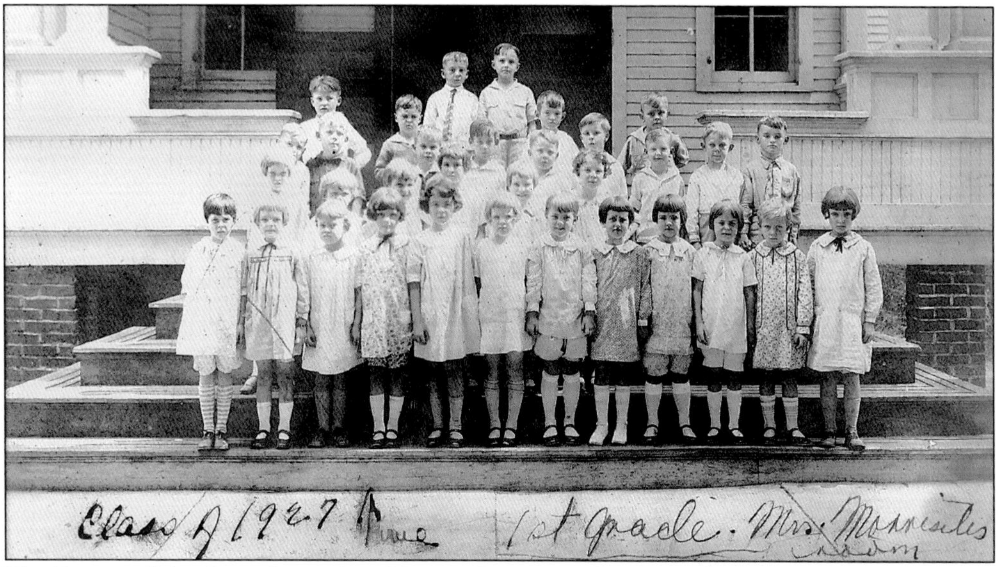

The Primary School was located on Harney Street. In this 1927 photo of the first grade class are the following: (first row) Margarite Ward, Ida Bland Overman, Bedie Palmer, Florence Woodley, Elizabeth Barnes, Jeanne Armstrong, Helen Kendrick, Elizabeth Hughes, Ruby Pritchard, Billie Seymore, Jan Tuttle, and Margaret ?; (second row) Madeline Spruill, Susie Umphlett, unidentified, Hazel Richly, Kathleen Shannonhouse, and Mary Whitfield; (third row) Phil Bauer, Almond Spence, Raleigh Griffin, Billy Sawyer, Thomas Markam, Fletcher Bailey, LaSalle Johnson, and Murphy Phelps; (fifth row) Don Campen, Glover Grice, Allen Taylor, and William Jackson; (sixth row) unidentified and C.B. Morrisette.

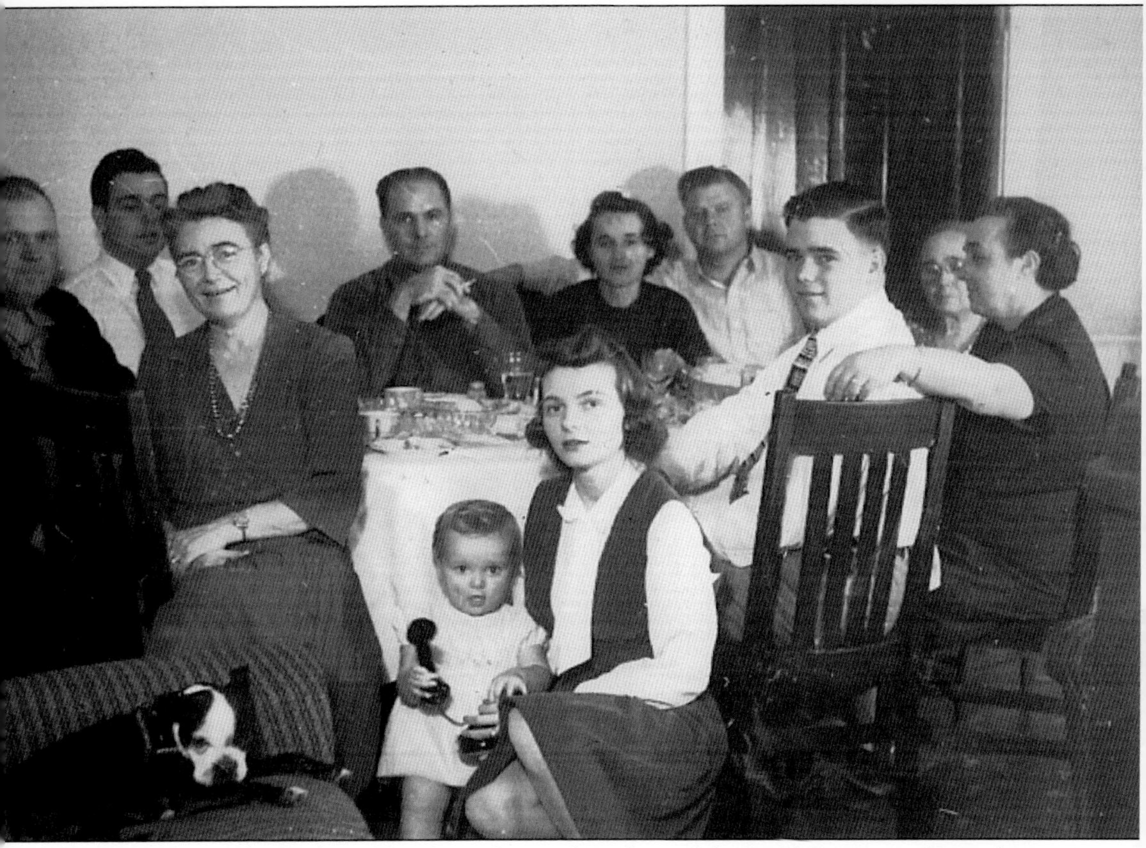

This photo shows the Walston Family as they gathered to celebrate Christmas on December 25, 1947. The gathering took place at Grandmother Walston's house, which was located on Pearl Street.

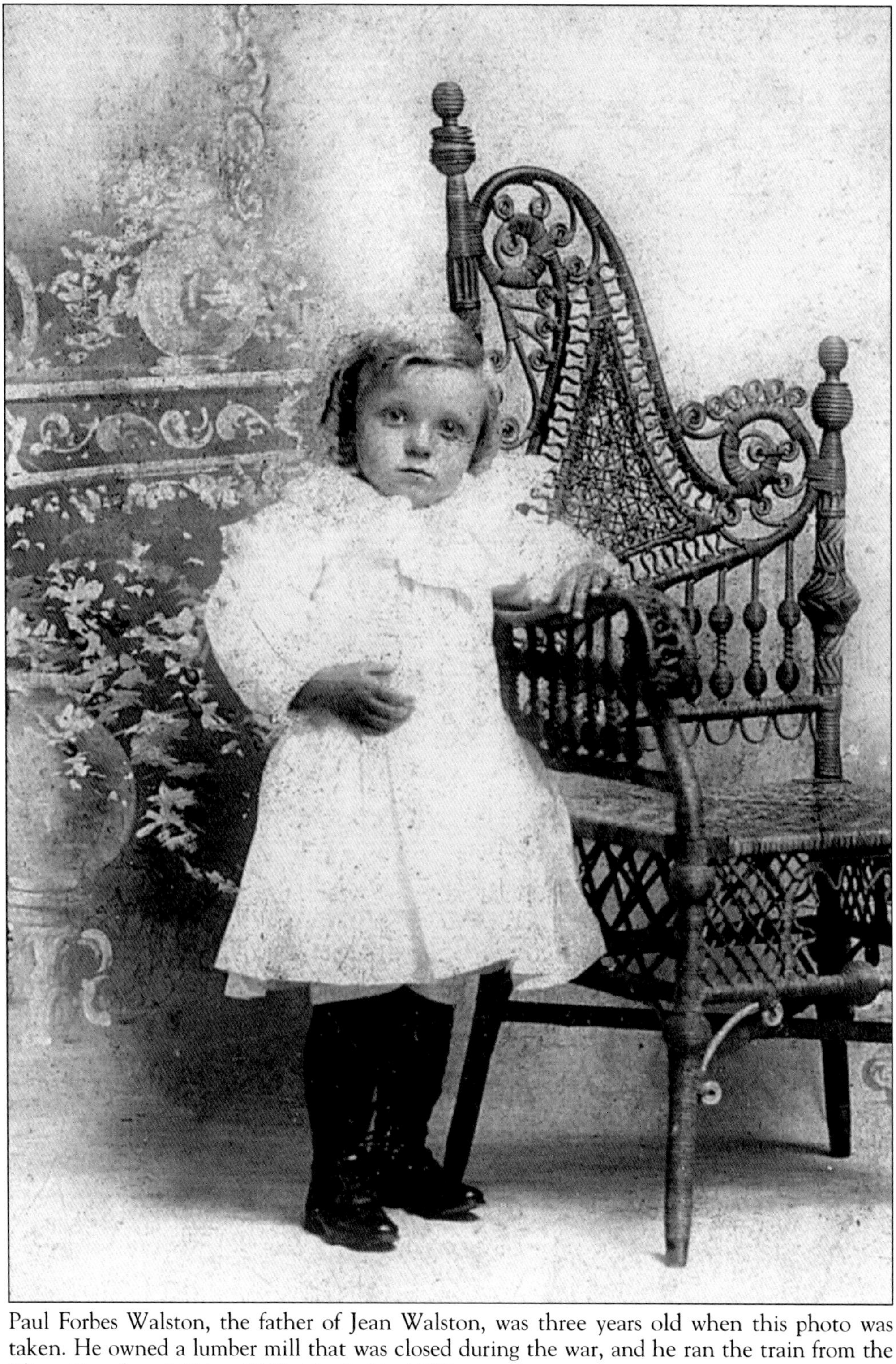

Paul Forbes Walston, the father of Jean Walston, was three years old when this photo was taken. He owned a lumber mill that was closed during the war, and he ran the train from the Blimp Base from 1944 to 1957. He died in 1957.

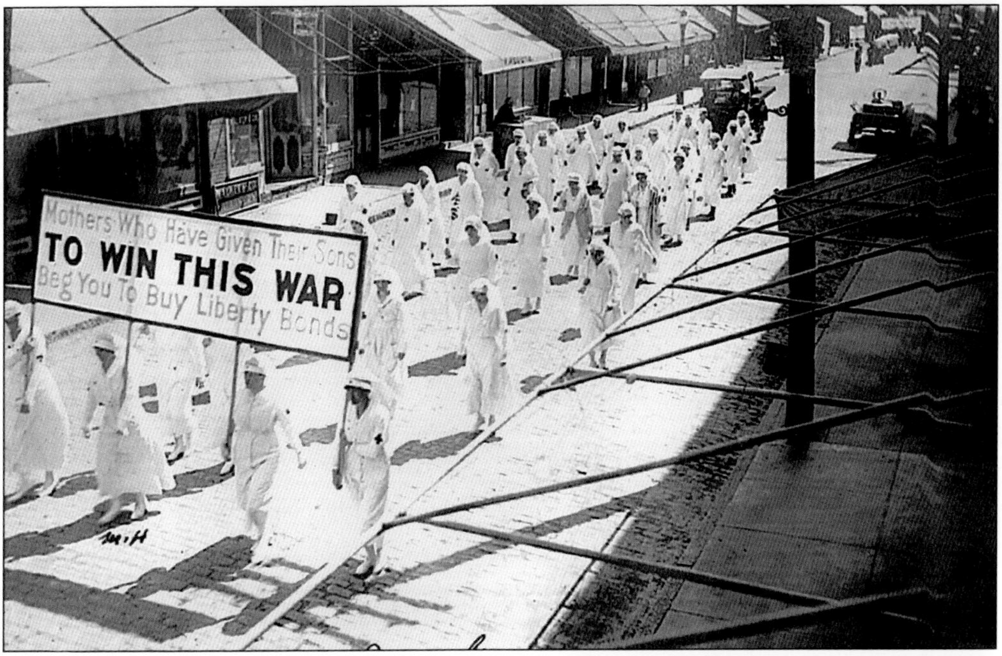

These women "beg you to buy liberty bonds to win the war." The first time women came together to march in the Peace Parade in Elizabeth City was on November 13, 1918. Pictured from left to right on the front row are Mae Worth, Margaret Hollowell, Mary Miller Lamb, and Bessie Stewart.

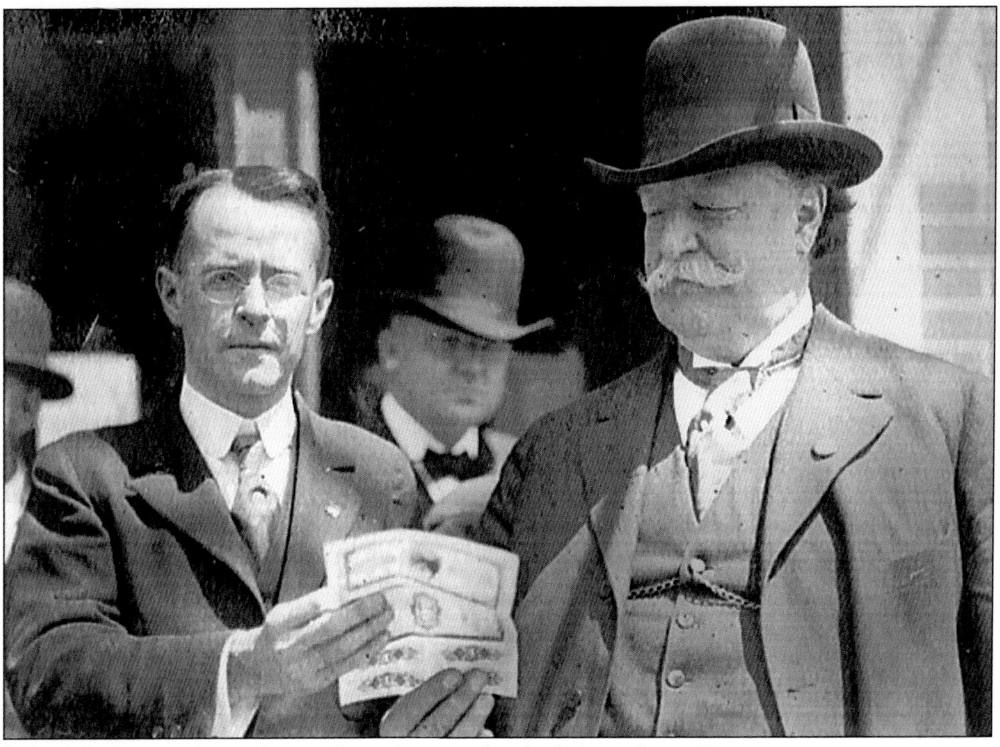

Judge Meekins, right, is shown doing his part for the Liberty Loan Drive.

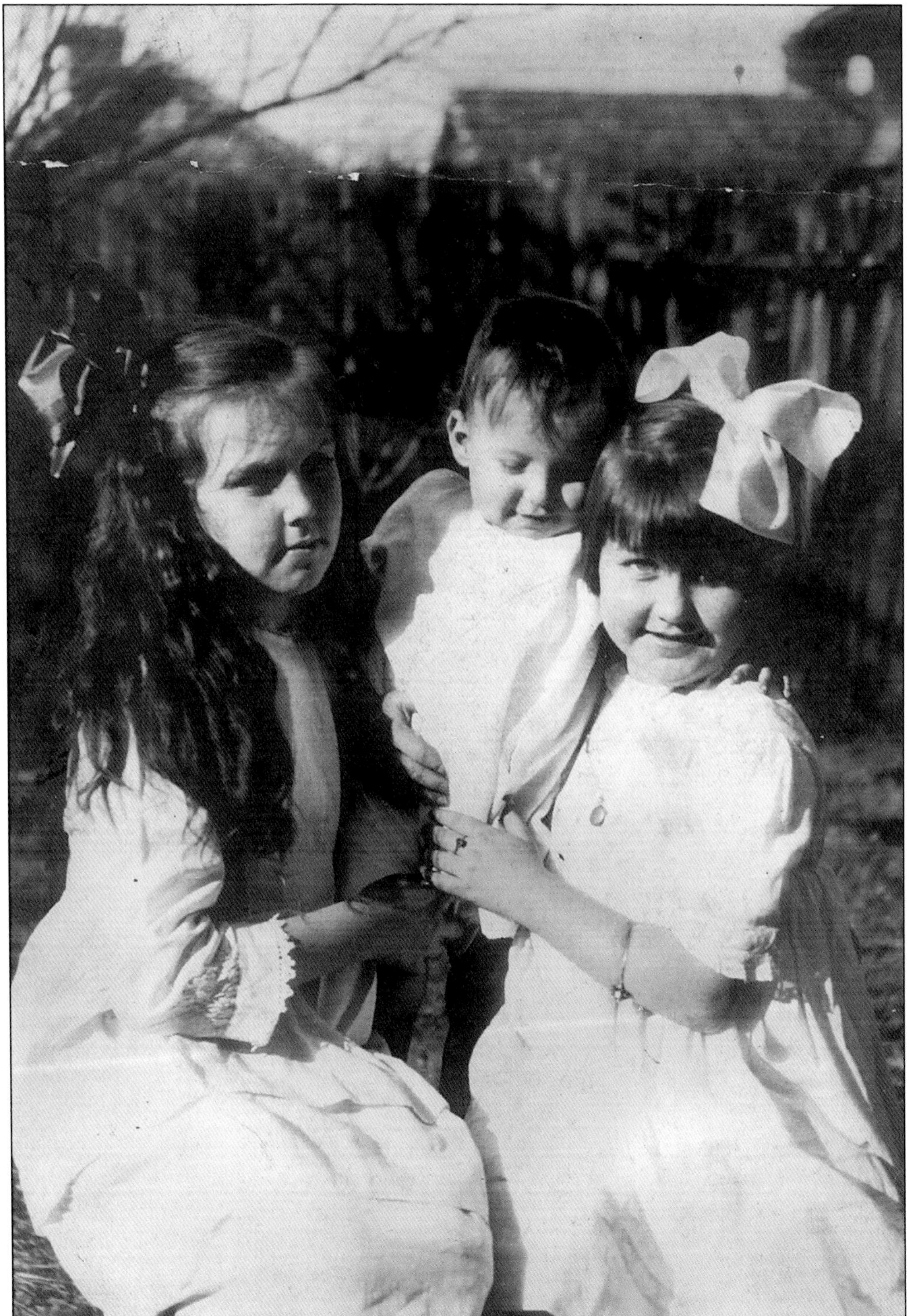

Pictured from left to right are Gwen Jones Madrin, R.C. Jones, and Lois Katherine Jones Peel.

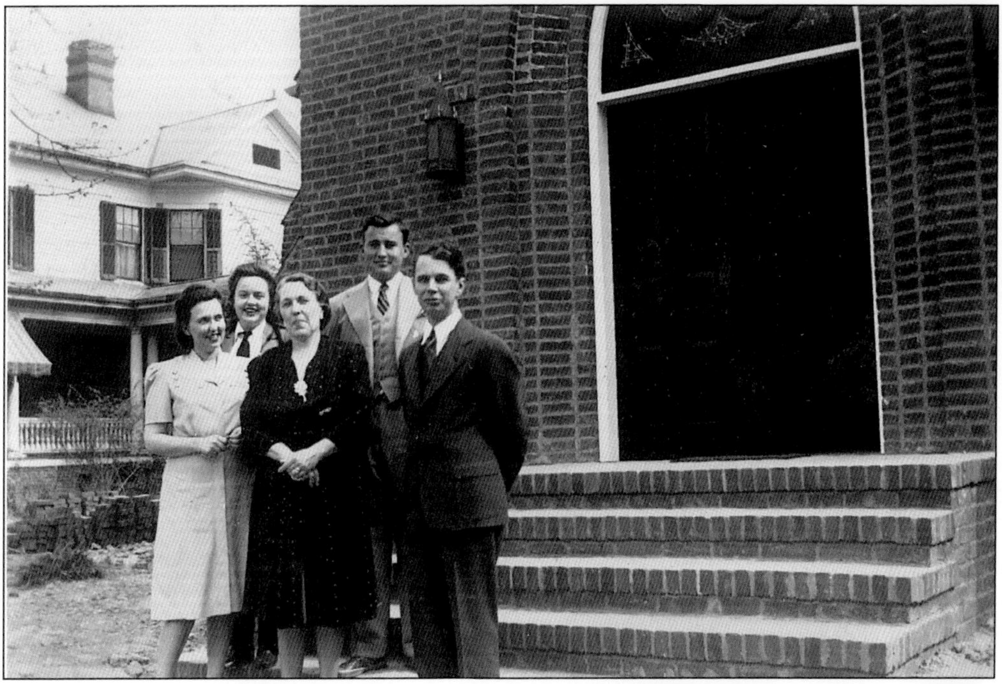

The picture above was taken at Cann Memorial Presbyterian Church on West Main Street. From left to right are the following members: (front row) Gwen Jones Madrin, Josephine Barrett Jones, and unidentified; (back row) Winnie Jones Wood and Everett Barrett Jones.

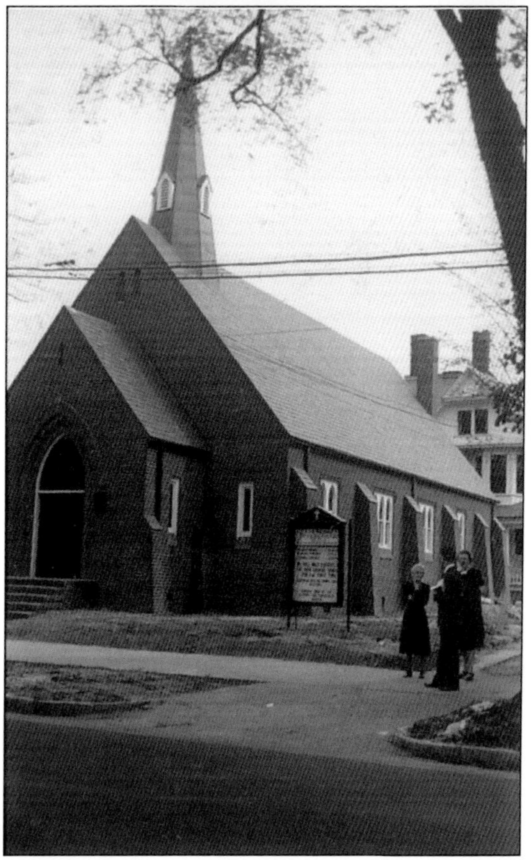

Shown in this image is Cann Memorial Presbyterian Church.

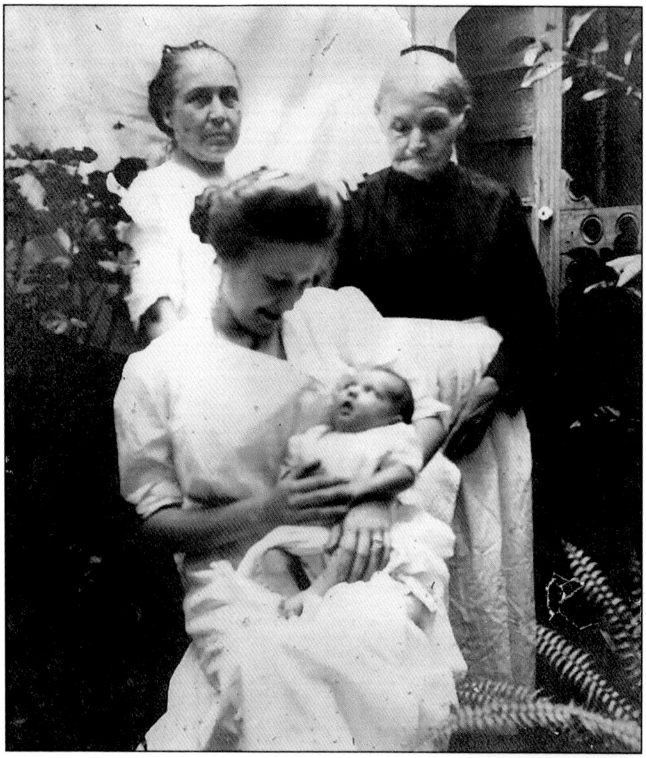

Four generations of the Jones family are shown in this photograph. The baby is Gwendolyn Jones (Madrin); she is held by her mother, Josephine Barrett Jones. In the top left is Grandmother Indiana Barrett and on the right is Great Grandmother Taylor.

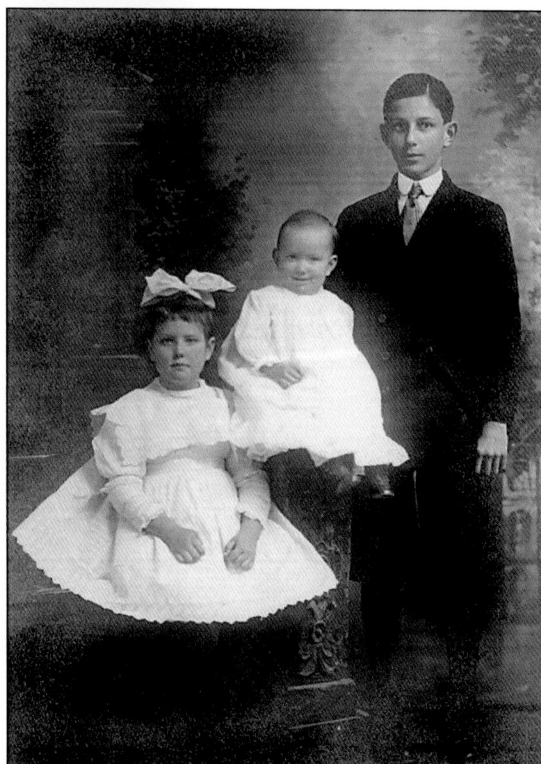

This 1909 picture includes, from left to right, Adelaide Josephine Augusta Dunstan (b. 1903), William Edward Dunstan Jr. (b. 1908), and Edmund Fleetwood Dunstan (b. 1896).

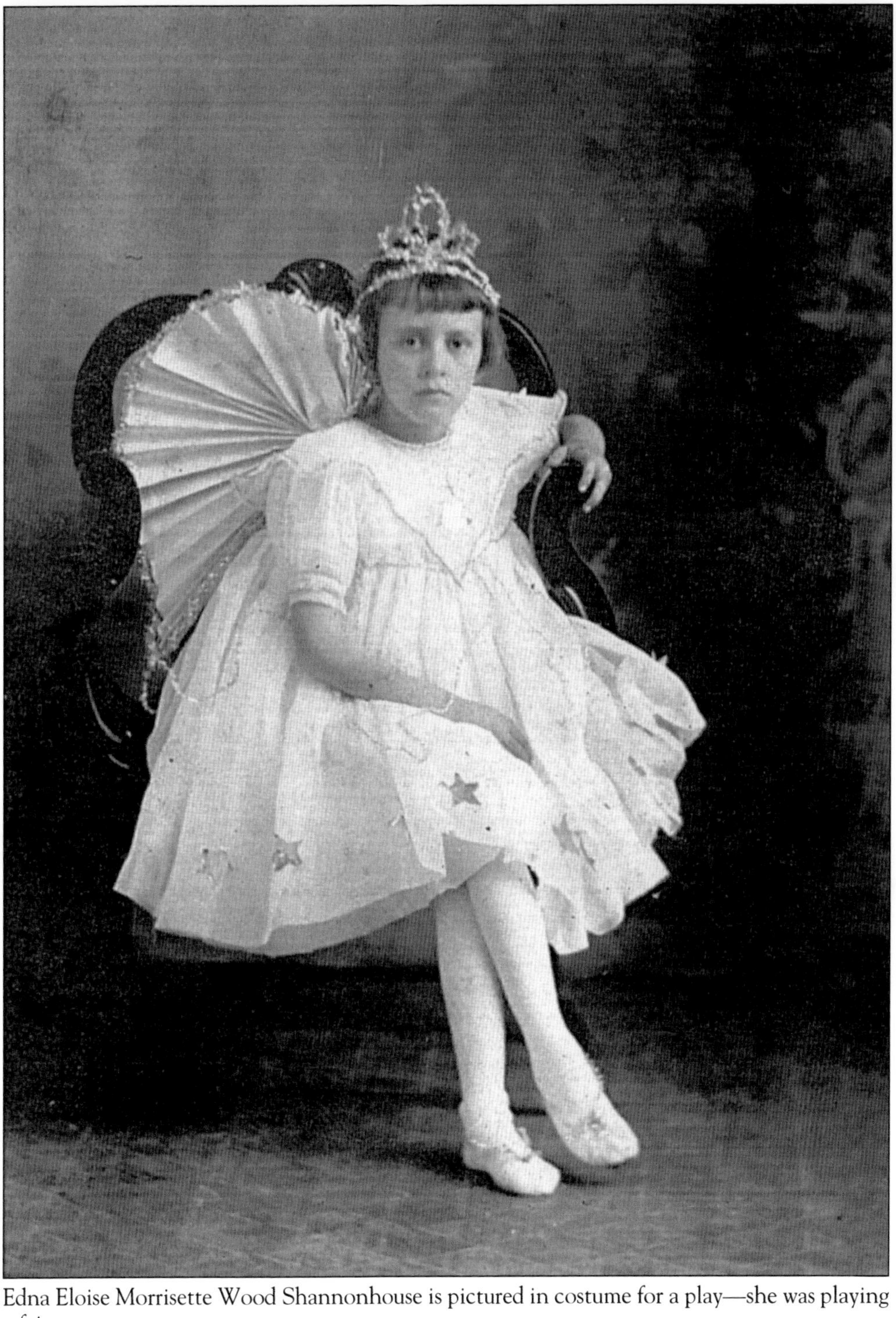

Edna Eloise Morrisette Wood Shannonhouse is pictured in costume for a play—she was playing a fairy.

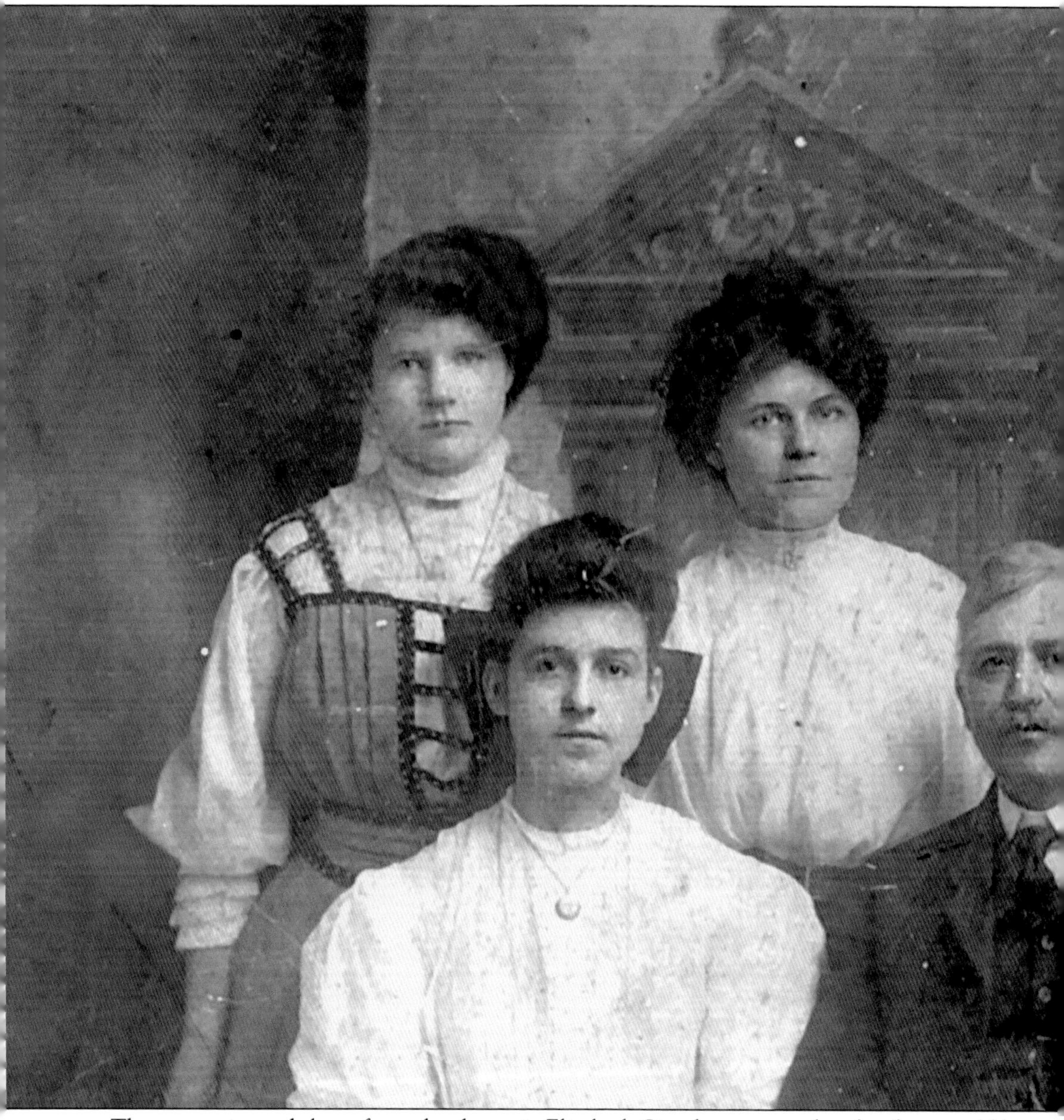

The group pictured above formed a chorus in Elizabeth City; however, only a few faces could be identified. Second from the left is Bertha Martin (Newby); her father designed and built City

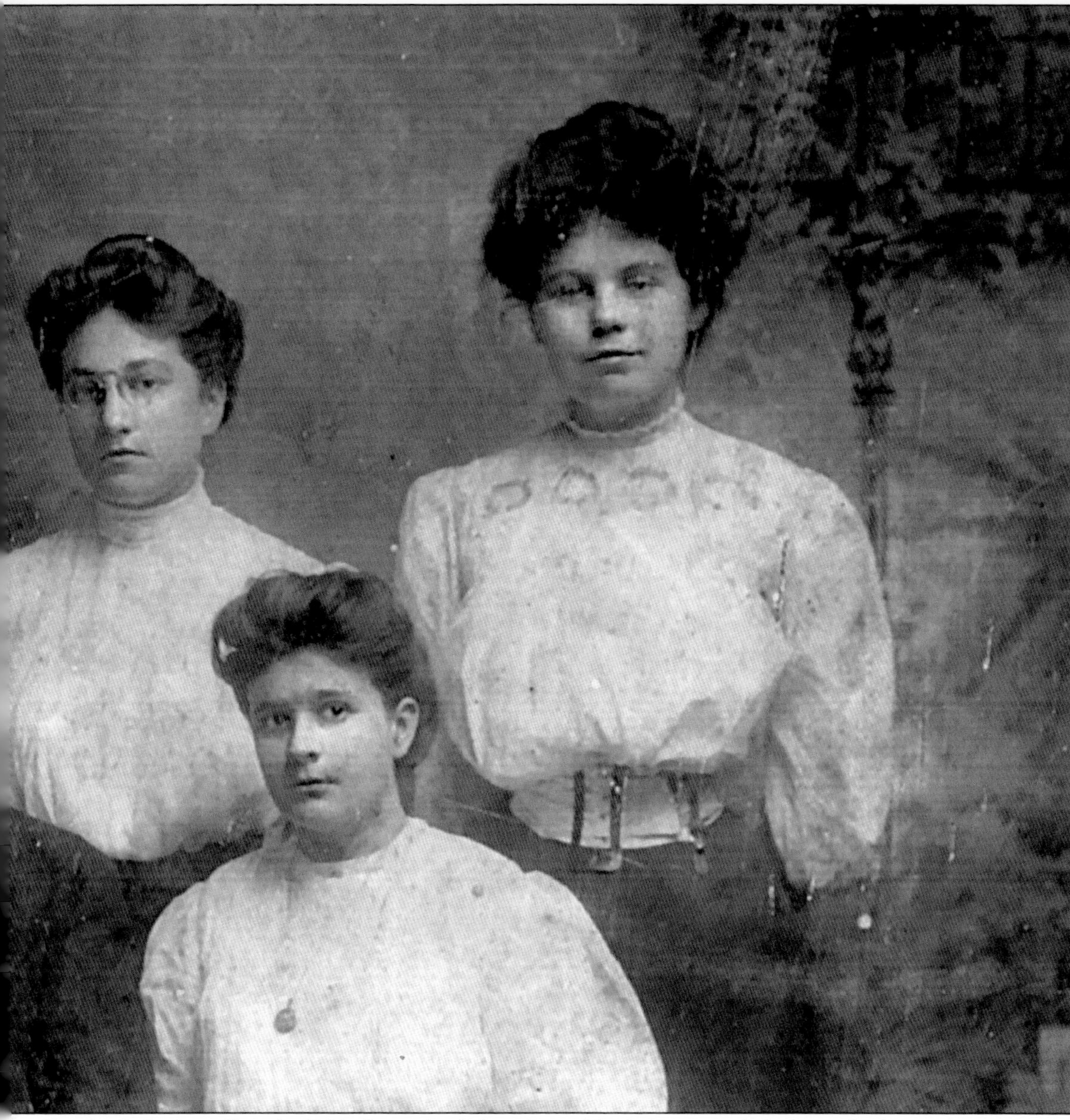

Road Methodist Church. Fifth from the left is Susie Emily Parsons (Morrisette); she is the mother of Maxine Morrisette Sweeney.

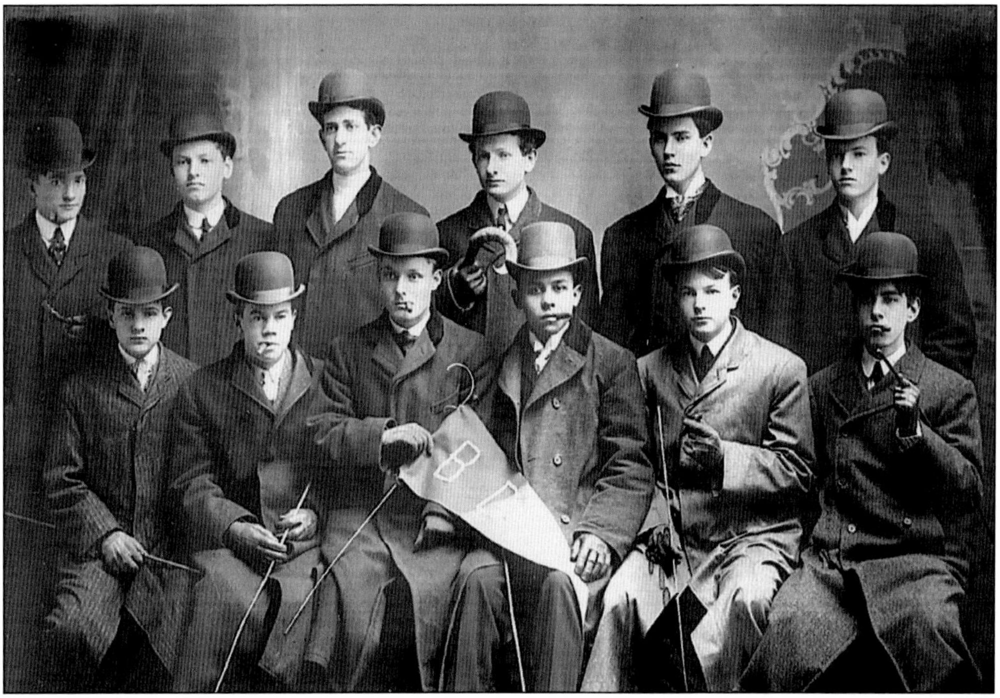

The group of men pictured above were members of the Brown Derby Club. From left to right are the following: (front row) Harold Overman, Charlie Robinson, George Cobb, William Cherry, Guy Pinner, and Tazwell Lamb; (back row) John Harney, Frank Scott, Willie Greenleaf, Ray Winder, Andrew Pendleton, and Maurice Griffin.

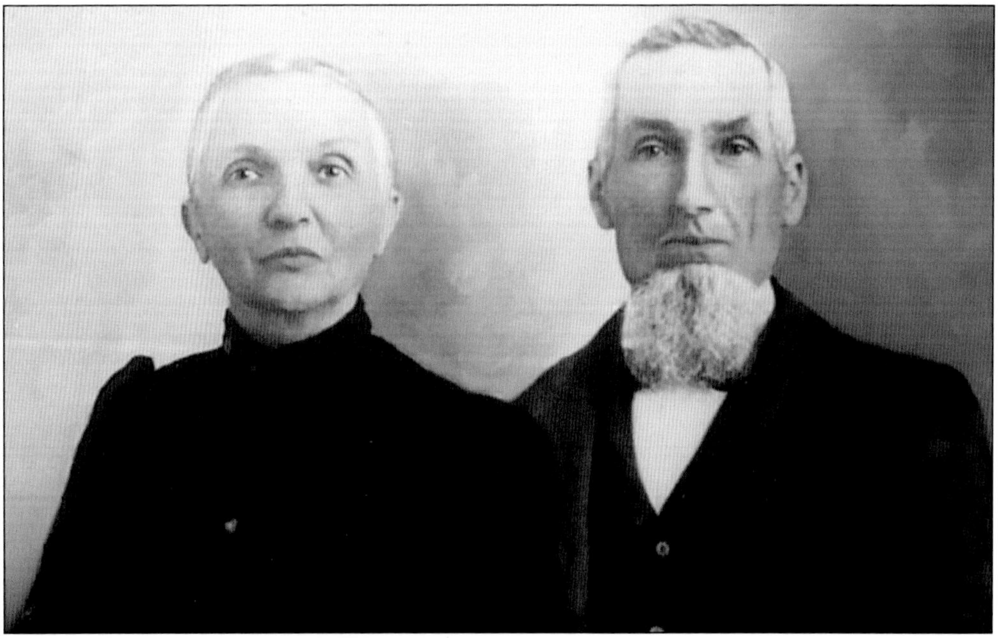

William Harney Harris (1842–1909) and Mary Morgan Harris (1846–1912) are pictured above. While a soldier in the Civil War, Mr. Harris obtained the scar on his face. He was the great-great-grandfather of Peggy McNaughton.

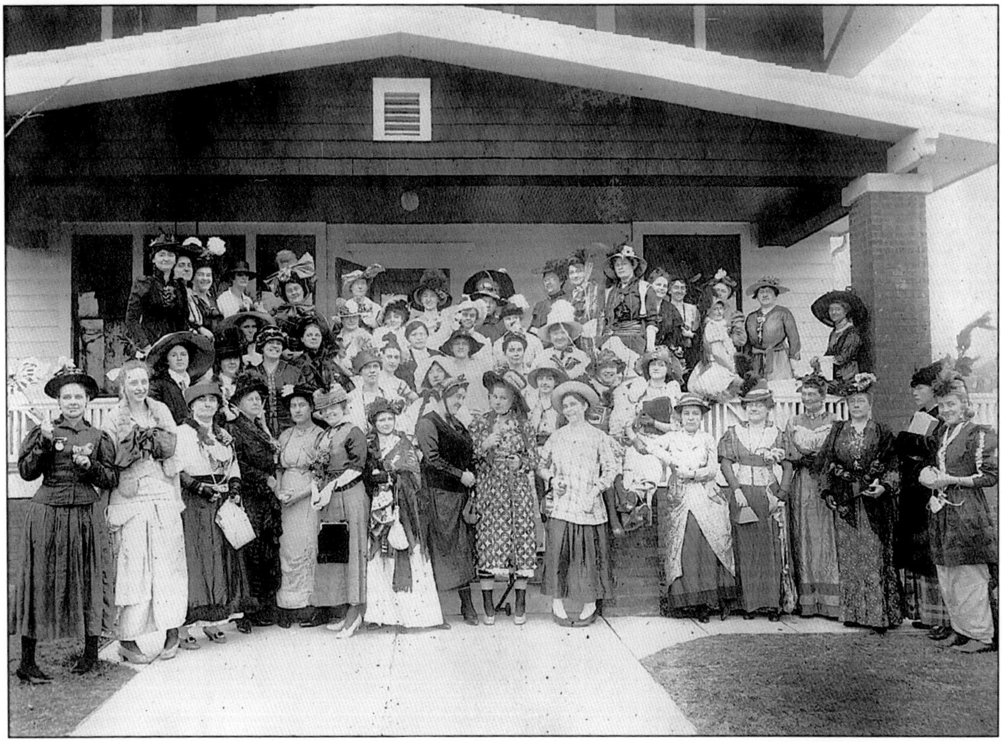

Many of the ladies donned their "finest" attire to attend a Tacky Party held at the home of Mary Fearing. The home is located at 806 West Church Street.

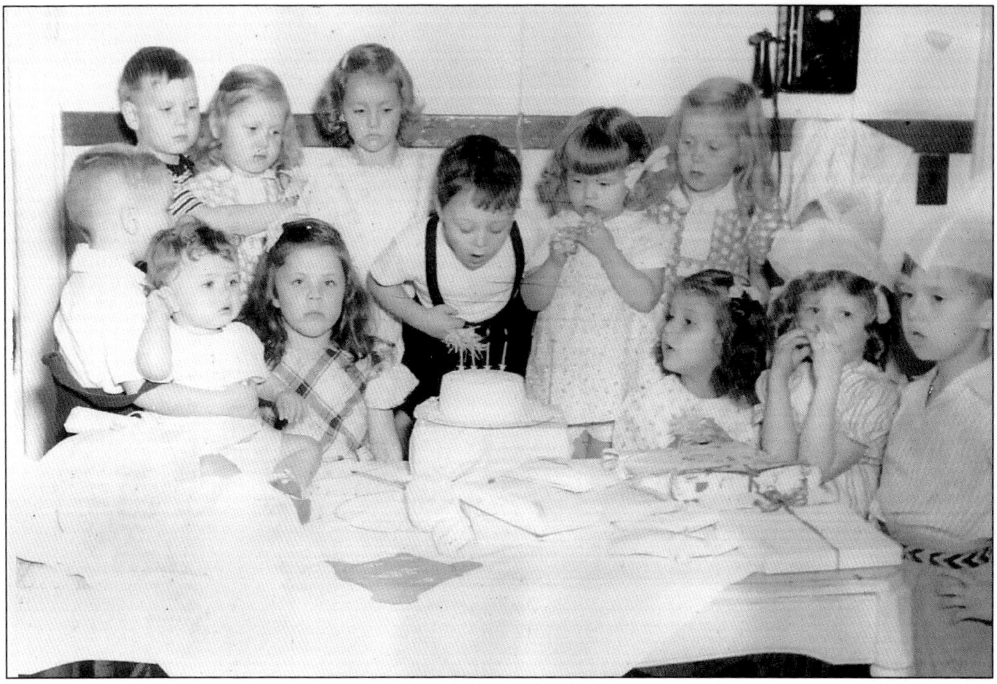

A birthday party was always fun. Notice the old telephone on the wall. The children are unidentified except for one girl in the top row, third from the left—Marilyn Madrin.

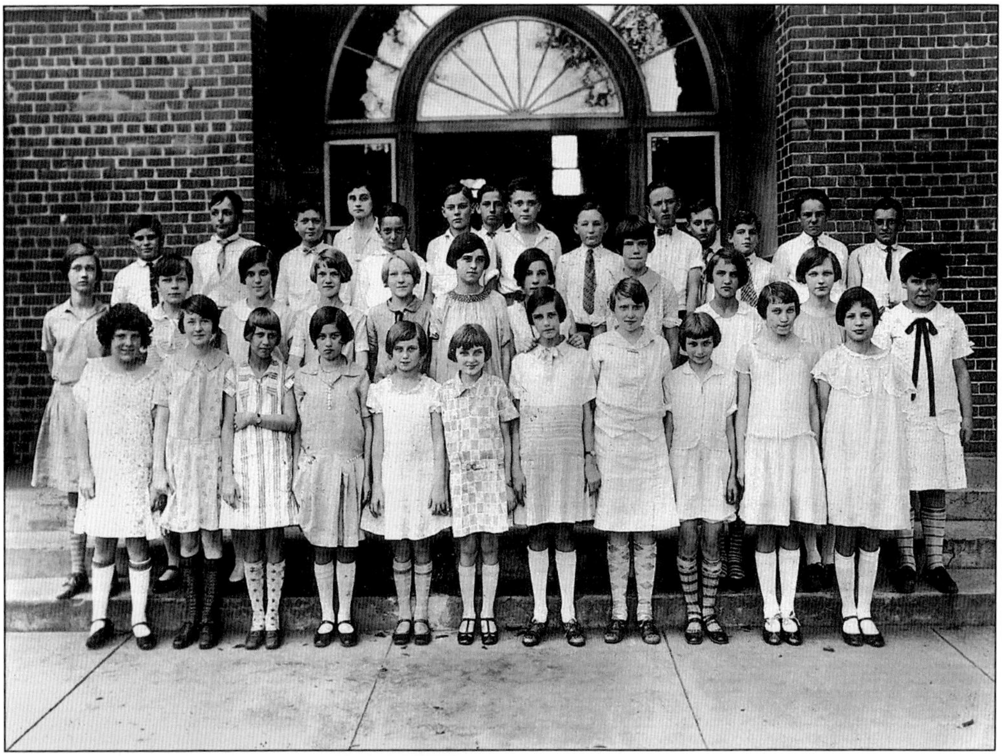

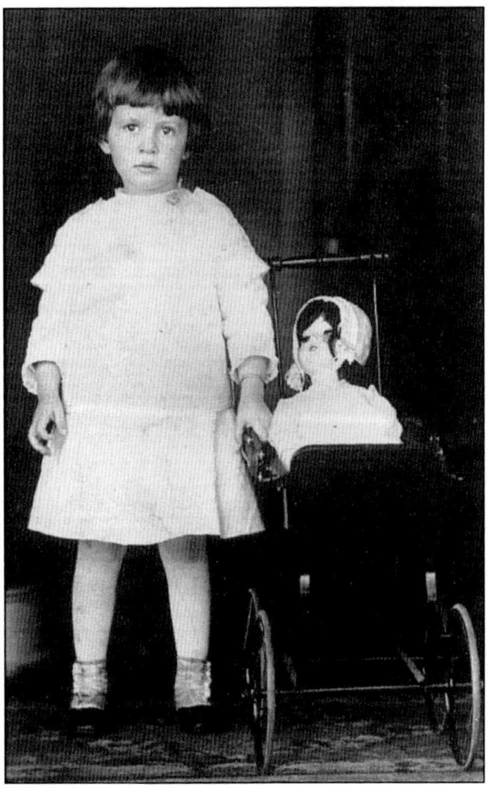

Miss Annie Feller taught seventh grade at Elizabeth City Grammar School in 1927. Her students were from left to right the following: (front row) Hazel Pendleton Dixon, Marguerite Sawyer Bateman, Marjorie Pritchard Funderburke, Edla Taylor, Selma Meads Cohoon, Maxine Morrisette Sweeney, Eleanor Aydlette, Doris Wilkins McCaskill, Elizabeth Munden, Lillian Dozier Collins, and Ruth Alice Ward Sloop; (middle row) Elizabeth Singleton Wood Smith, Willie Hill, Edith Midgette, Margaret Lee Seymour Sanders, Mildred Mann Ames, Kathleen Bray, Eleanor Goodwin Marshall, Mary Leigh Sheep, Evelyn Corbett, Stella Overman Virts, and Louise Willey; (back row) Charlie Toxey, Bill Daniels, Campbell Connery, John Peele, Carrol Price, Haywood Sawyer, Frances Jennings, Lindsay Hopkins, Richard Thompson, Clarence Barclay, Blades Forman, J.C. Sawyer, and Thomas Seeley.

Edna Morrisette Shannonhouse poses with her doll and carriage. Edna is the sister of Maxine Sweeney.

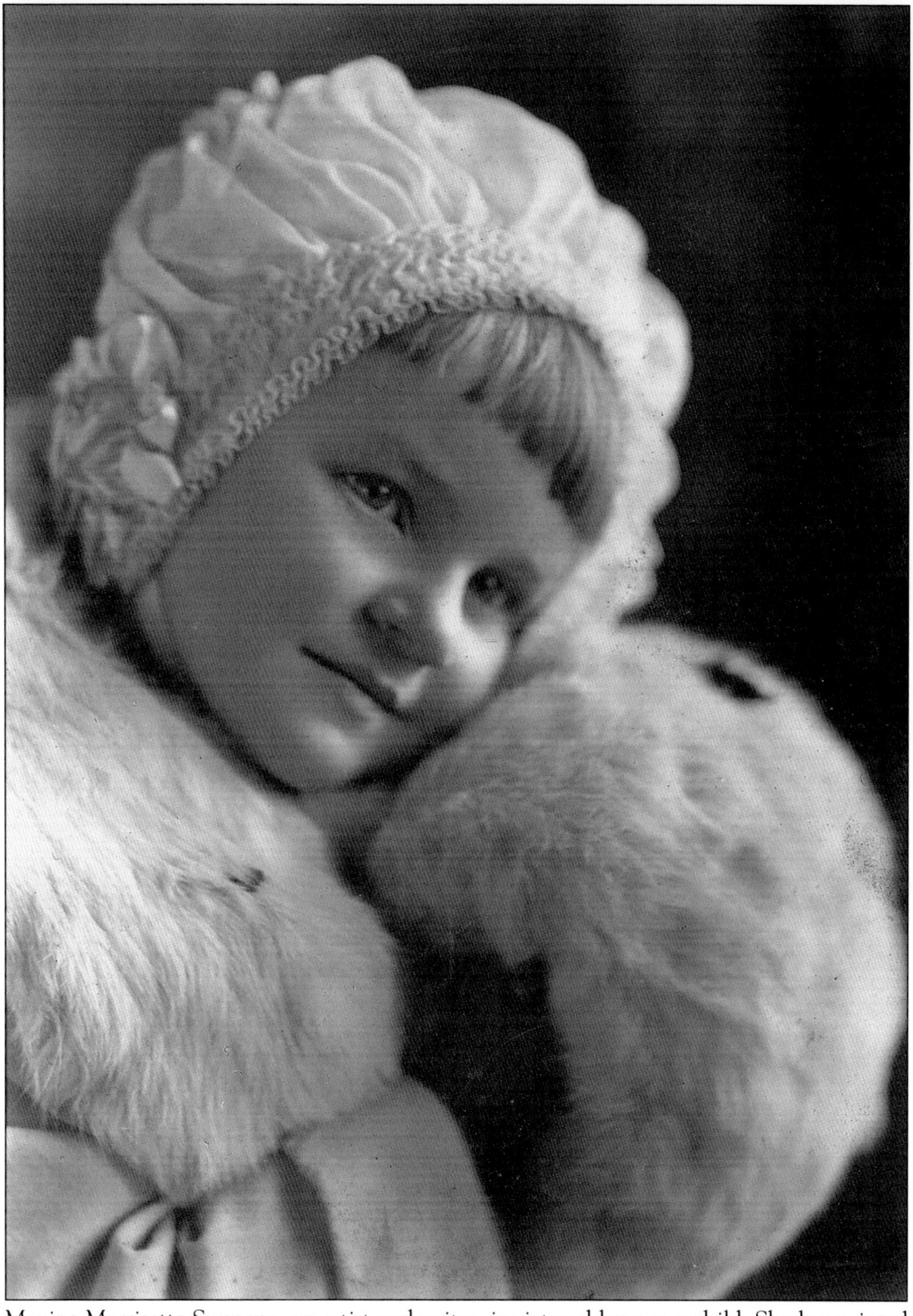

Maxine Morrisette Sweeney, an artist and writer, is pictured here as a child. She has painted many of the older homes in Elizabeth City and is well known for her outstanding portraits. She has also written and illustrated several children's books: two were recently published.

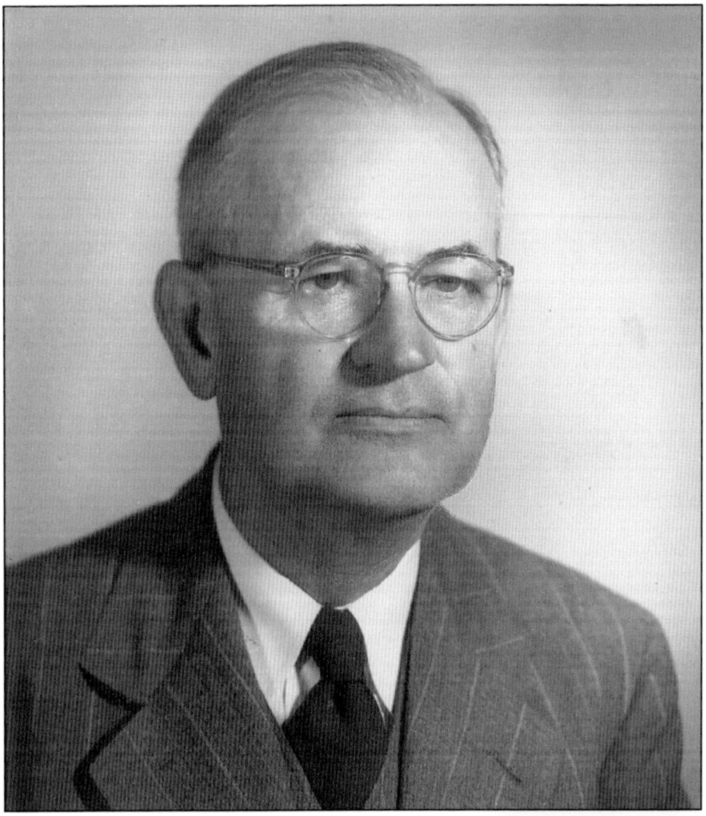

Mack Garrett Morrisette owned and operated M.G. Morrisette & Son Furniture Company located at the corner of Main and Water Streets, which is now the site of Centura Bank.

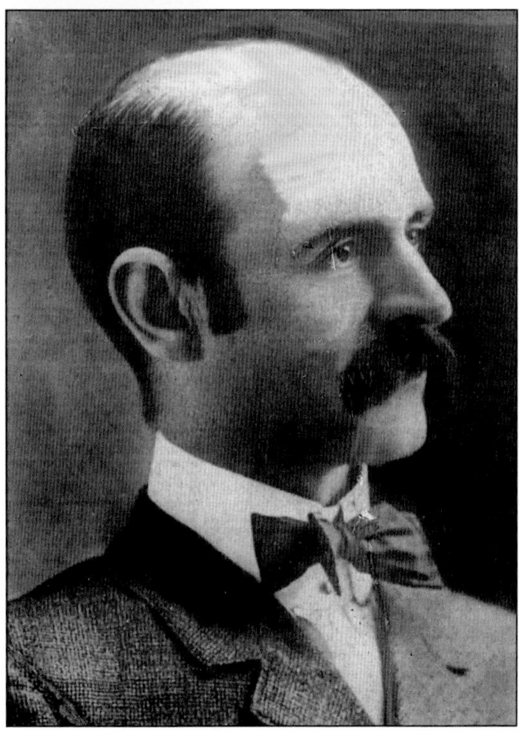

Dr. Oscar McMullen was a well-known and loved physician in Elizabeth City.

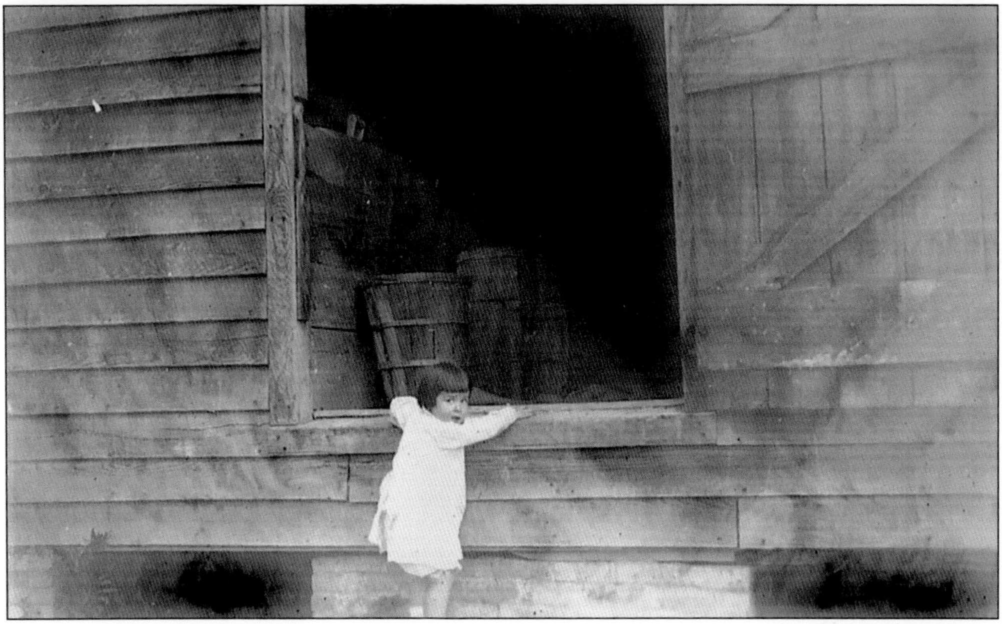

Virginia Hollowell plays by the barn door at Bayside Plantation.

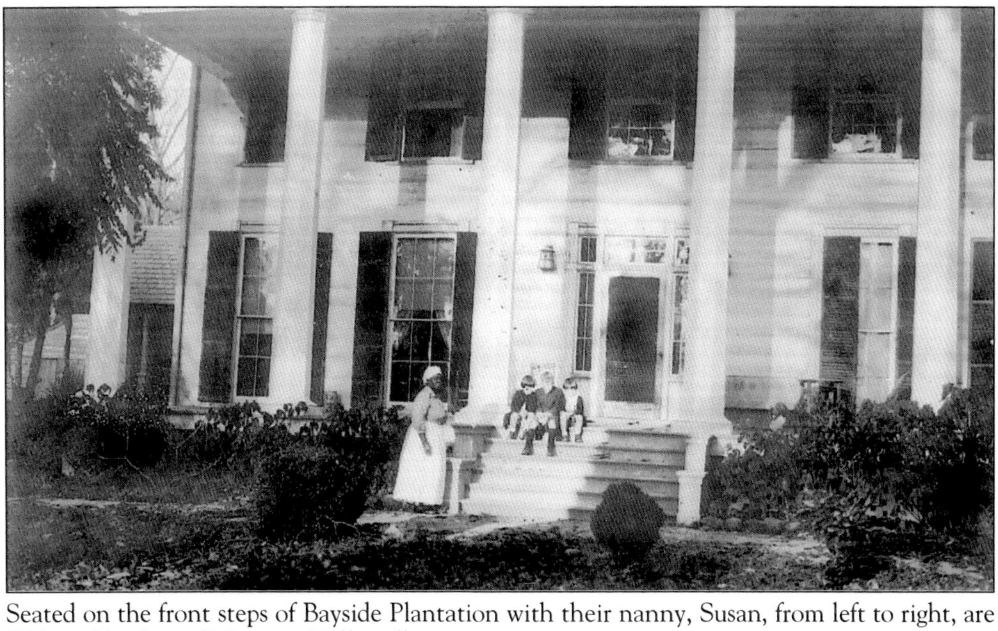

Seated on the front steps of Bayside Plantation with their nanny, Susan, from left to right, are Wilson, Frank, and Virginia Hollowell.

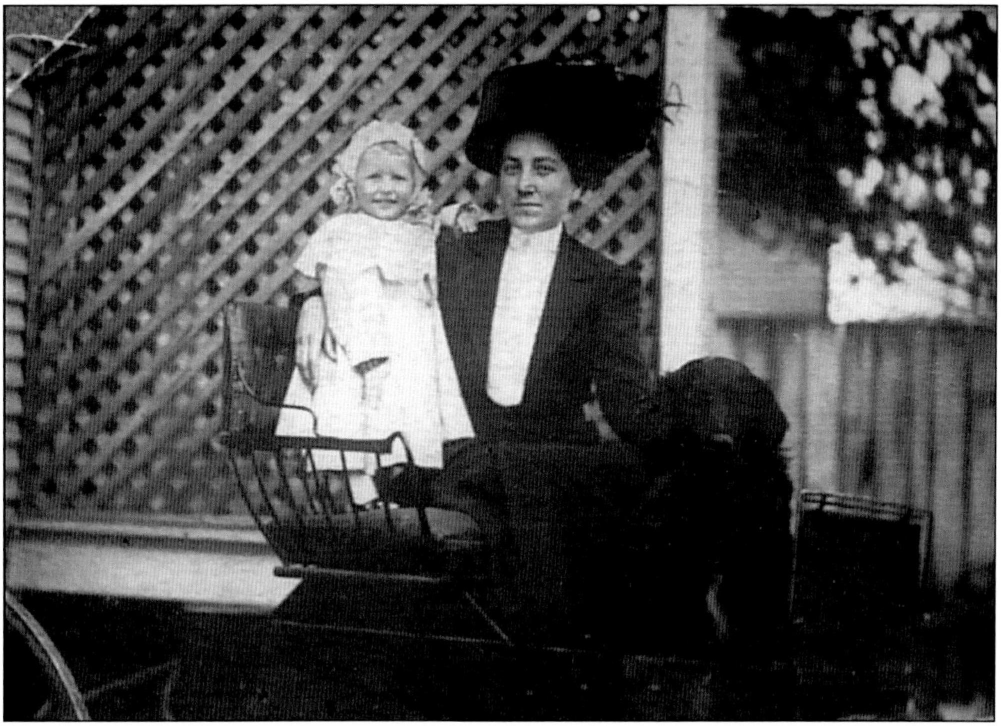

Edna Morrisette, left, and her mother, Susan Parson Morrisette, are seen in this photograph. Their dog was named Bruno. Susan Morrisette would put a note in Bruno's mouth listing the groceries she needed and Bruno would go to the store and bring them home.

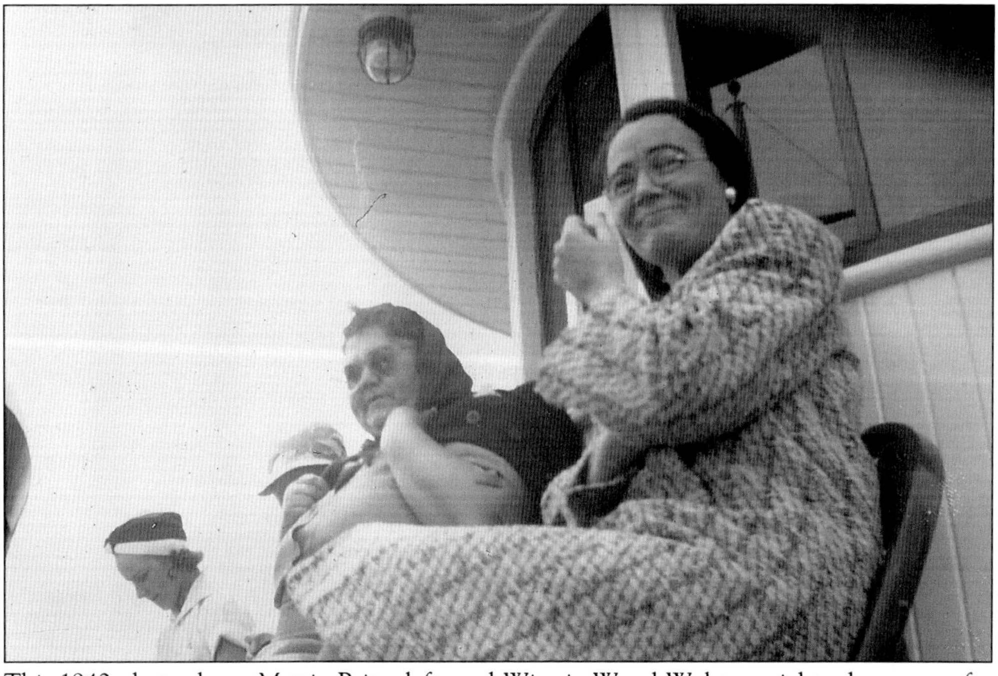

This 1940 photo shows Mattie Brite, left, and Winnie Wood Walston, right, chaperones for the junior-senior boat trip for Central High School.

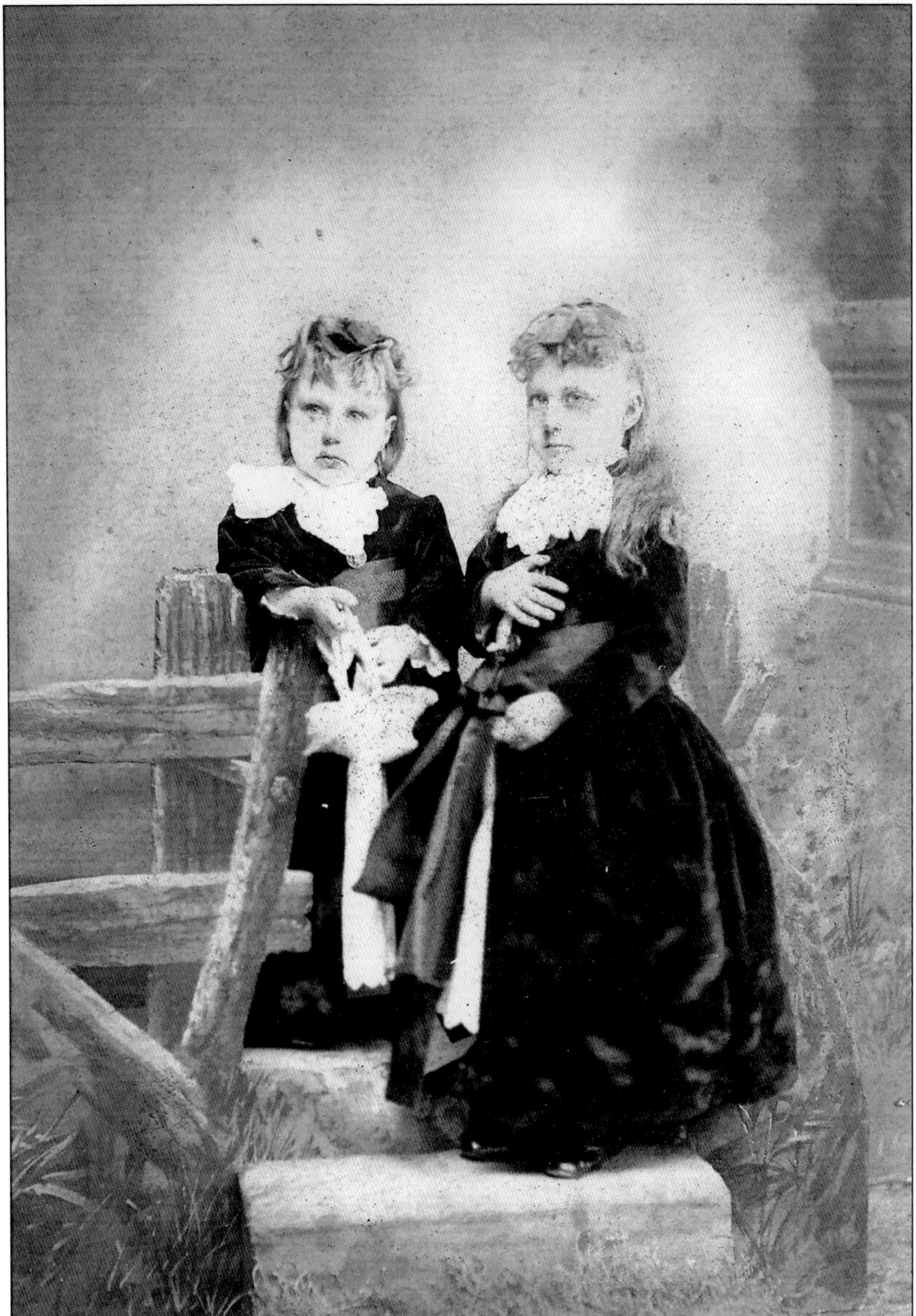

Sisters Josephine Barrett Jones (left) and Sarah Catherine Barrett (right) are shown in the photo above. They had planned a double wedding; however, Sarah died of pneumonia prior to the wedding date. Josephine was the mother of Winifred Jones Wood.

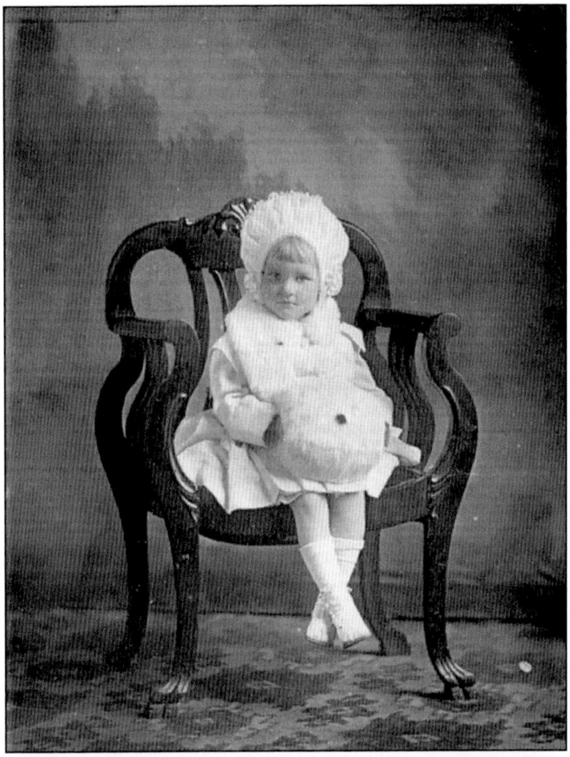

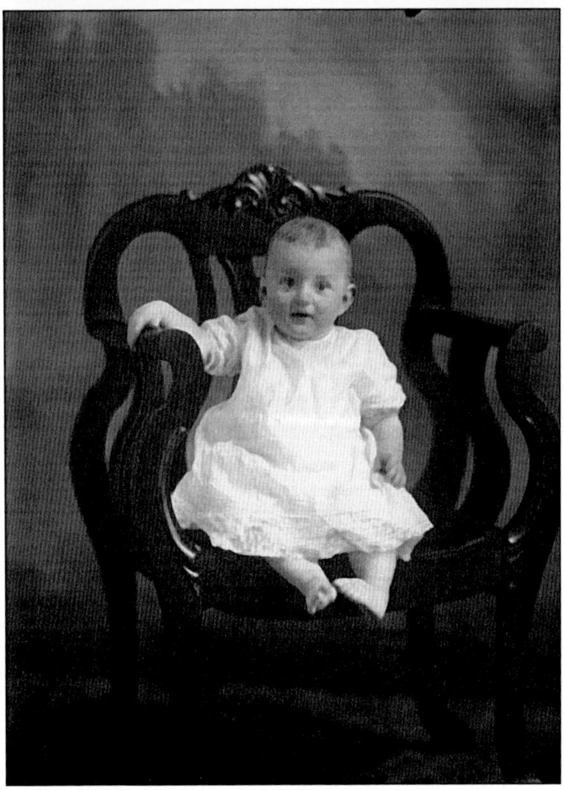

Maxine Morrisette Sweeney, shown in the top photograph, and her brother Mack Morrisette Jr., pictured in the bottom image, were born and raised in Elizabeth City. They lived on Road Street.

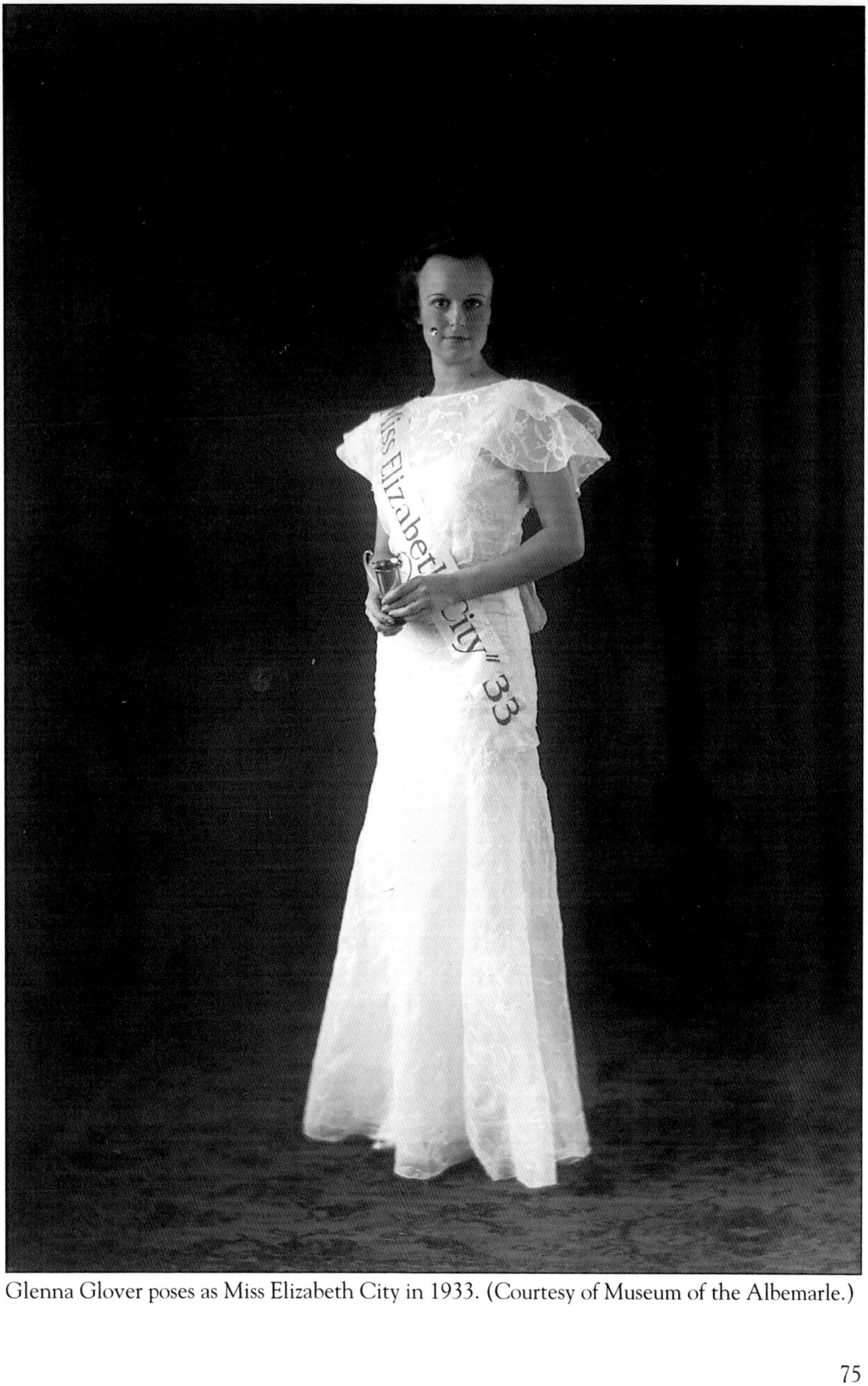

Glenna Glover poses as Miss Elizabeth City in 1933. (Courtesy of Museum of the Albemarle.)

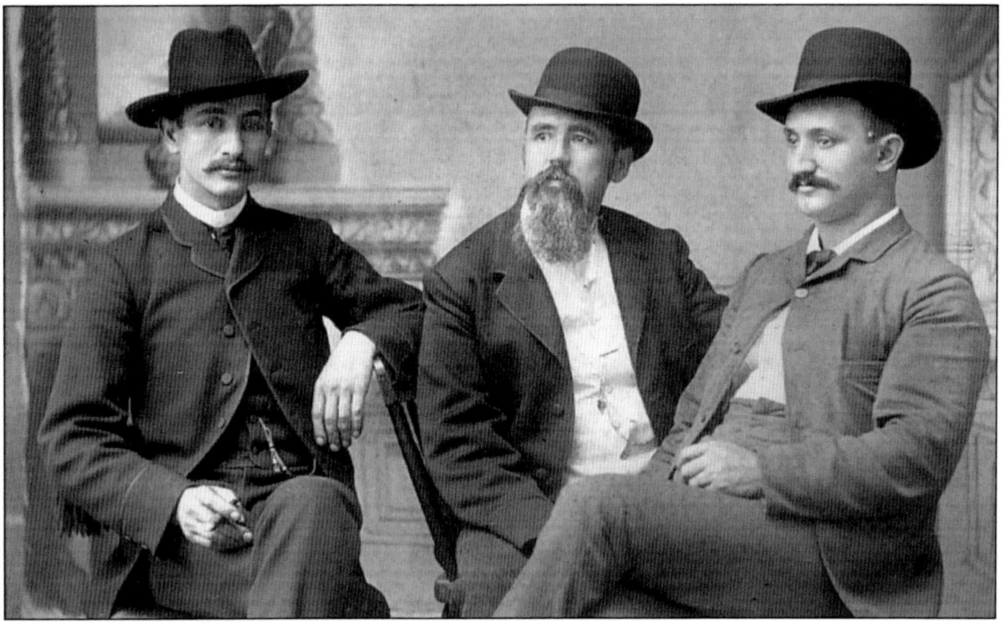

From left to right are Robert Engle, John Forman Engle (partner with Zoeller Photo Gallery and great-grandfather of Florence Stevens), and an unidentified friend.

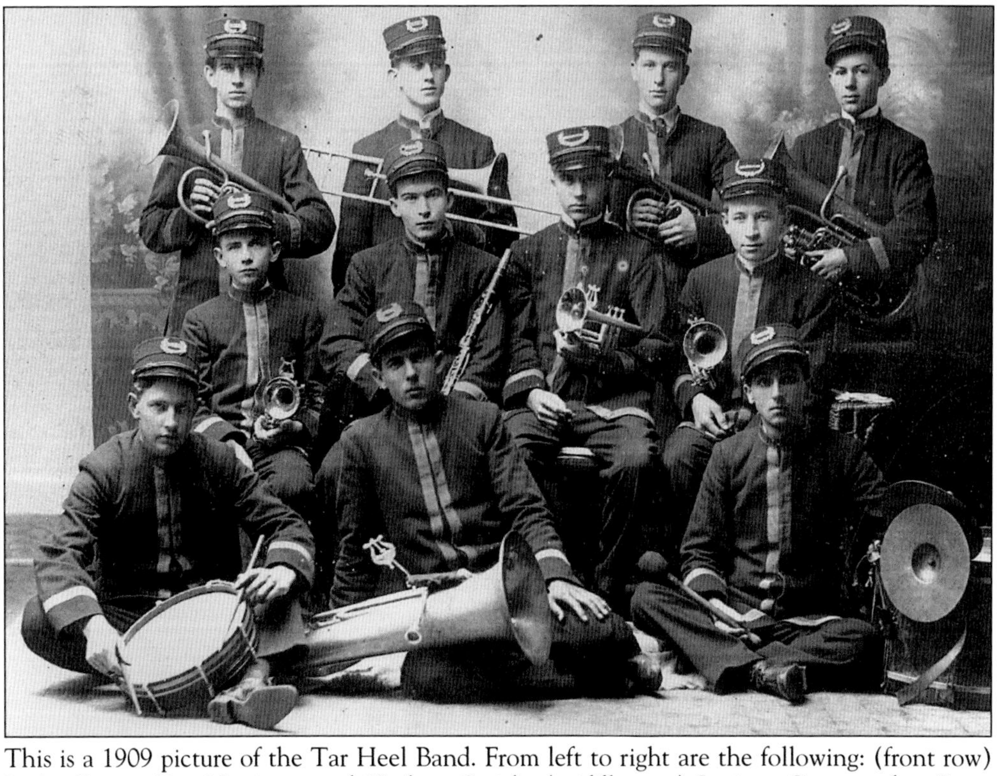

This is a 1909 picture of the Tar Heel Band. From left to right are the following: (front row) Leslie Davis, Guy Harrison, and Herbert Smith; (middle row) Latiner Commander, Scott Lister, Henry Hardison, and Howard Nettrick; (back row) Graham Trueblood, Ken Davis, unidentified, and Lutrell Glover. (Courtesy of Museum of the Albemarle.)

These two photos show the children of Elizabeth City dressed in their Sunday best for Easter. Pictured from left to right in a 1952 photo (top) are Kay Pyle, Marilyn Madrin, Buddy Madrin, and Connie Pyle. Below, Buddy and Marilyn Madrin strike a pose for the camera as they sit on their front porch.

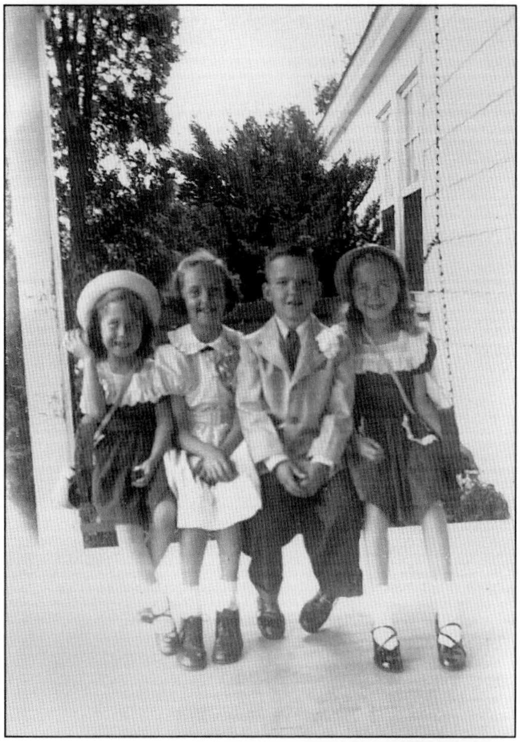

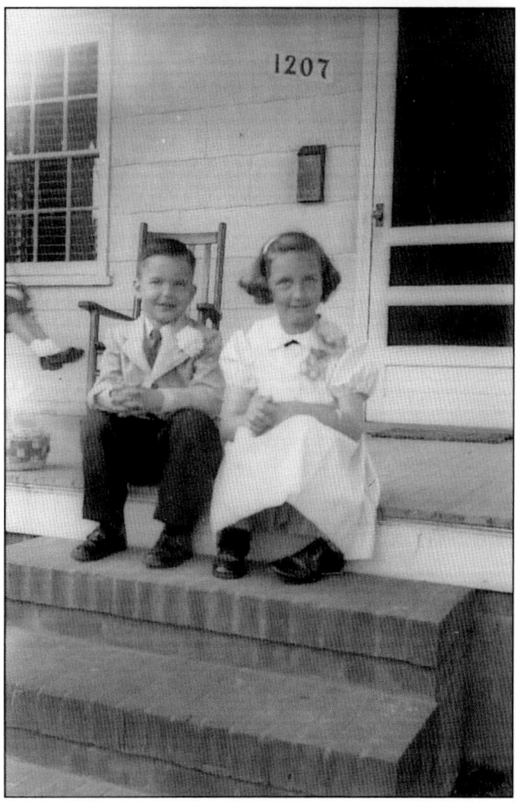

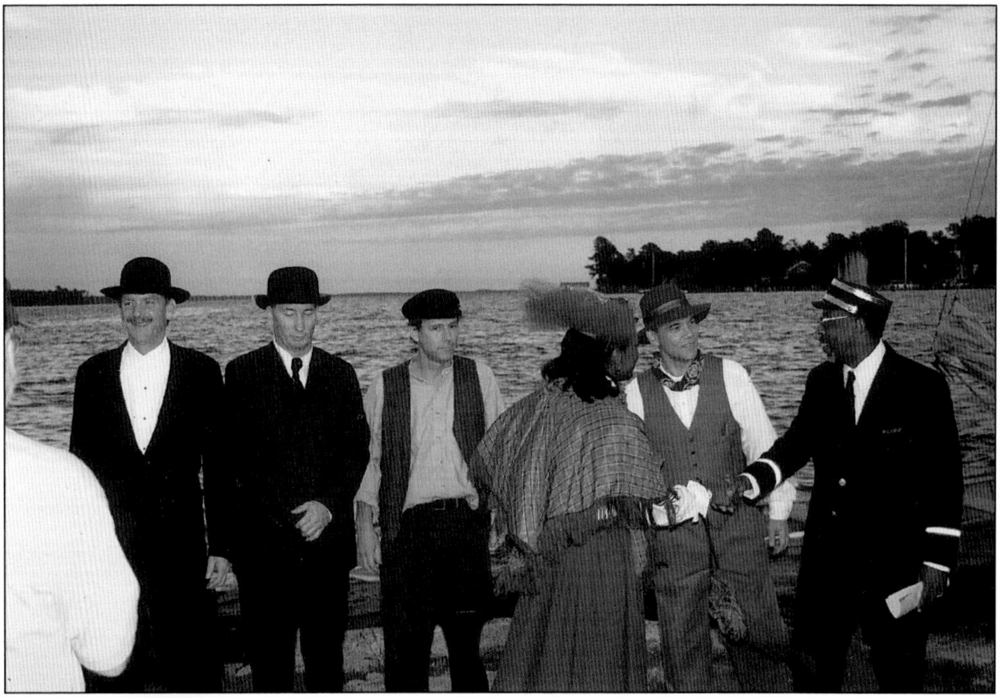

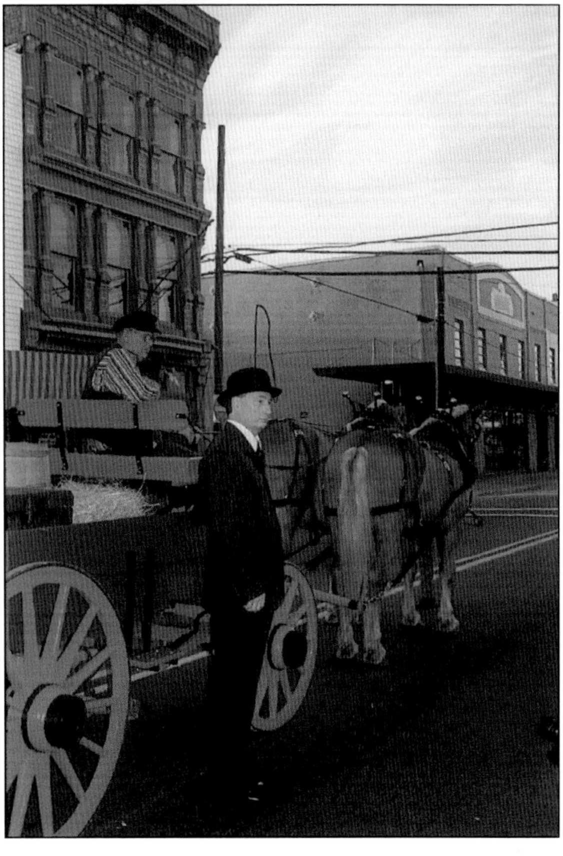

The Wright Brothers came to Elizabeth City on their way to Kitty Hawk. They had a difficult time finding someone to guide them to Kitty Hawk since most residents did not know how to get there. Below, actors portray the Wright Brothers on their first trip to Elizabeth City.

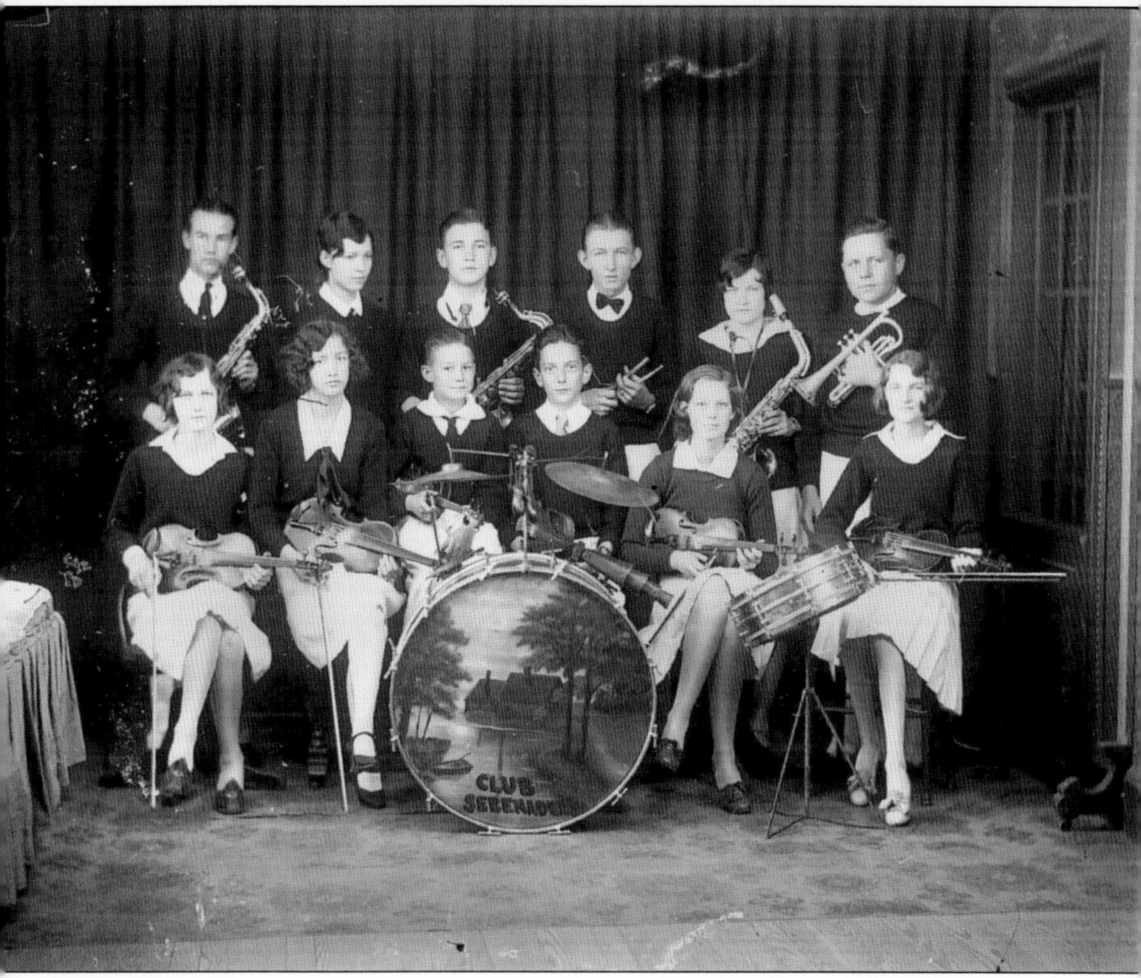

The Club Serenaders was made up of local students in the Elizabeth City High School Band. The following members are, from left to right, (front row) unidentified, Nancy Reid Love, Bobby Elliot, John Peele, Martha Outten, and Maxine Morrisette (Mrs. John Sweeney); (back row) Wilford Dail, Alice Davis, Elliott Cooke, "Frog" Swain, unidentified, and Robert Spence. (Courtesy of Museum of the Albemarle.)

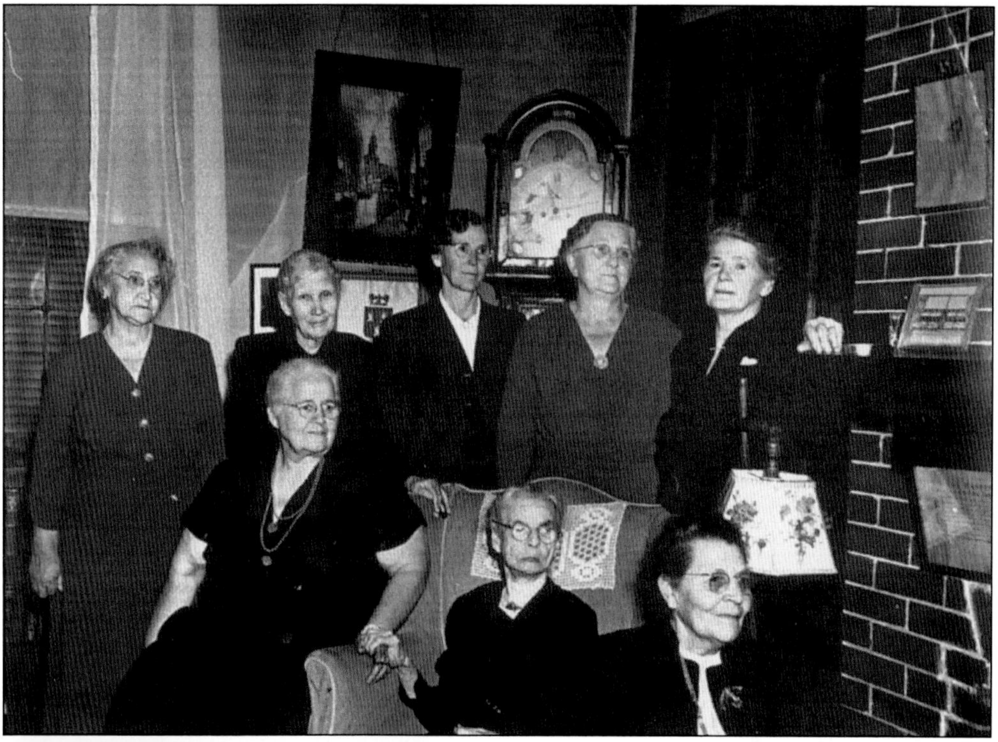

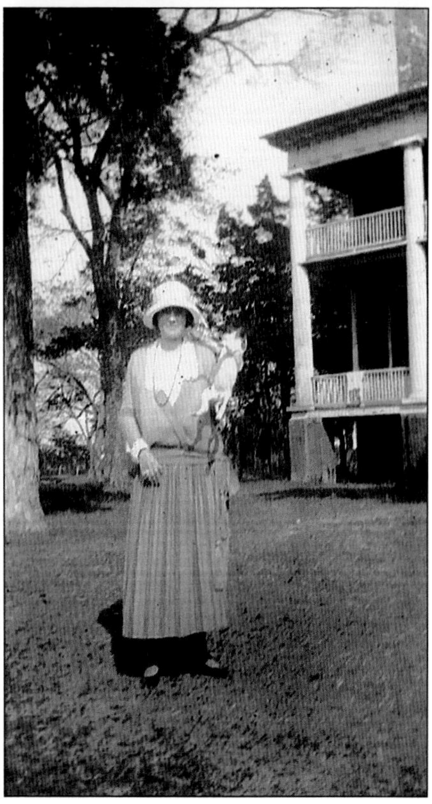

The first Home Demonstration Club started in Pasquotank County in April of 1917 and was called the Dry Ridge Club. It was later combined with the Newbegun Club and called Marcia Albertson Home Demonstration Club. The members are, from left to right, the following: (front row) Mrs. W.J. Hobbs, Miss Marcia Albertson (first Home Demonstration agent for Pasquotank County), and Mrs. W.T. Jackson Sr.; (standing) Mrs. Sam Wilson Sr., Mrs. J.L. Palmer, Mrs. J.M. Wilson, Mrs. Haywood Morris, and Mrs. C.L. Ball. Not pictured is Mrs. Mae Commander. (Courtesy of Museum of the Albemarle.)

Tillie Ehringhaus, wife of Gov. J.C.B. Ehringhaus of Elizabeth City, is shown visiting the Leigh House at Lands End Plantation in Perquimans County in 1923.

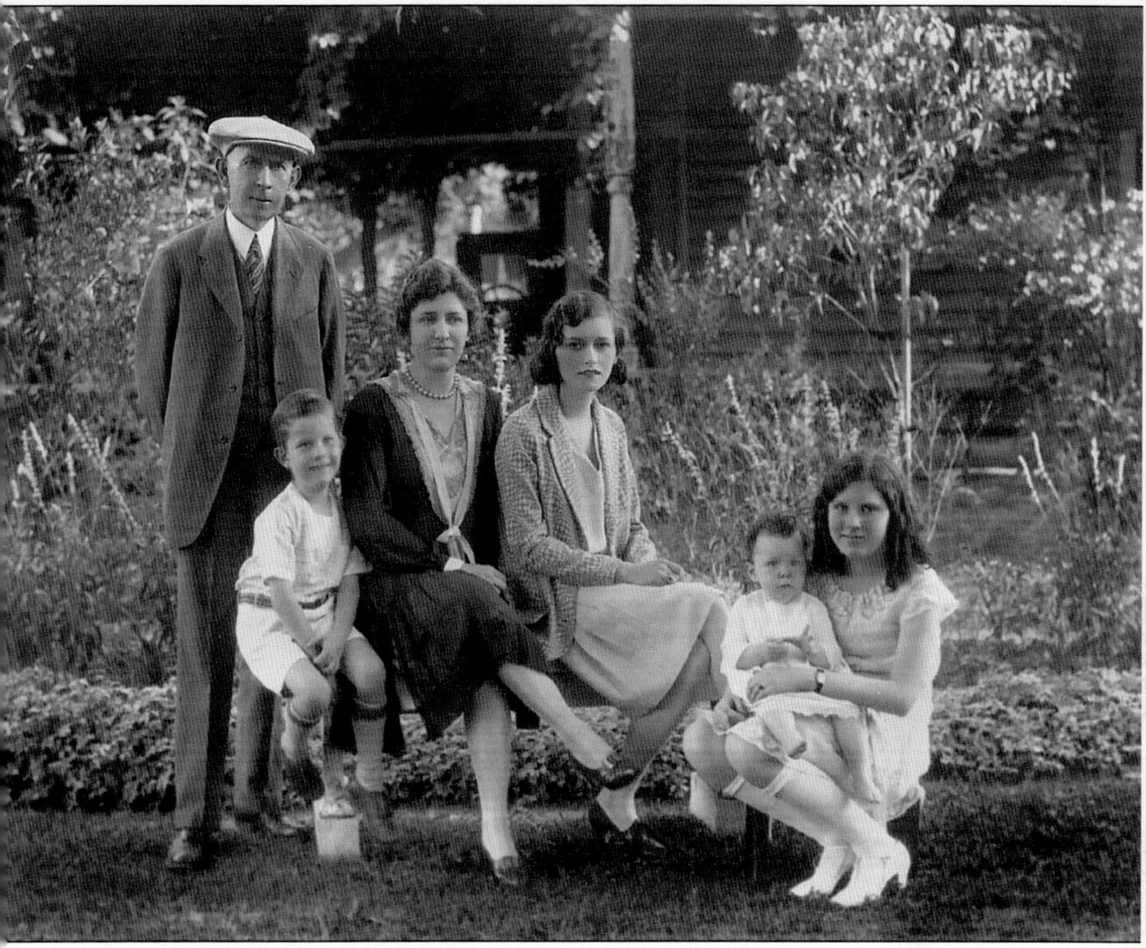

This 1930s picture showcases the Pendleton family in their backyard at 503 West Main Street. The family members are, from left to right, Dr. Andrew Lewis Pendleton, Andrew Lewis Pendleton Jr., Hazel Williams Evans Pendleton, Mary Francis Pendleton London, Nancy Ross Pendleton Owens, and Hazel Evans Pendleton Dixon.

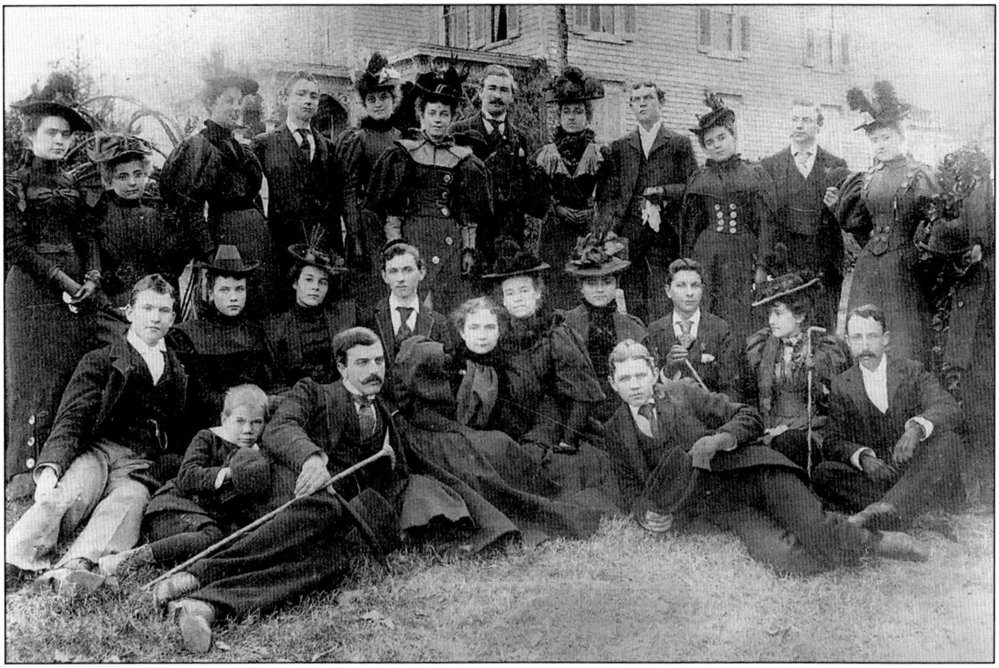

In 1892 the members of the C.H.I.C. Club gathered for this photo. (Courtesy of Museum of the Albemarle)

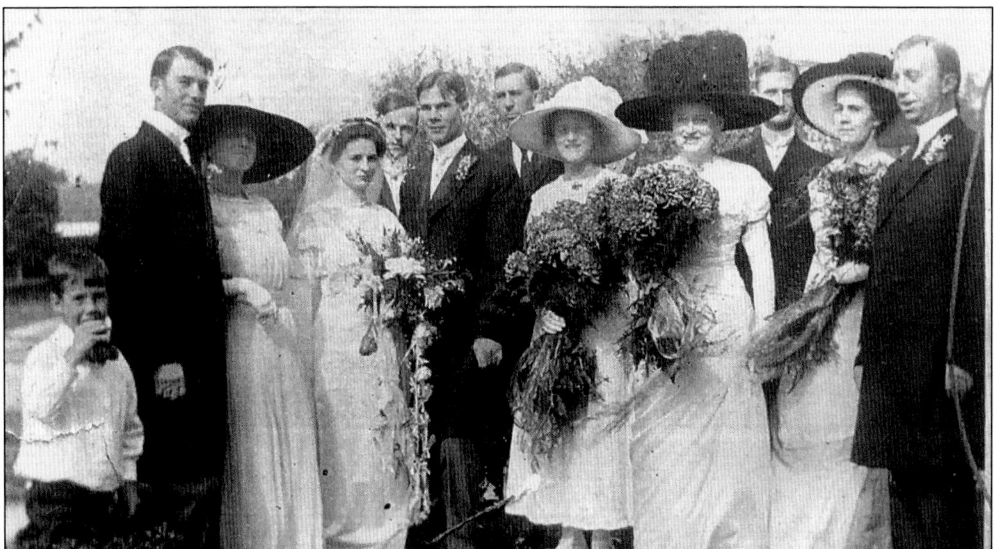

In 1911, Evelyn Etheridge married Frank Vaughan Scott. The "new" organ at the Episcopal Church was first played at the wedding. From left to right are the following: Selden Lamb; Baxter Bell; Evelyn Aydlett (later Mrs. Phil Sawyer), organist; "Eva" Evelyn Etheridge Scott (bride); Tazwell Lamb (editor of the *Virginian Pilot*); Frank Vaughan Scott (groom); Winfield Wort; Nell Etheridge Covington (Wadesborough); Rebia Ethel Etheridge Worth (Mrs. Winfield Worth); Walter P. Wood; Mrs. Ethel Scott Lamb (sister of Frank Scott); Malvern Tillett (lawyer, teacher, son of the Mrs. Tillett who had a local school, tutored one of the Rockefeller children, and married Amie Pinner). (Courtesy of Museum of the Albemarle.)

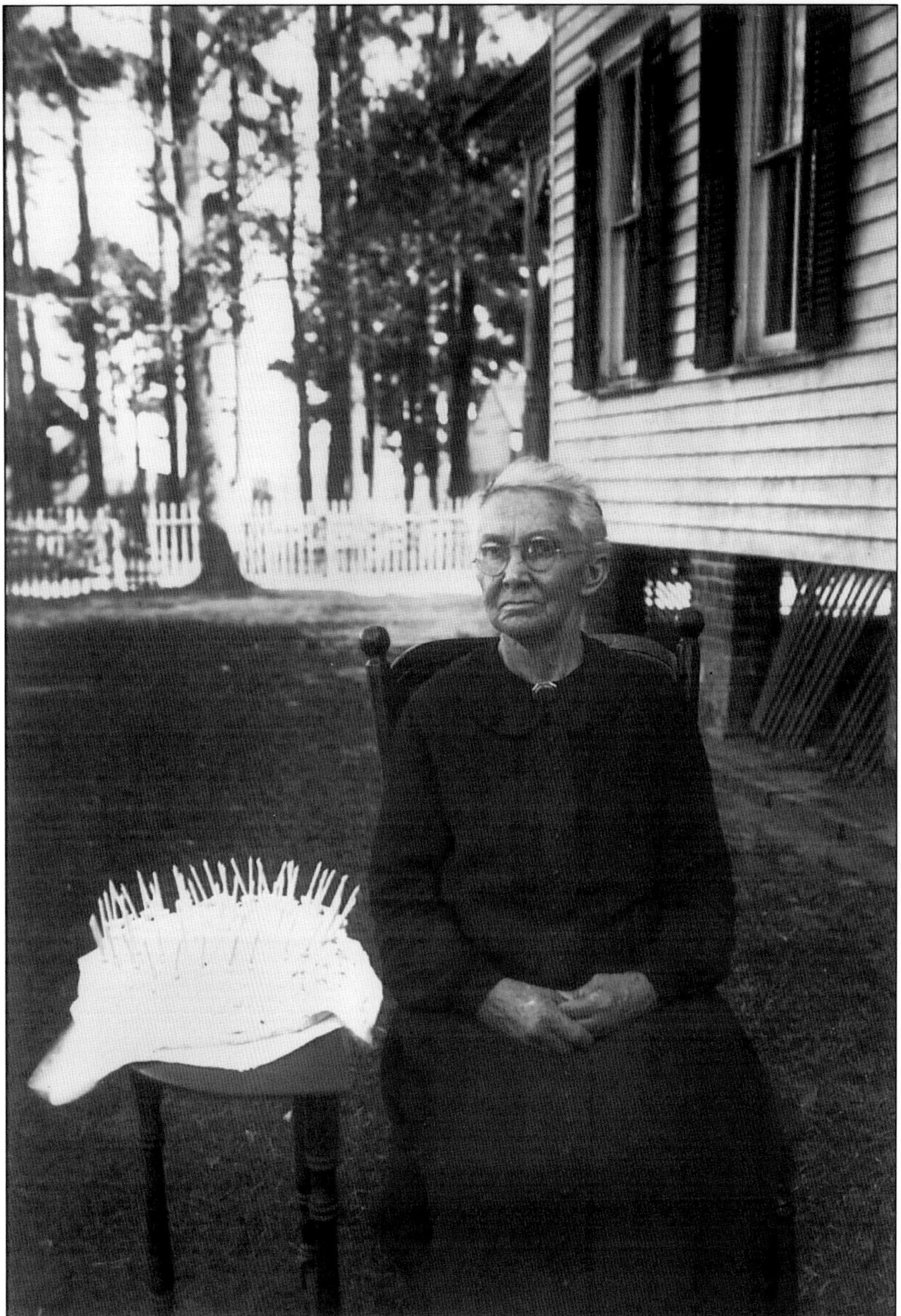

Mary Louise Davis (Ms. Myles Lowrey Davis) was 65 in 1933. (Courtesy of Museum of the Albemarle.)

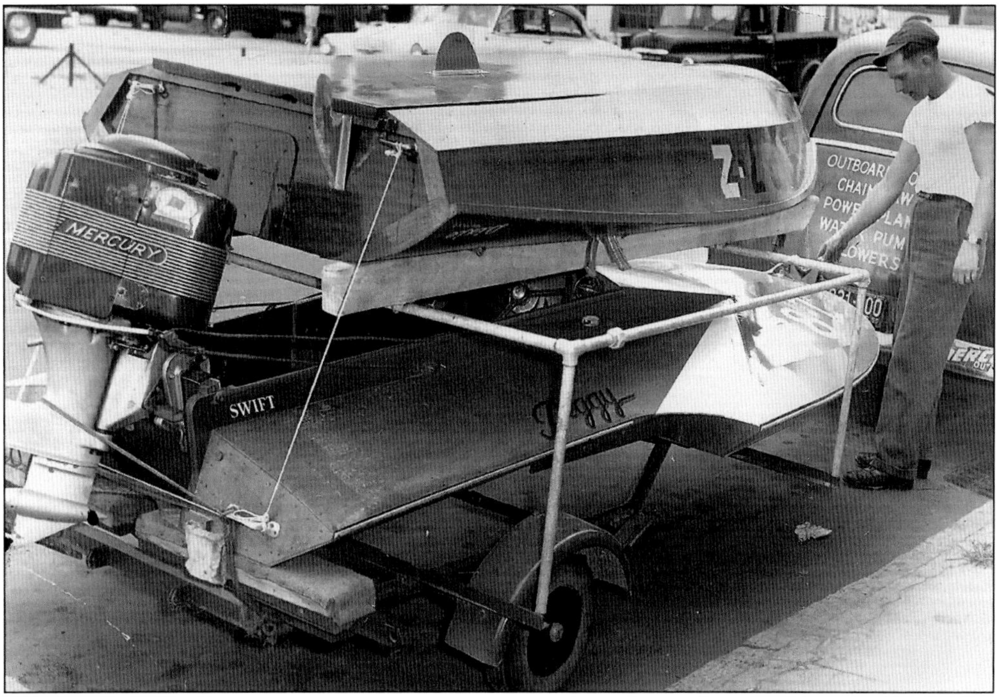

C. Frank McNaughton Jr., shown with his race boats, owned an outboard motor business. He set international world records with his racing.

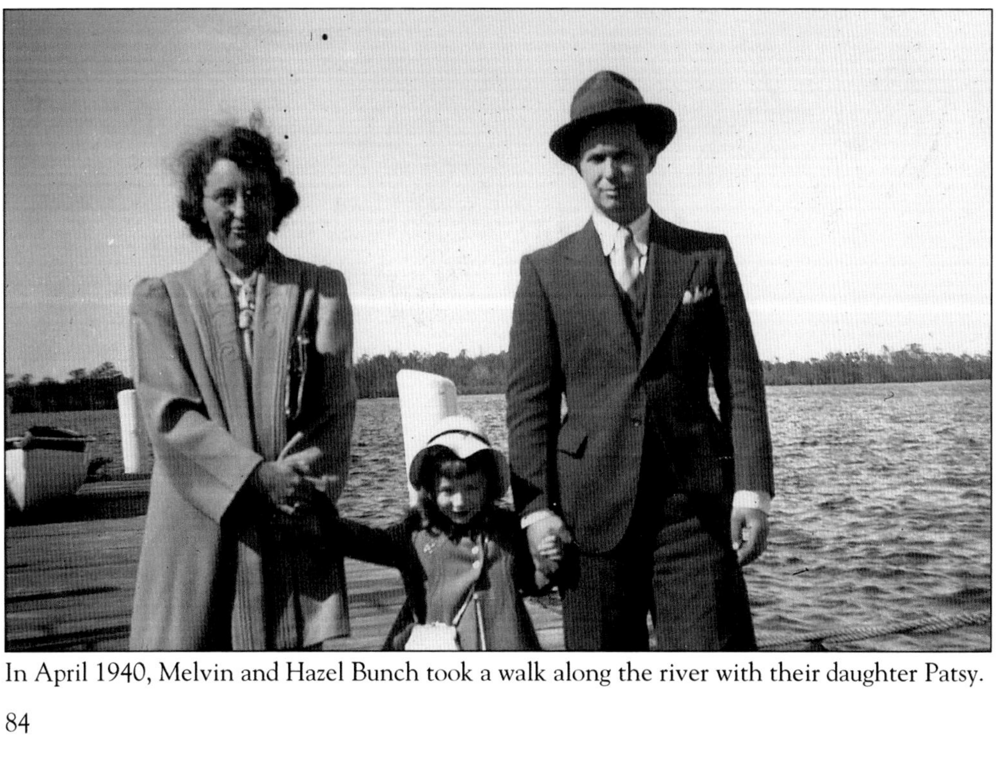

In April 1940, Melvin and Hazel Bunch took a walk along the river with their daughter Patsy.

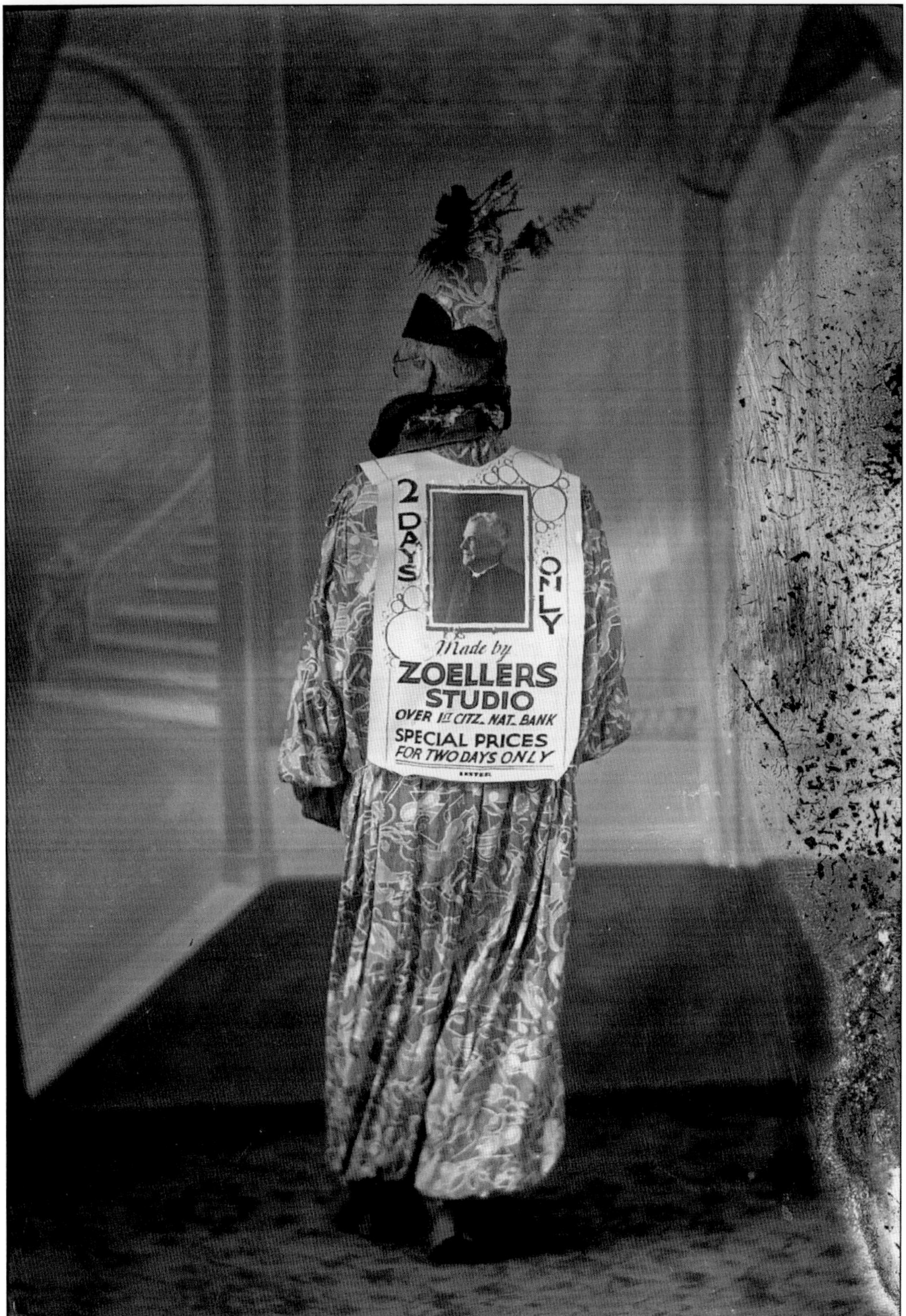

William Zoeller used this "human billboard" to advertise his two-day special. His studio was located over the First Citizens National Bank. (Courtesy of Museum of the Albemarle.)

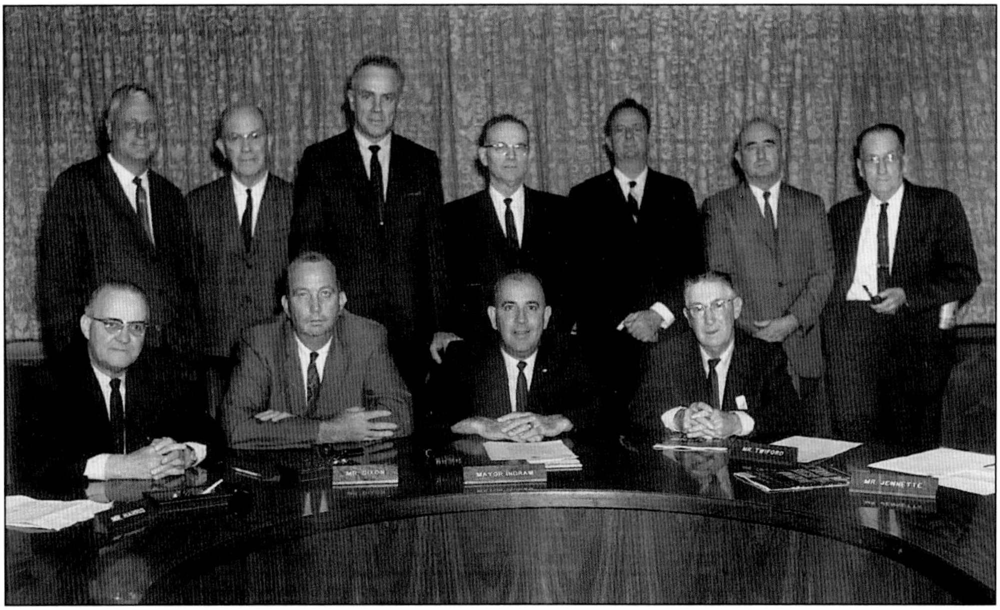

The city council for Elizabeth City was comprised of the following elected officials in 1967. From left to right are (standing) Kenyon Wilson, Bob Luther, Cader Harris, Parker Midgett, John W. Foreman, Bertram Jennette, and Cecil Richardson; (seated) Harry Tunstall, Potter Dixon, Mayor Emmett Ingram, and Kurt Twiford.

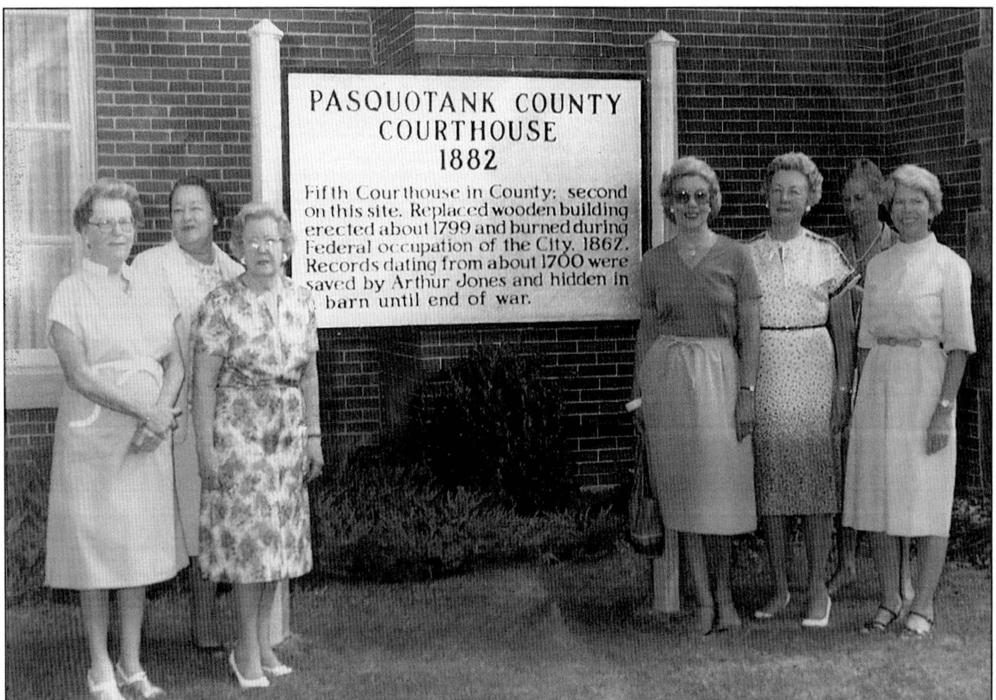

The Colonial Dames presented this plaque to the Pasquotank County Courthouse in the summer of 1983. From left to right are Hazel Dixon, Louise Peters, Mary Meekins Gilbert, Ann Dunston, unidentified, Sis Hall, and Betty Gaither.

Three

COUNTRY

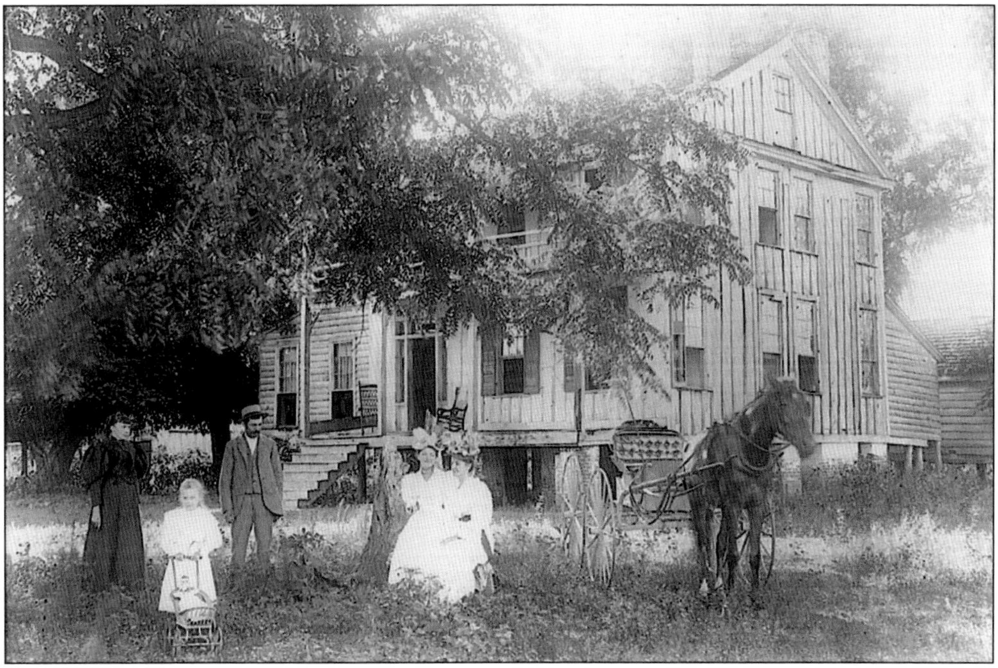

Crocker Hill, the home of Mr. and Mrs. A.J. Jennings, was located near Newbegun Creek. Pictured on the left is Mrs. A.J. Jennings, the child with the doll is Birdie, next is Mr. A.J. Jennings, followed by Birdie's sisters. This picture was taken around 1895. Mr. and Mrs. Jennings were the grandparents of Bill Small.

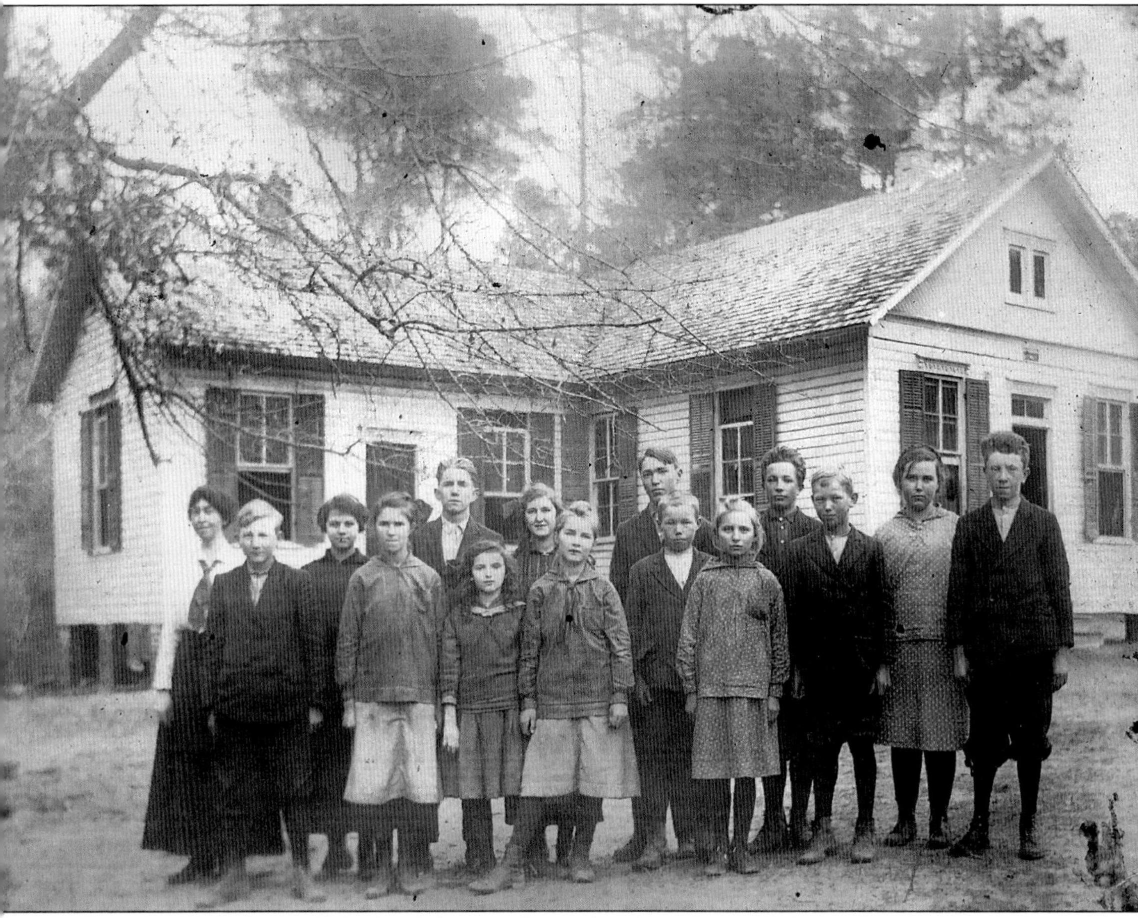

This is an unidentified school that was located within Pasquotank County.

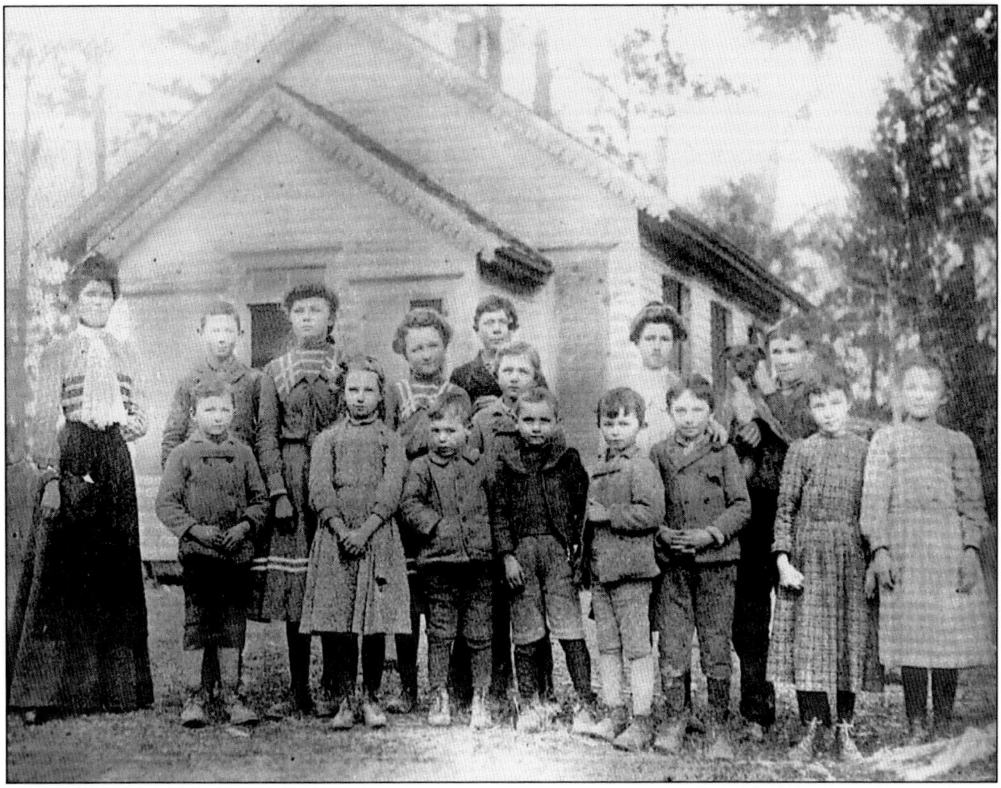

Small's School was a one-room schoolhouse located near Rabbits' Corner. Maggie Harrell was the teacher.

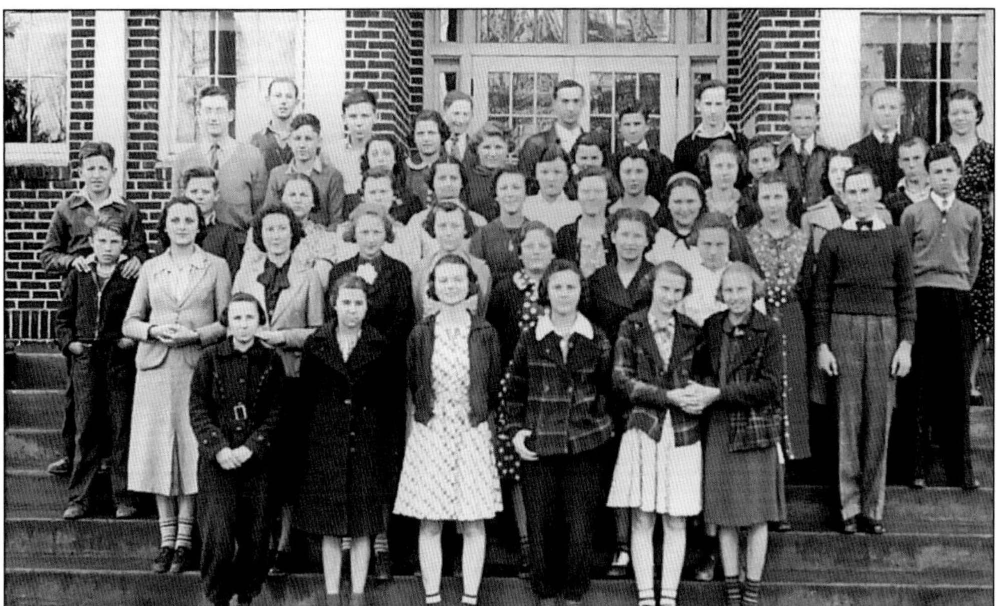

The Class of 1937–1938 of Central High School's Glee Club posed for this picture. Betty Earp was the director. She was the public school music teacher for Pasquotank County.

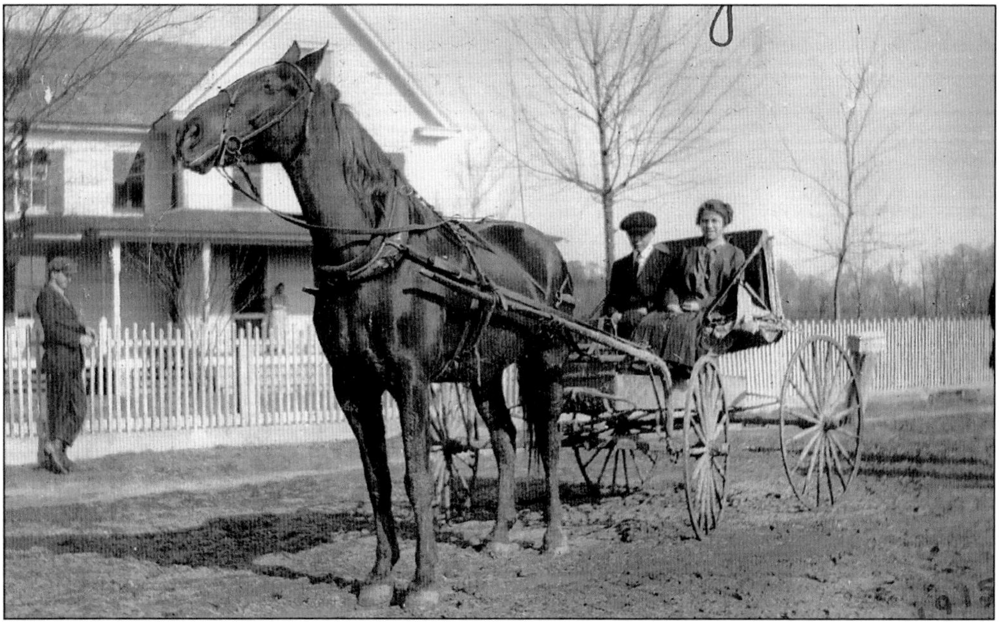

Wilma Tuttle and Guy Wood are shown here in 1915 at the home of Henry Wood.

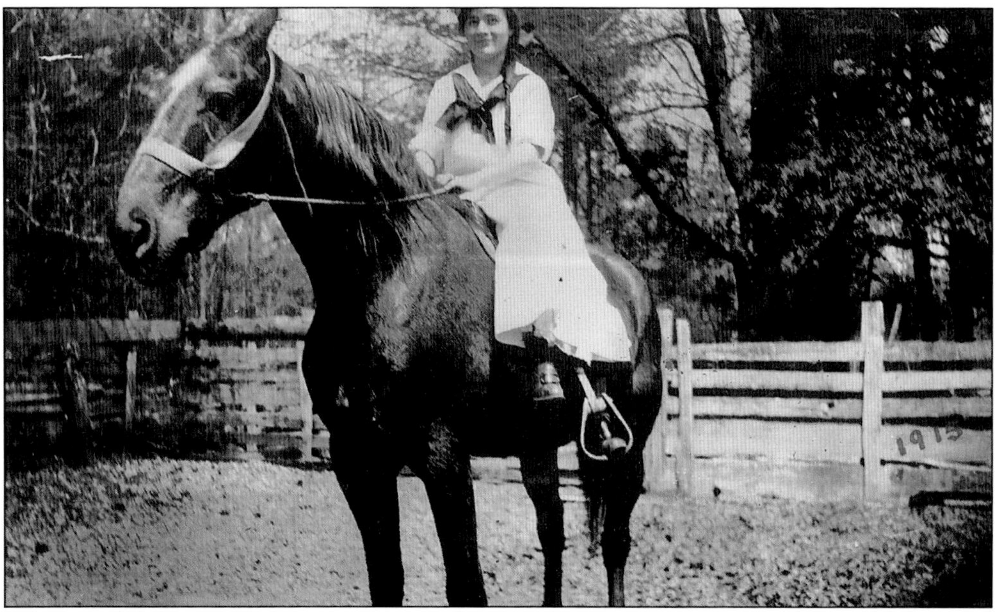

This is Winnie Wood Walston with her horse Winks in 1915.

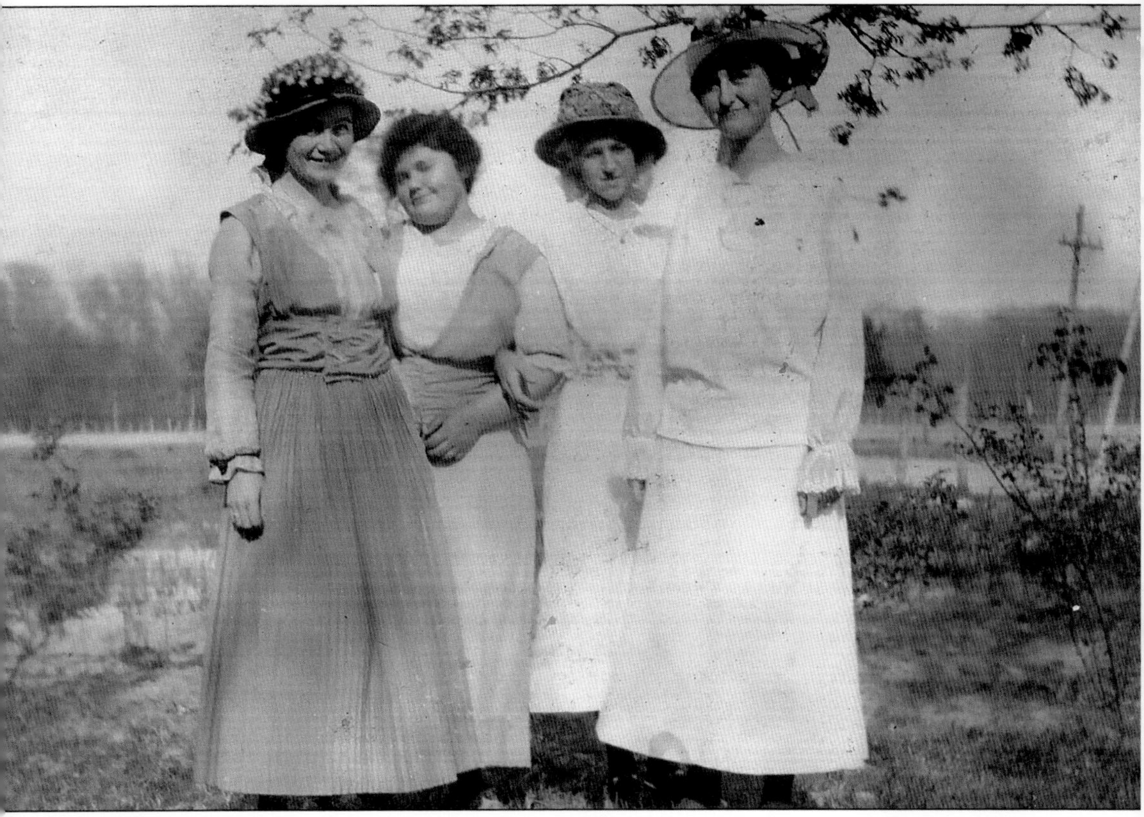

These ladies, from left to right, are Winnie Wood Walston, Mattie Brite, unidentified, and Nan Wood (half-sister of Winnie Wood Walston). The picture was taken in 1915.

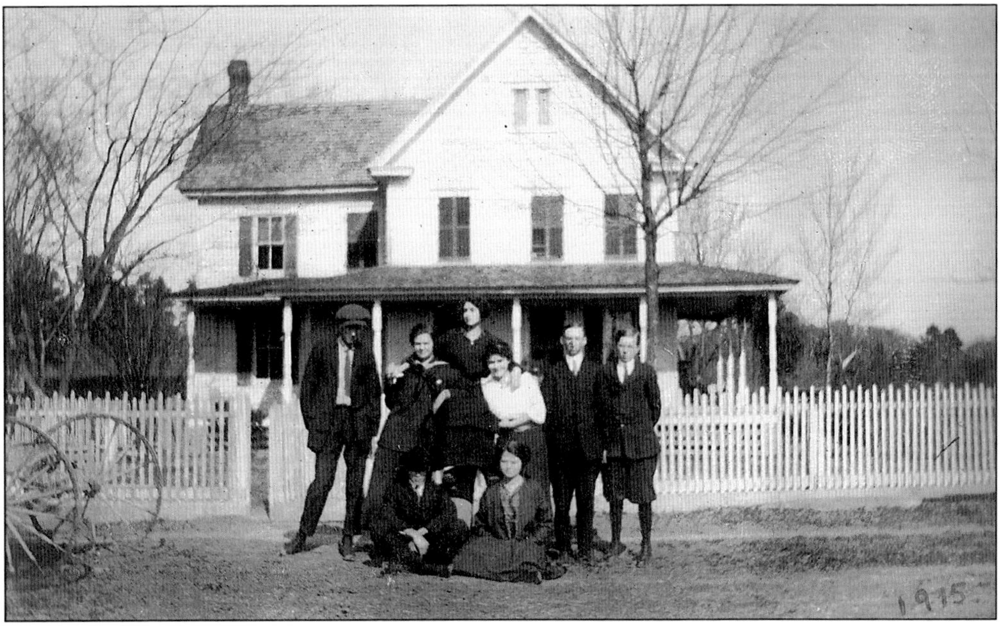

These pictures show the Wood farm in 1915. The house stood on the site of the present-day Pizza Inn.

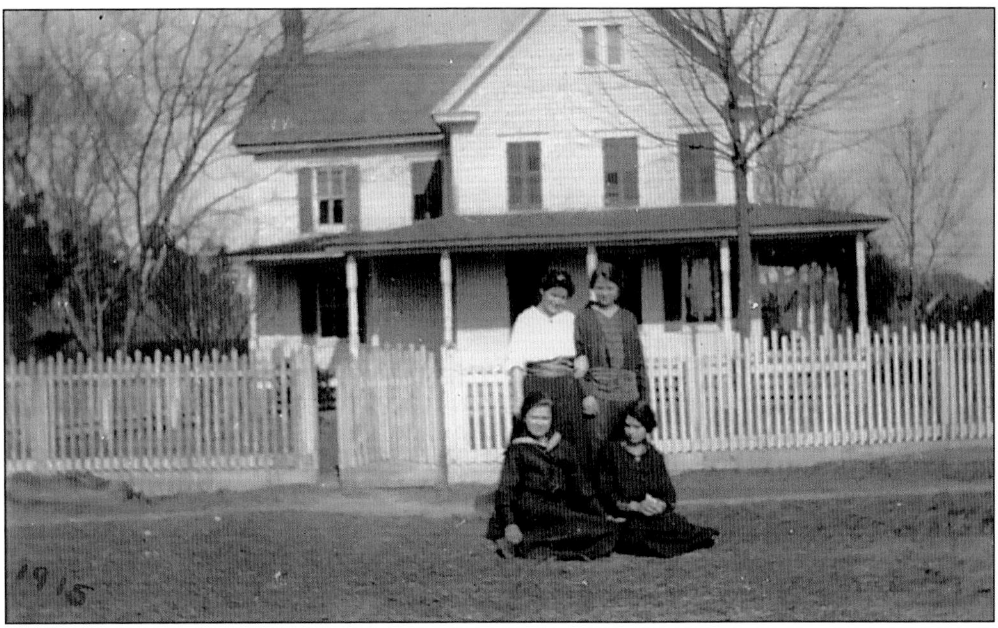

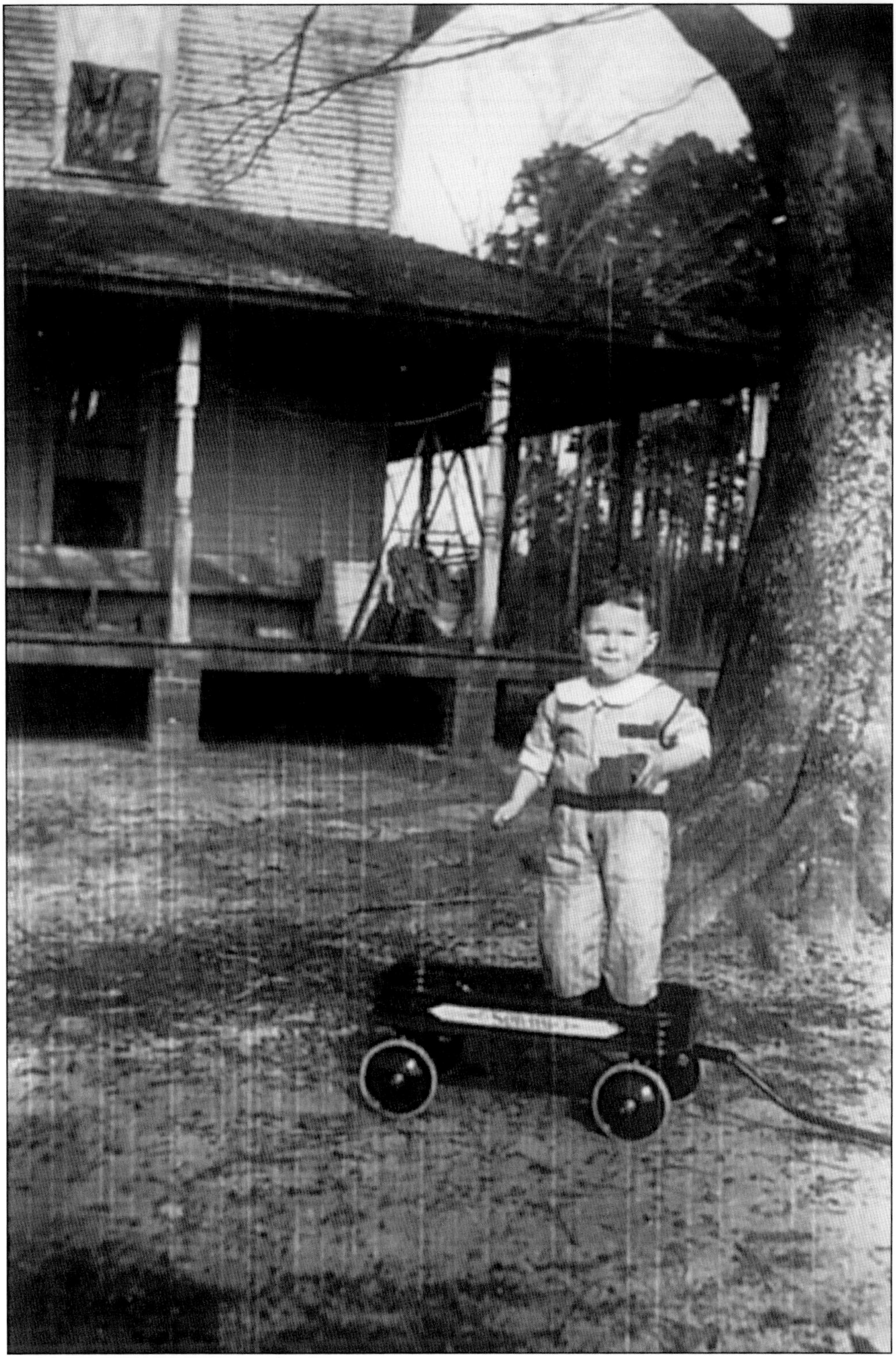

This is an unidentified boy with his wagon.

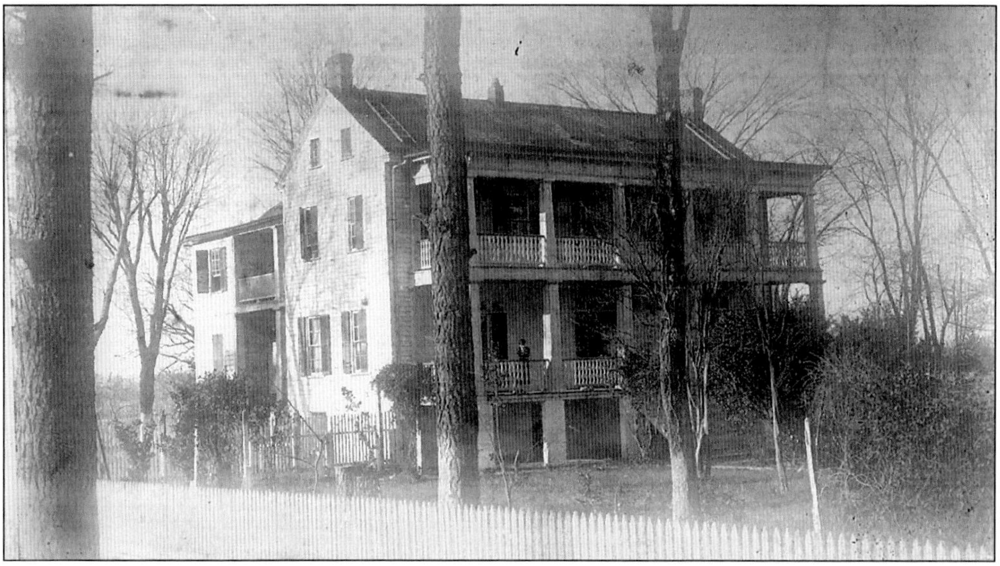

Florence Stevens's great-grandparents, the Engles, came from Trenton, New Jersey, after the Civil War and resided at the Messenger-Fearing-Morrisette Plantation located at 911 Riverside Avenue. The family had four girls and one boy. Florence Engle, one of the daughters, was the grandmother of Florence Stevens.

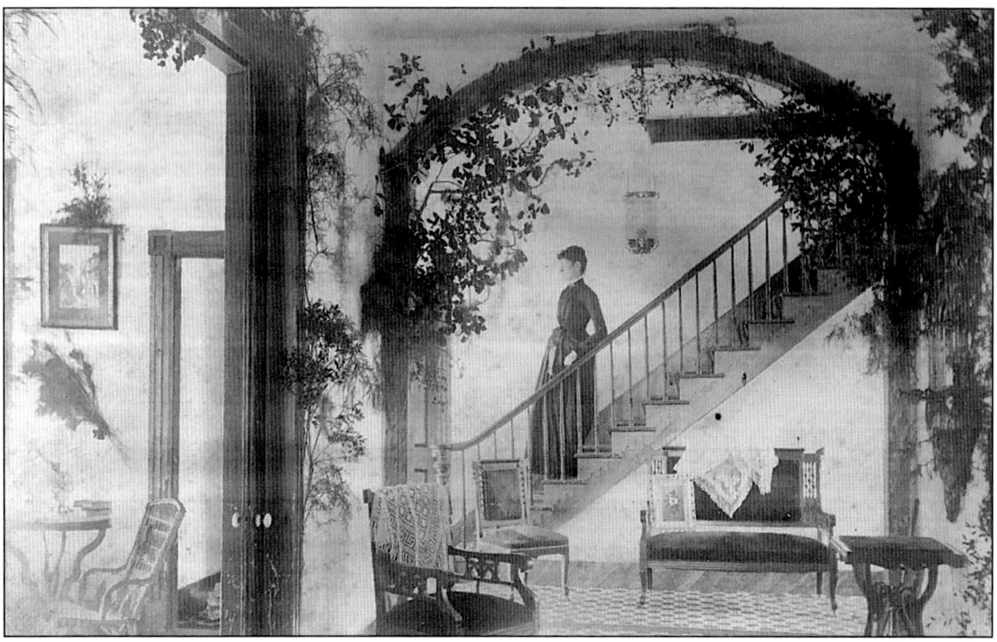

An interior photo of the Messenger-Fearing-Morrisette home shows Florence Engle on the staircase. Florence used to tell the story of the headless horseman that rode in the basement and "bumped" up the steps.

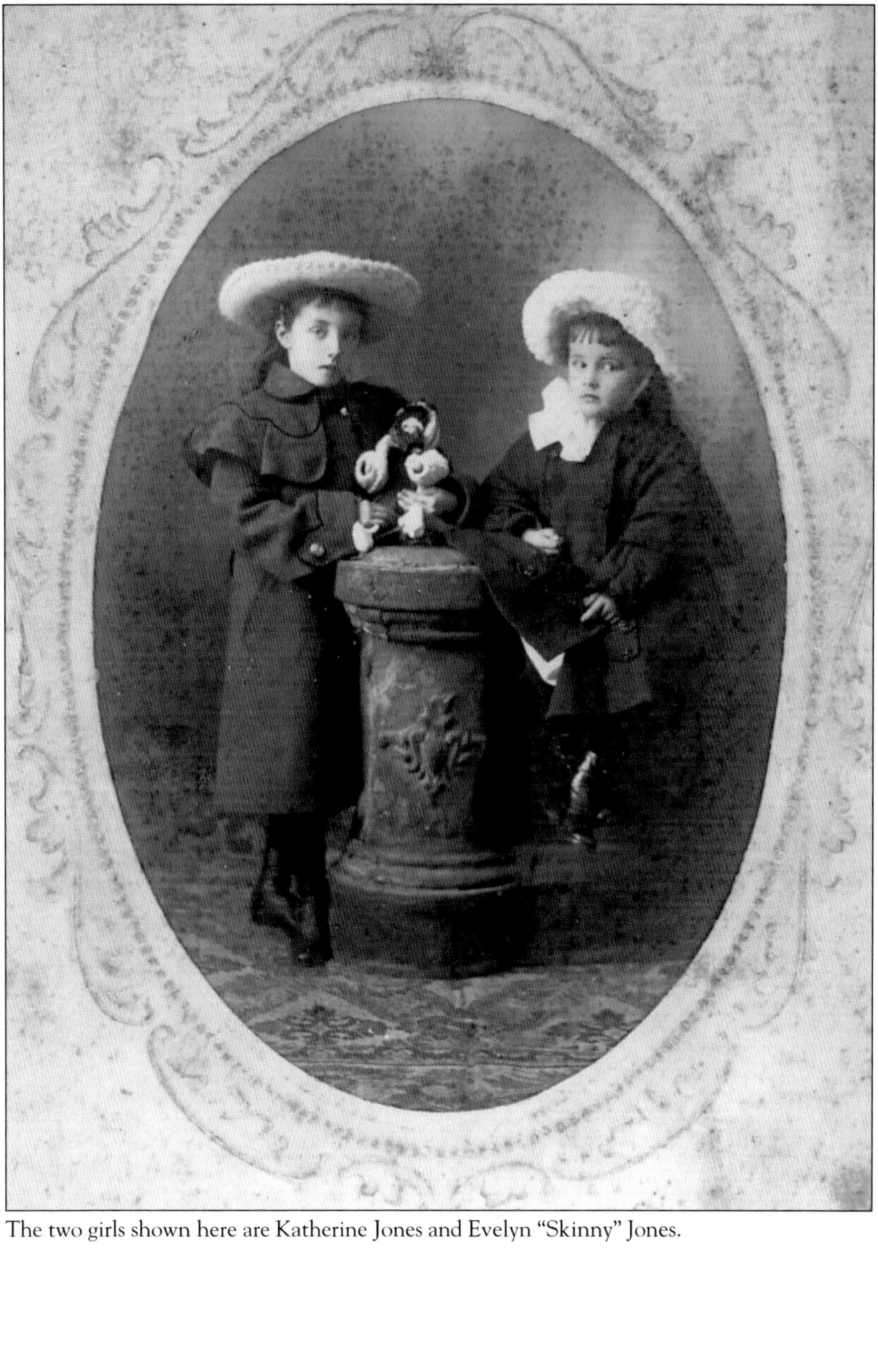

The two girls shown here are Katherine Jones and Evelyn "Skinny" Jones.

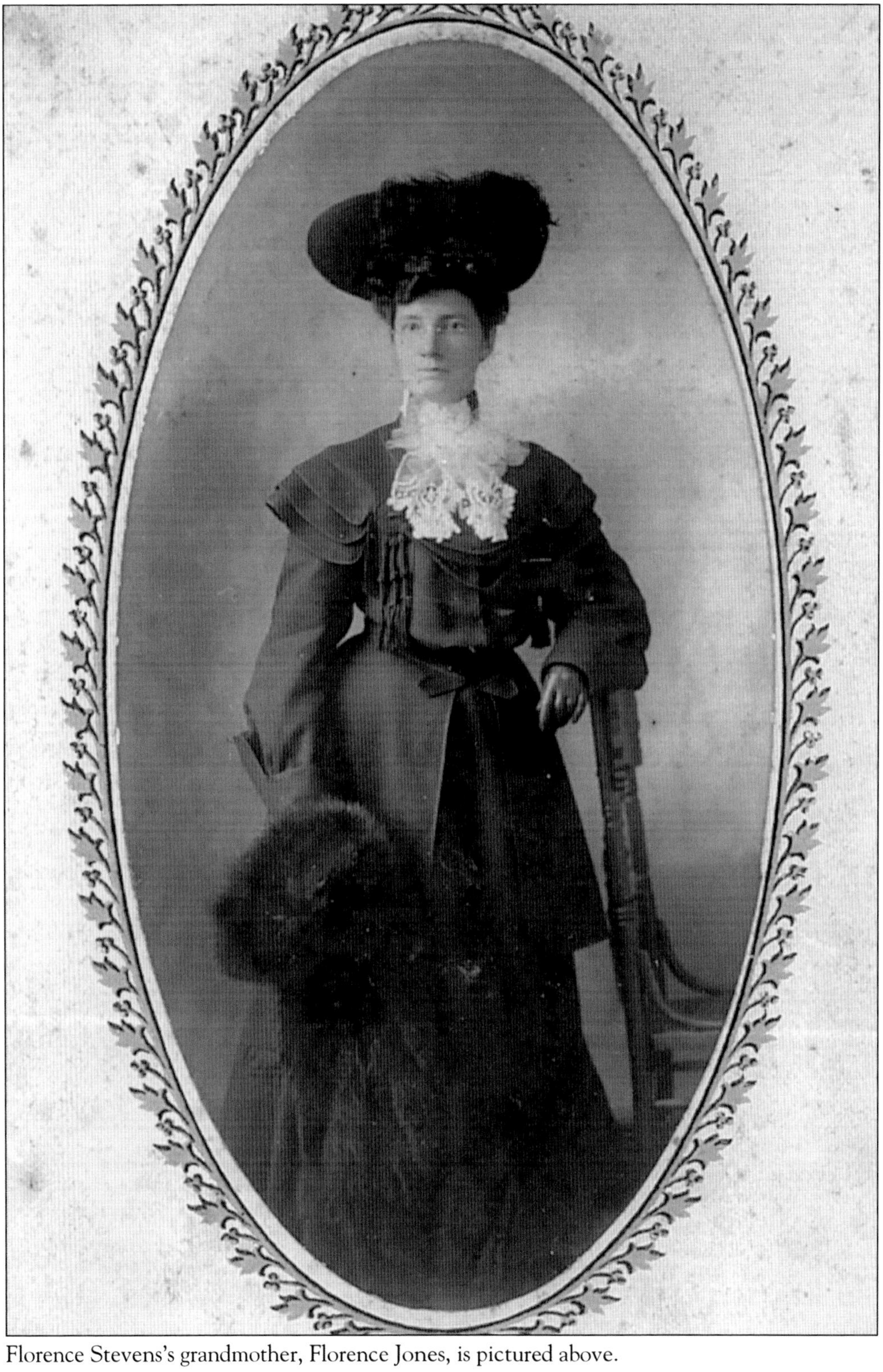

Florence Stevens's grandmother, Florence Jones, is pictured above.

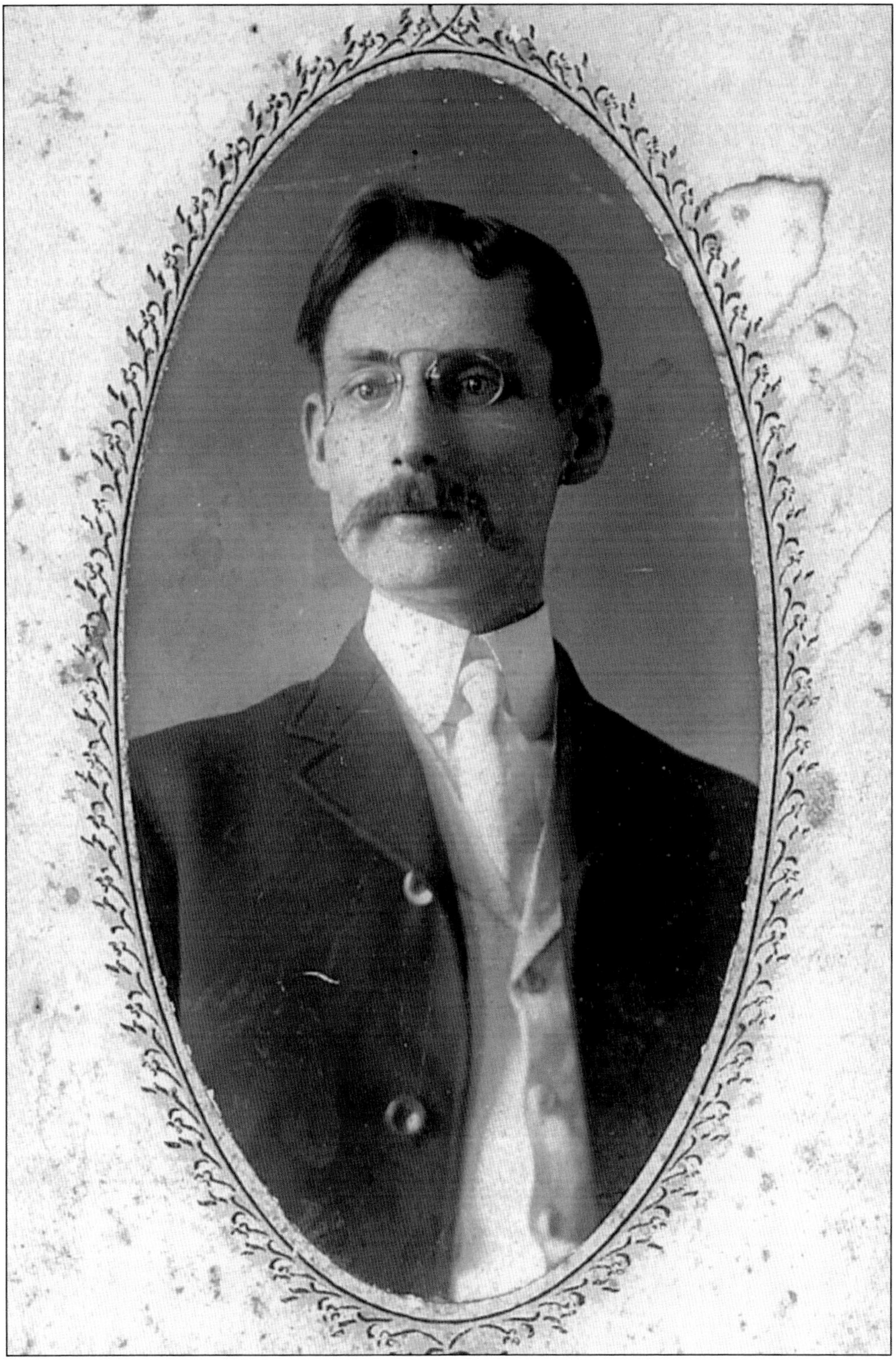

Tom Jones, a traveling salesman, is pictured above.

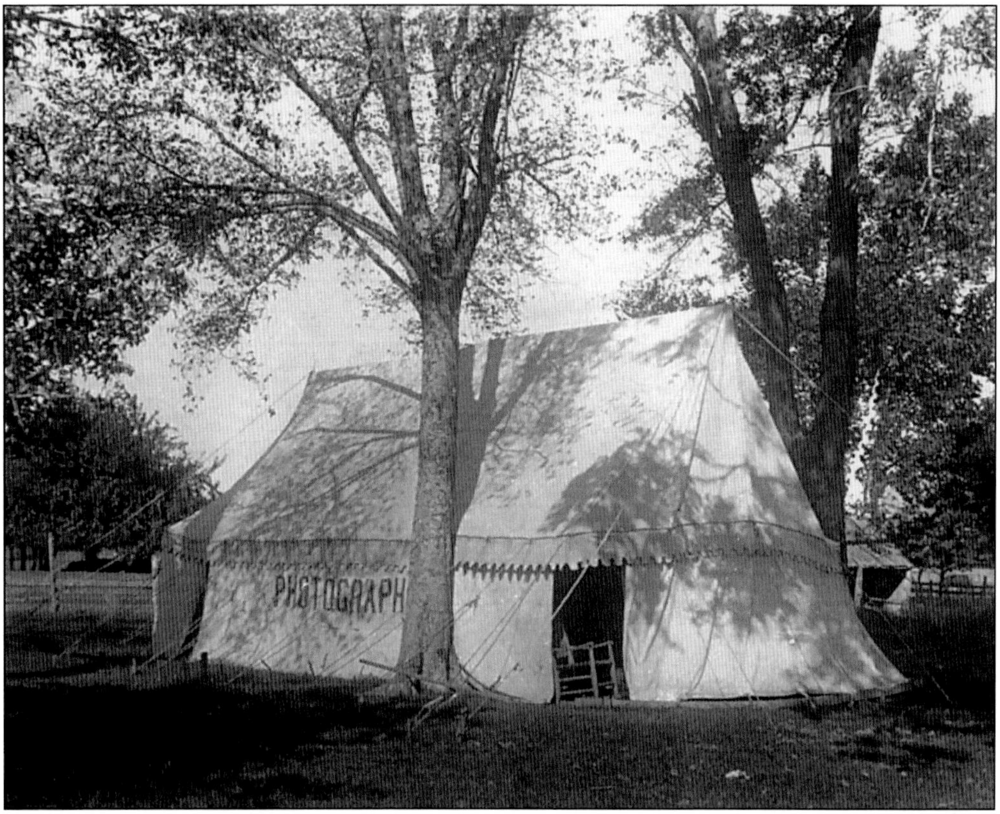

John Engle was a traveling photographer whose tent is shown in these images. He traveled to the North, the West Coast, and Mexico to take photographs. Engle lived in the Messinger-Fearing-Morrisette Home, and is seen seated outside of his tent in the photo below.

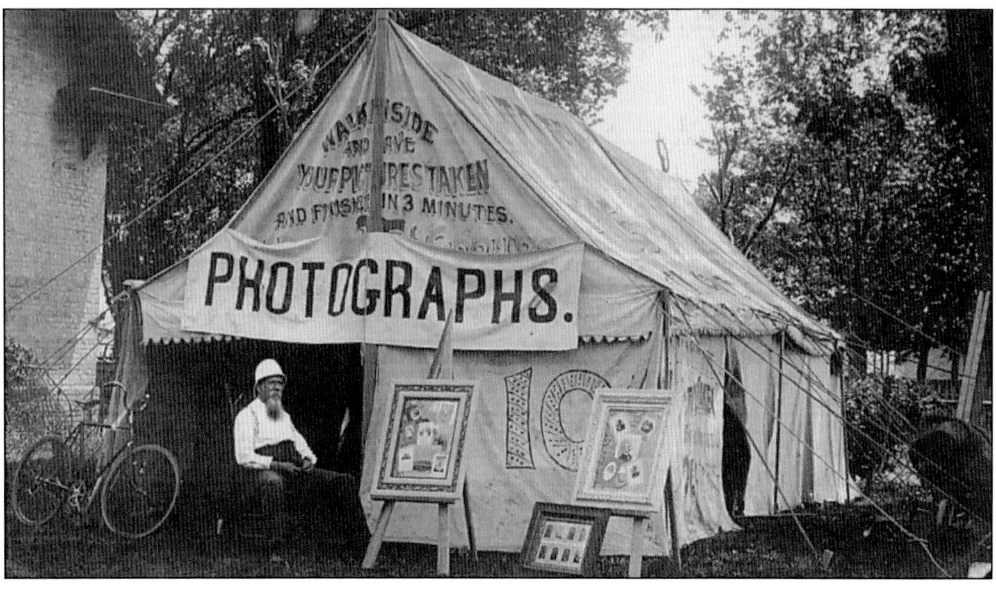

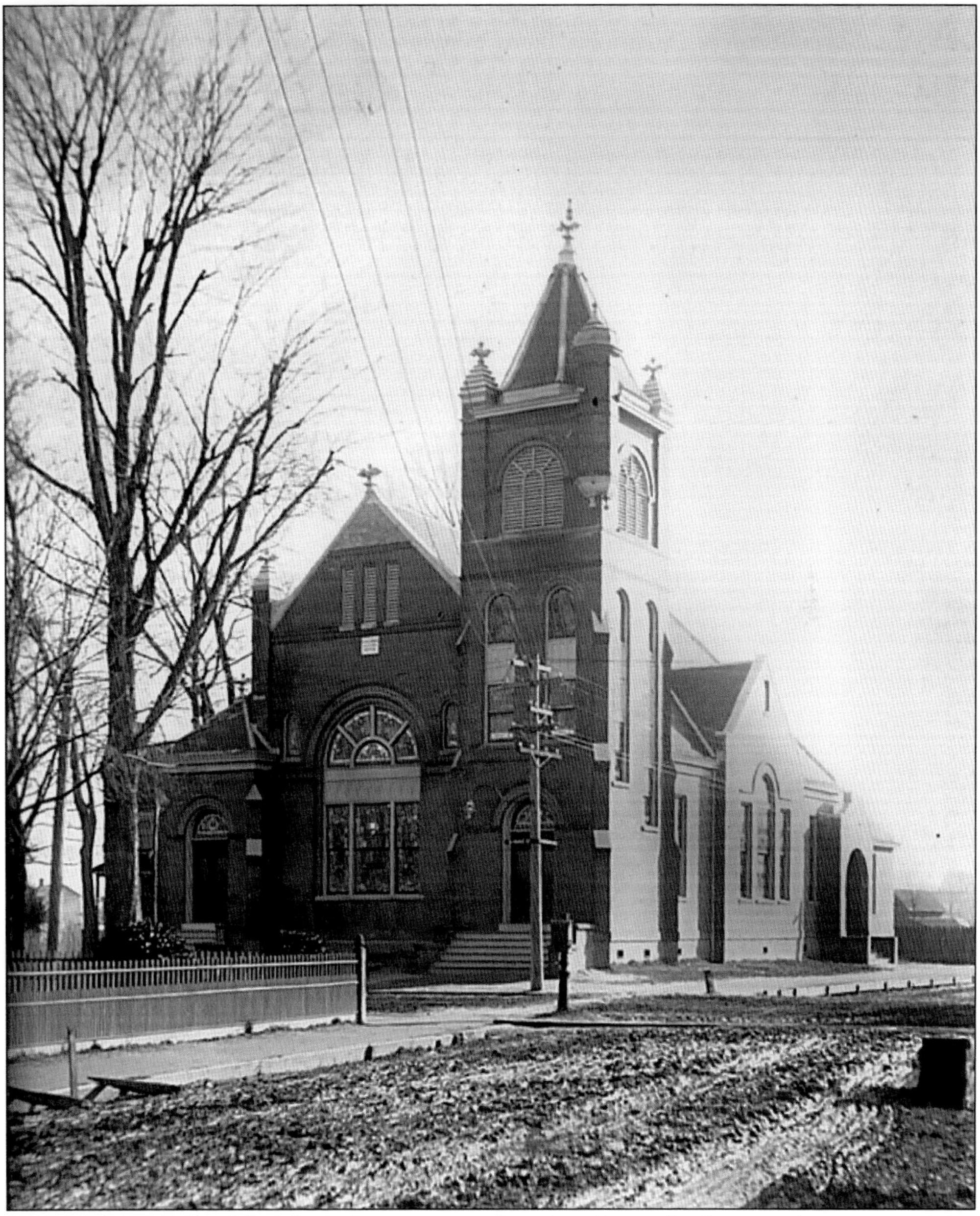

City Road Methodist Church sits on an unpaved road in this early photograph.

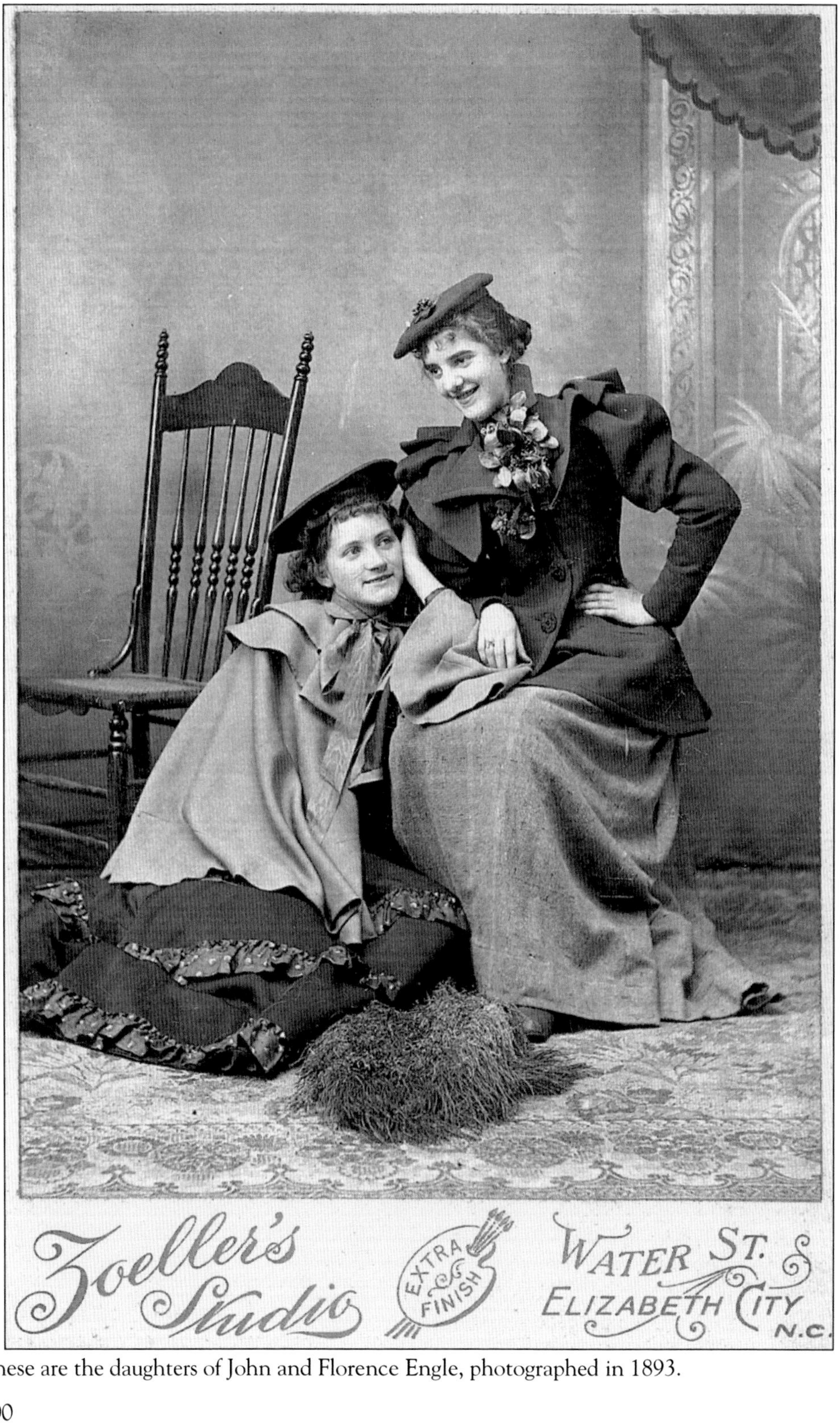

These are the daughters of John and Florence Engle, photographed in 1893.

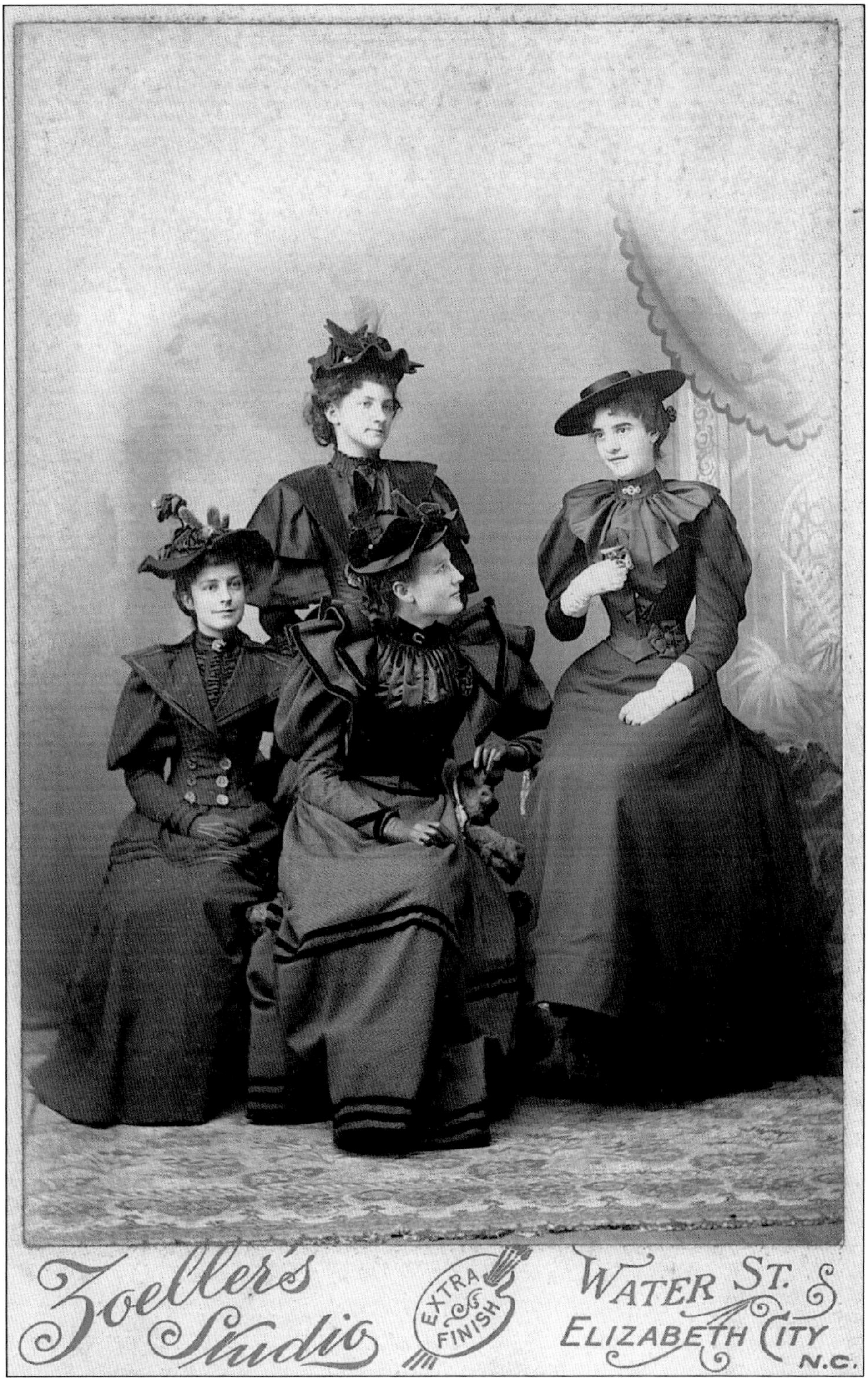

John and Florence Engle's daughters are shown in this photo during Christmas of 1892.

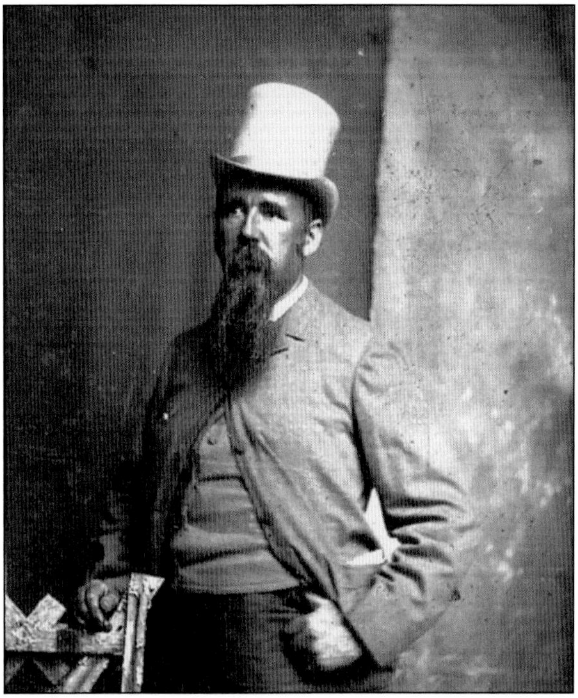

When photography was in its infancy, a kind of picture called the tintype was used. This is a picture of John Engle.

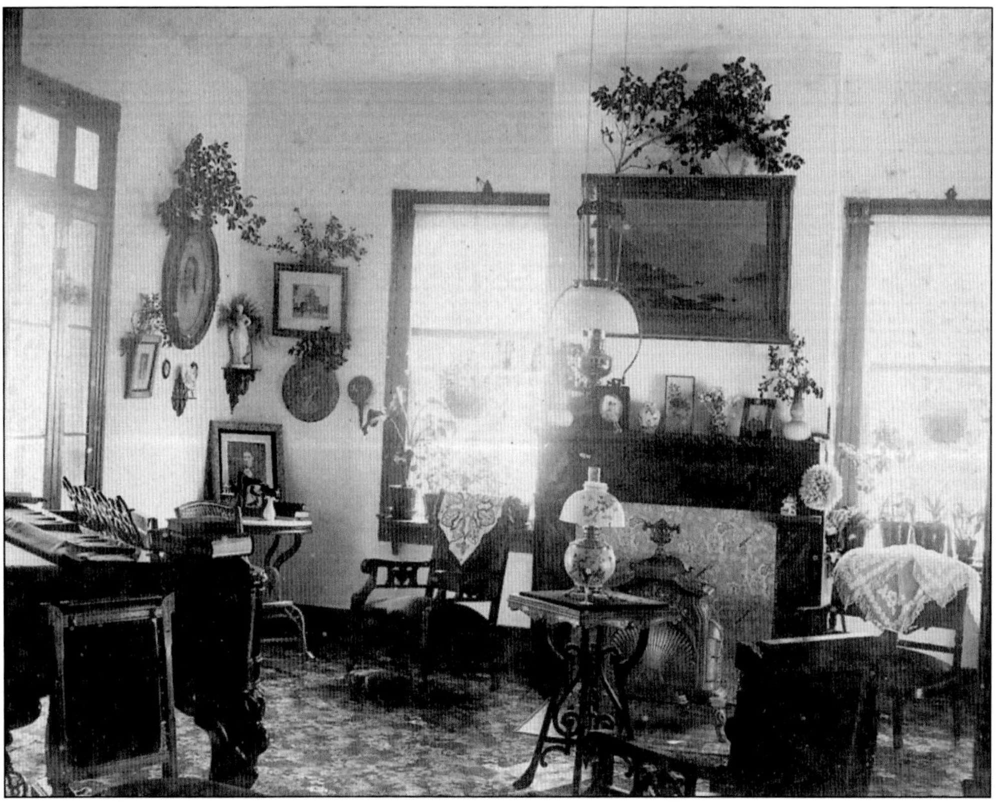

The Engles's Christmas decorations are seen at the Messenger-Fearing-Morrisette home.

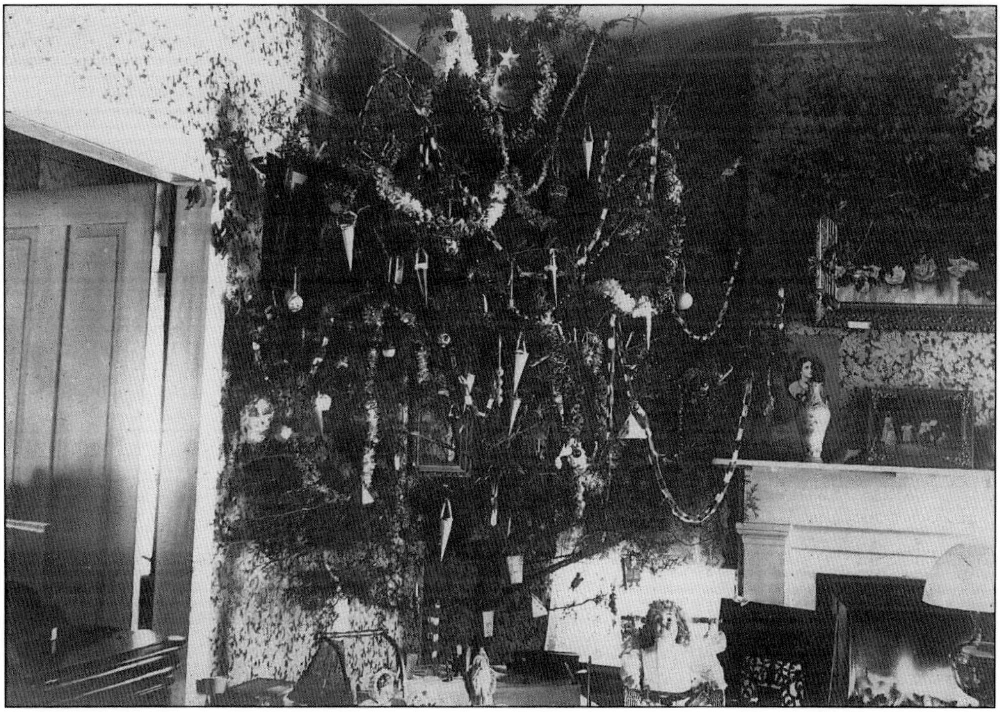

Florence Engle Jones always left her Christmas tree up until Easter. They rarely had heat in the room so that made the tree last longer.

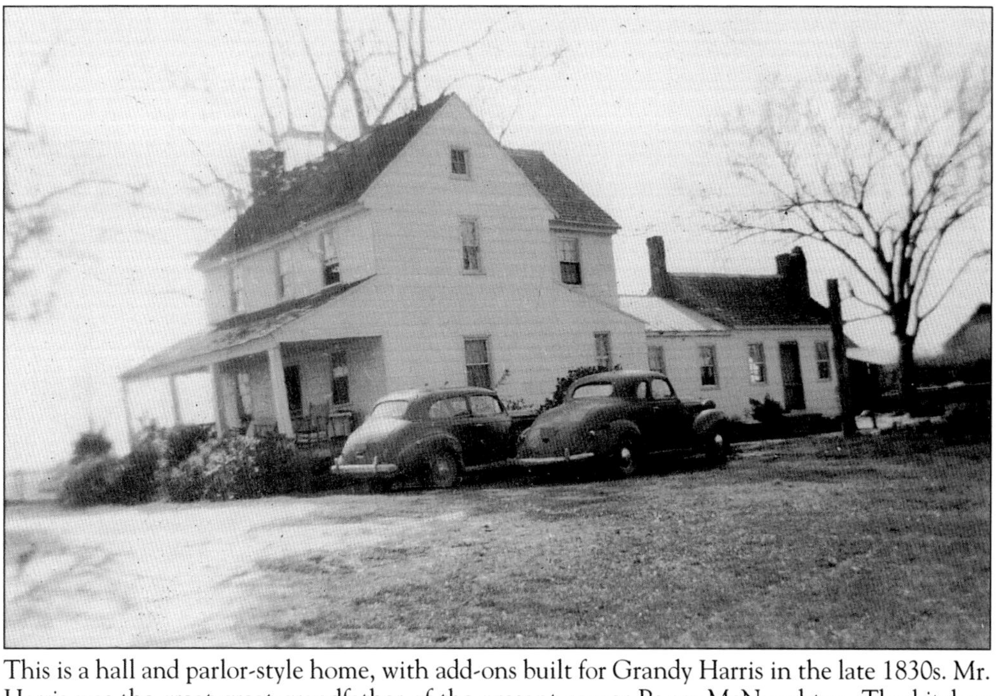

This is a hall and parlor-style home, with add-ons built for Grandy Harris in the late 1830s. Mr. Harris was the great-great-grandfather of the present owner Peggy McNaughton. The kitchen at the far end was moved from another home that burned on the plantation. The home is located on West Main Street Extended.

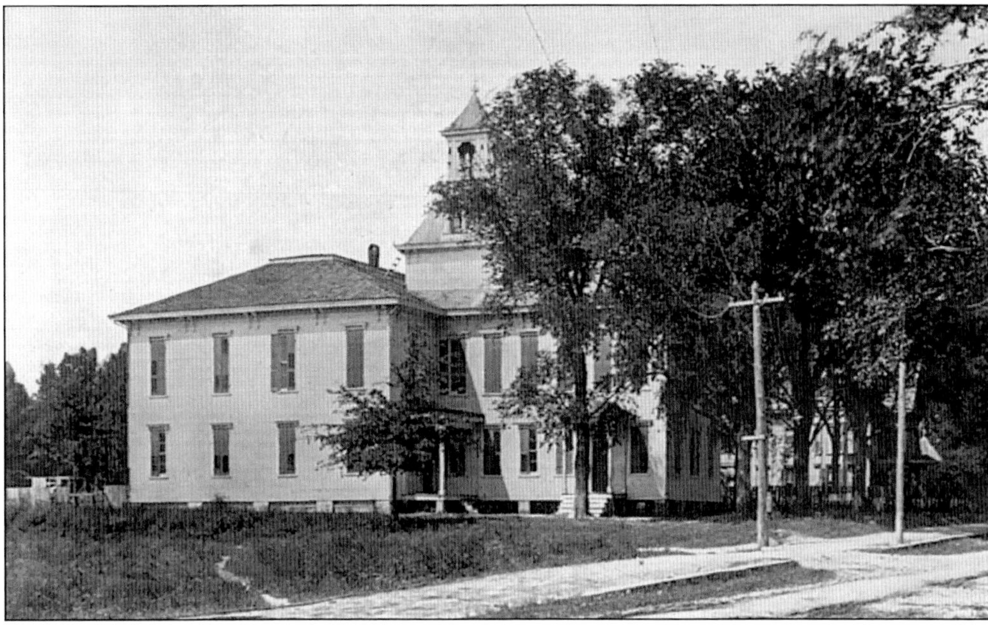

Atlantic Collegiate Institute was opened in 1878 as Elizabeth City Academy. There were three departments. The Primary Department taught reading, spelling, writing, language lessons, arithmetic, geography, singing, drawing, and calisthenics. The Preparatory Department taught reading, spelling, writing, geography, grammar, arithmetic, U.S. history, physiology, Latin, and French. The Collegiate Department taught classical and English. Students were required to study each night—Primary for one hour, Intermediate for two-and-a-half hours, and Advanced for three hours.

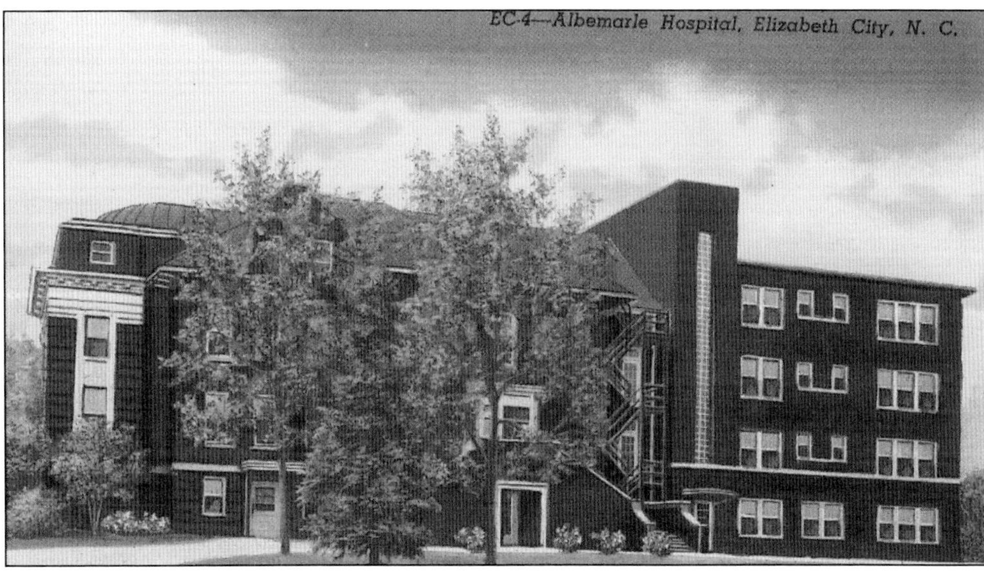

Albemarle Hospital, created in 1914, was located in Riverside on the Pasquotank River. It was the first established hospital building in the Albemarle area, designed by Wilson, North Carolina architects Benton and Moore. The building was later sold and became College of the Albemarle. Today it is Riverwind Apartments.

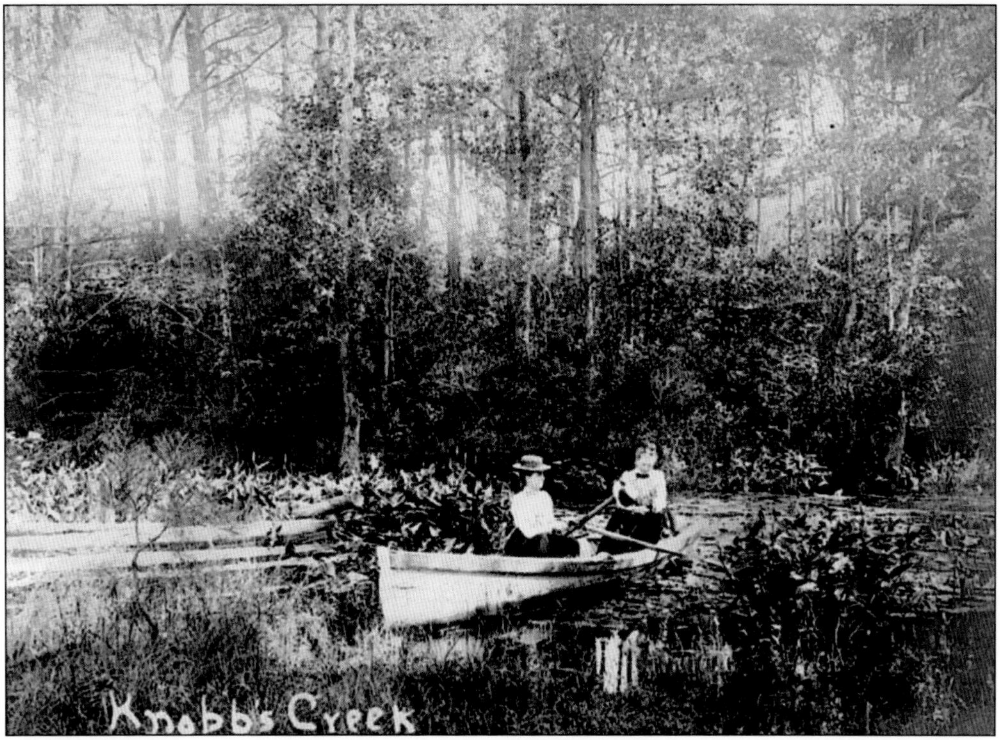

Knobbs Creek was a wonderful place for a boat ride adventure.

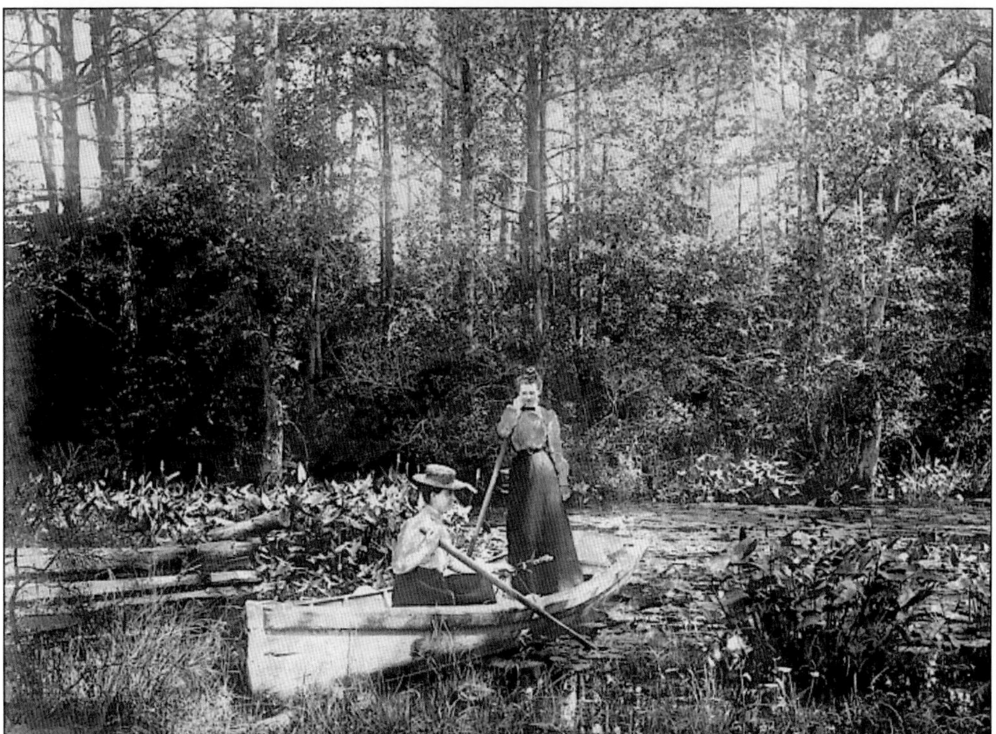

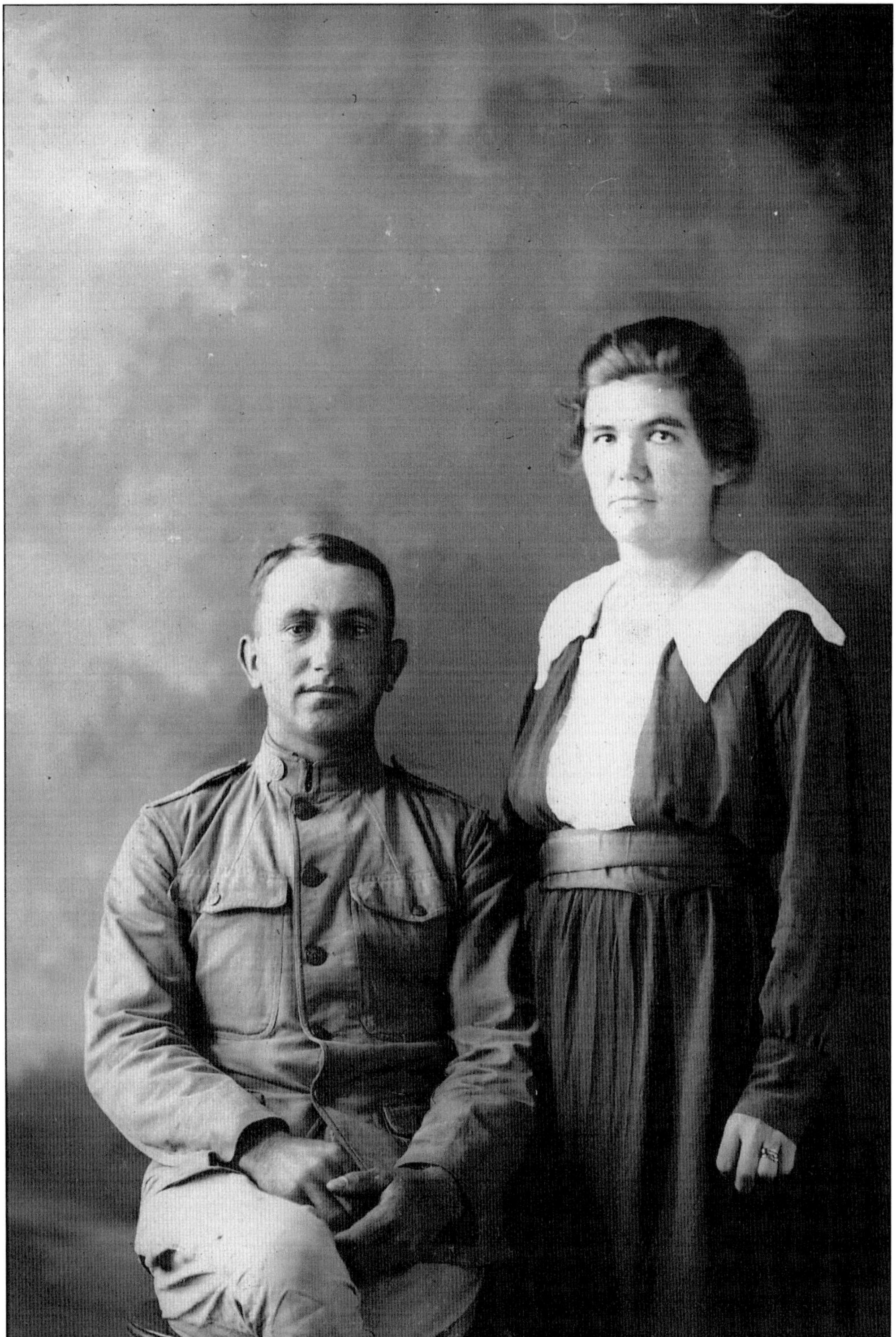

The couple in this early 1900s photo are unidentified; he wears a World War I uniform.

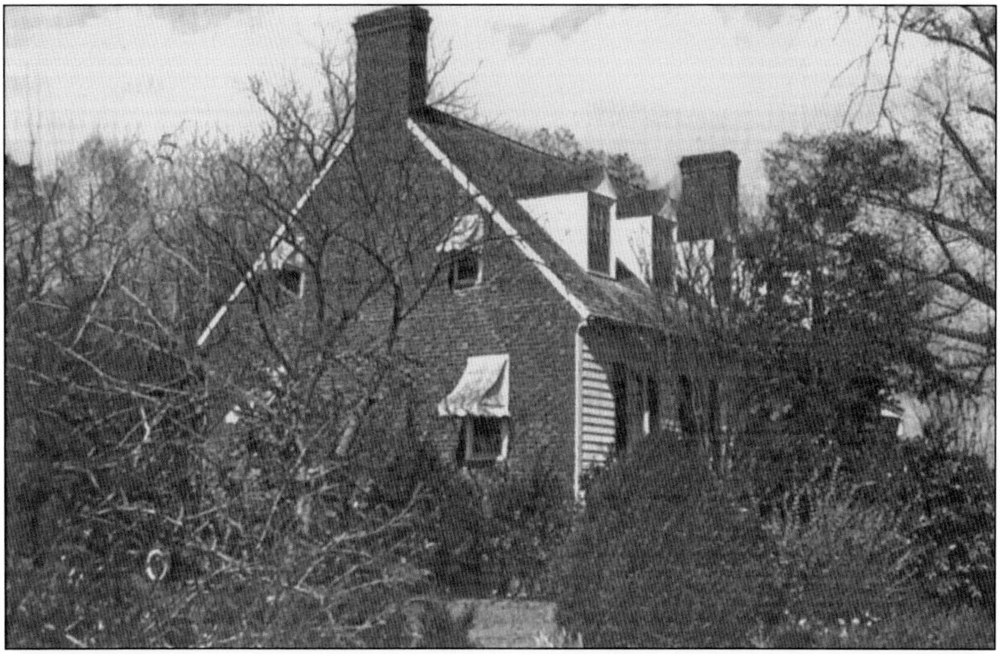

The old Brick House is located three miles from Elizabeth City. It was built in 1750 by Robert Munden. He served in the House of Commons from 1754 to 1759, and had 19 slaves and more than 2,700 acres. The house stayed in the Munden family until 1841 and was sold. In 1935 Charles A. McLellan bought the house and sold the interiors. In 1936 Paul Jackson and his wife, Carrie, bought the house and re-built the interiors. In 1943 Eleanor and John Stuart bought the house.

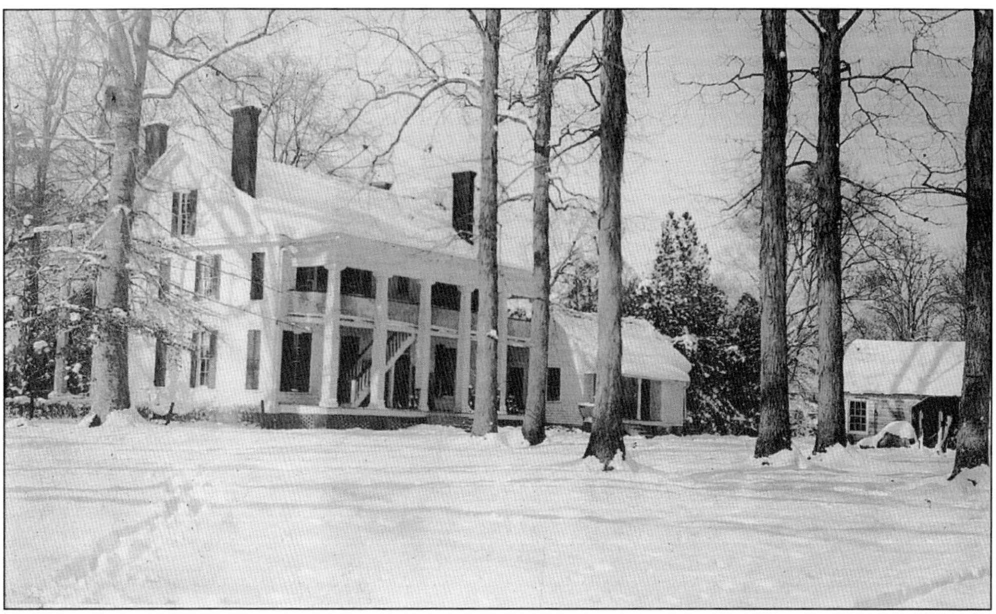

Christopher Wilson Hollowell built Bayside Plantation in 1856 around the time he married Alpine Bodine. This snow scene shows the rear of the home with its Doric pillars and second-story porch.

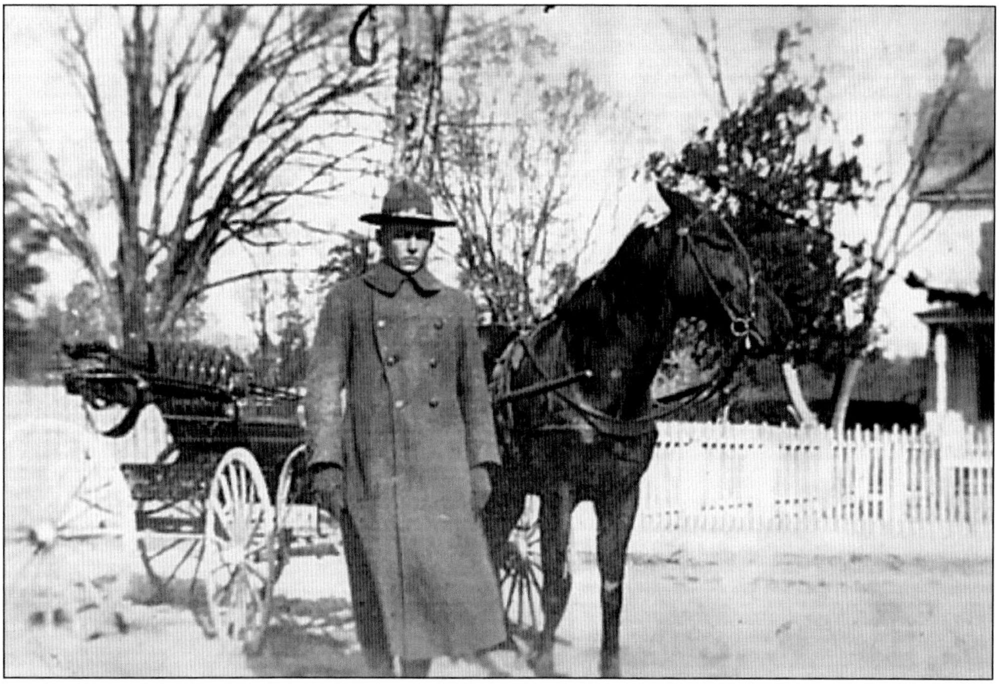

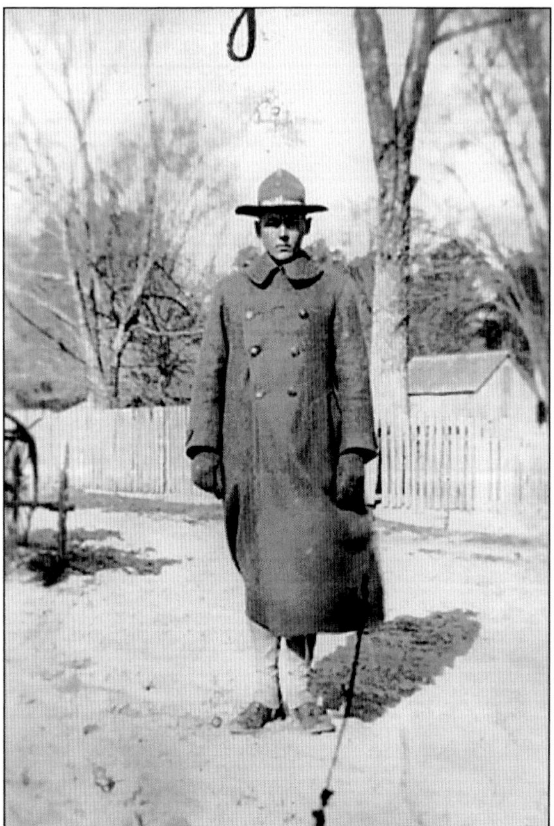

Lloyd Tuttle was the father of Audrey Tuttle who lived on Oak Stump Road. He is shown here in his World War I uniform.

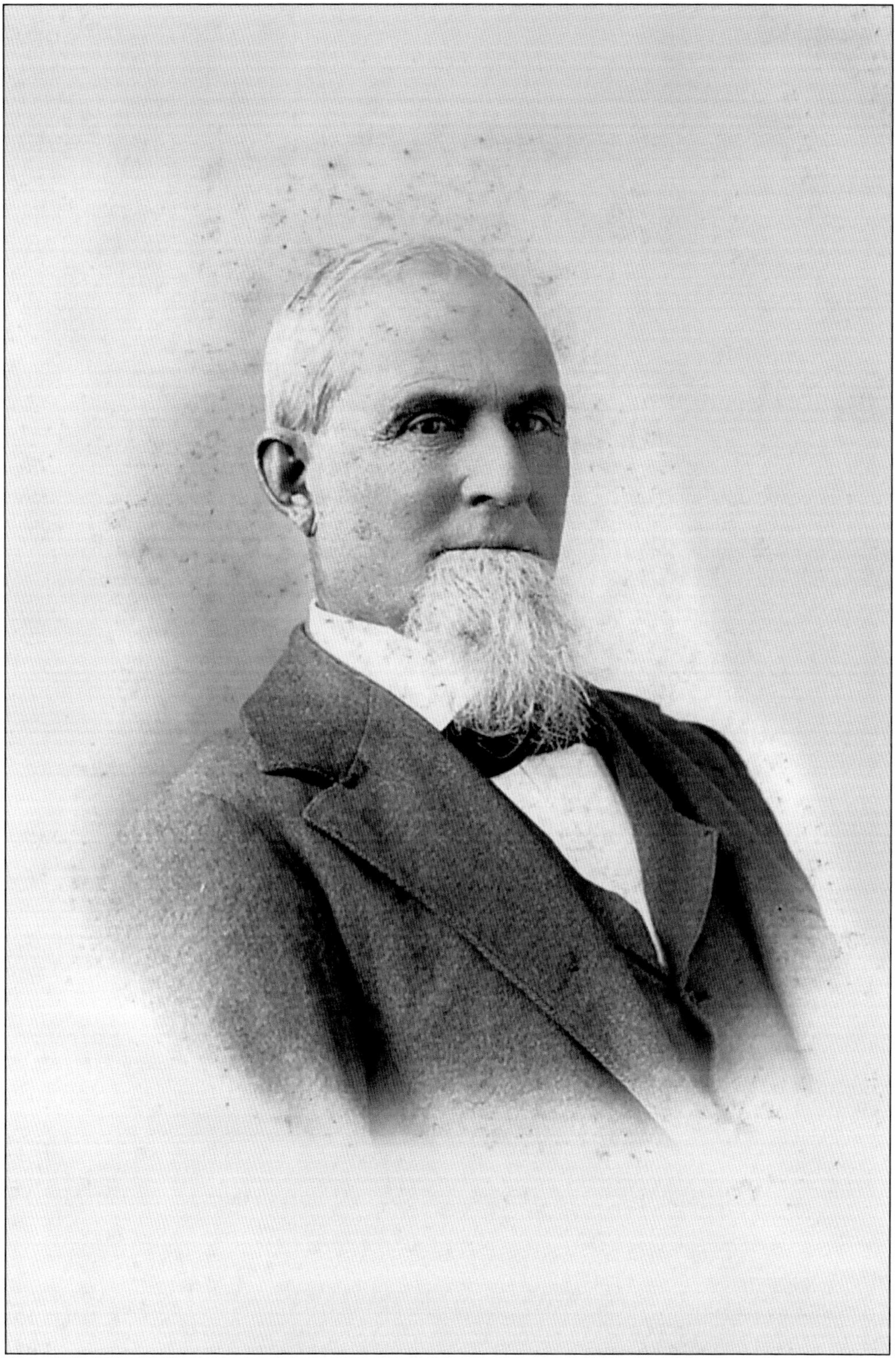

Henry Clay Wood was born in 1836. He was the grandfather of Jean Walston.

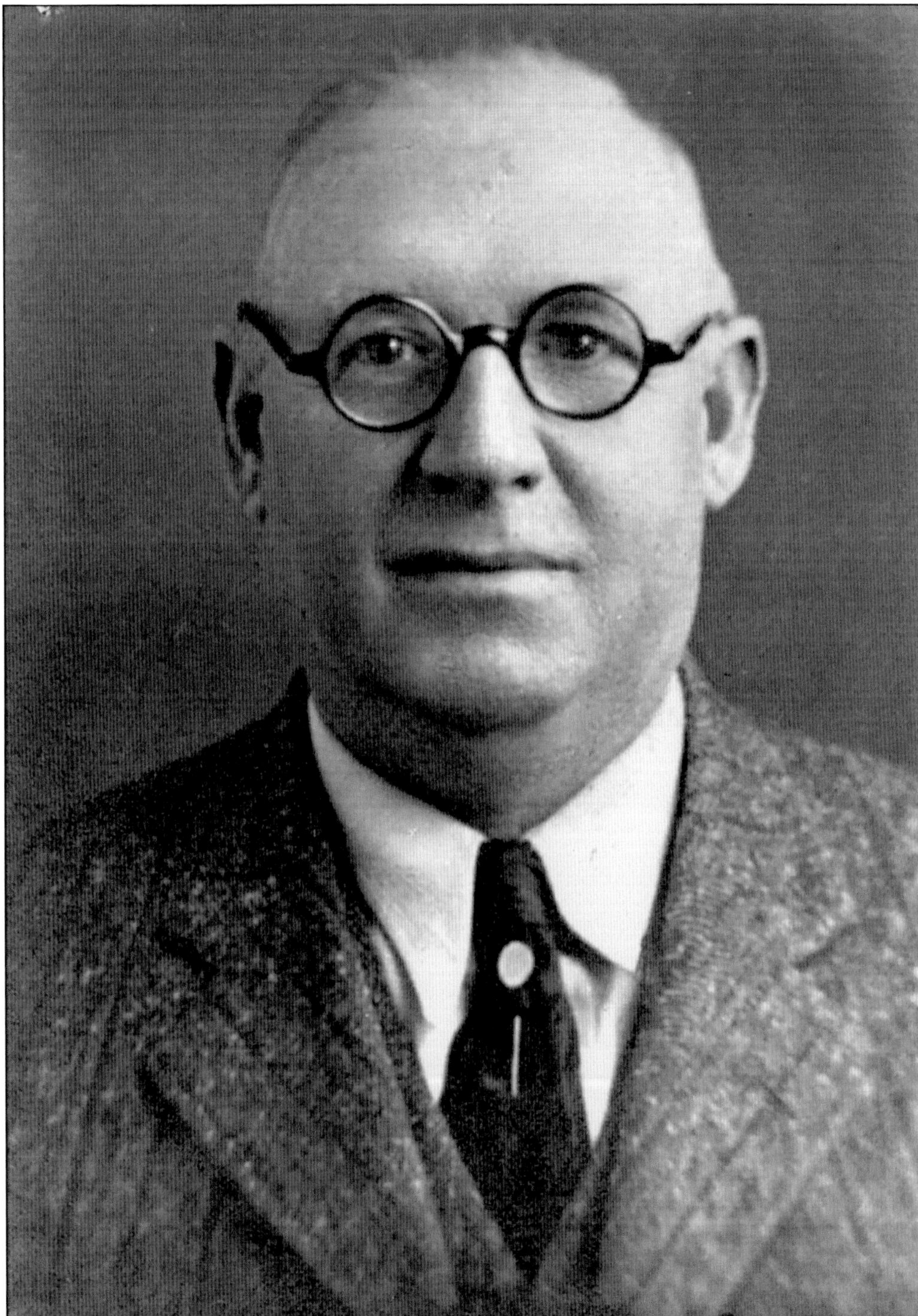

Ambrose Barco Walston was the grandfather of Jean K. Walston; he sold logs for a living. He died in 1937.

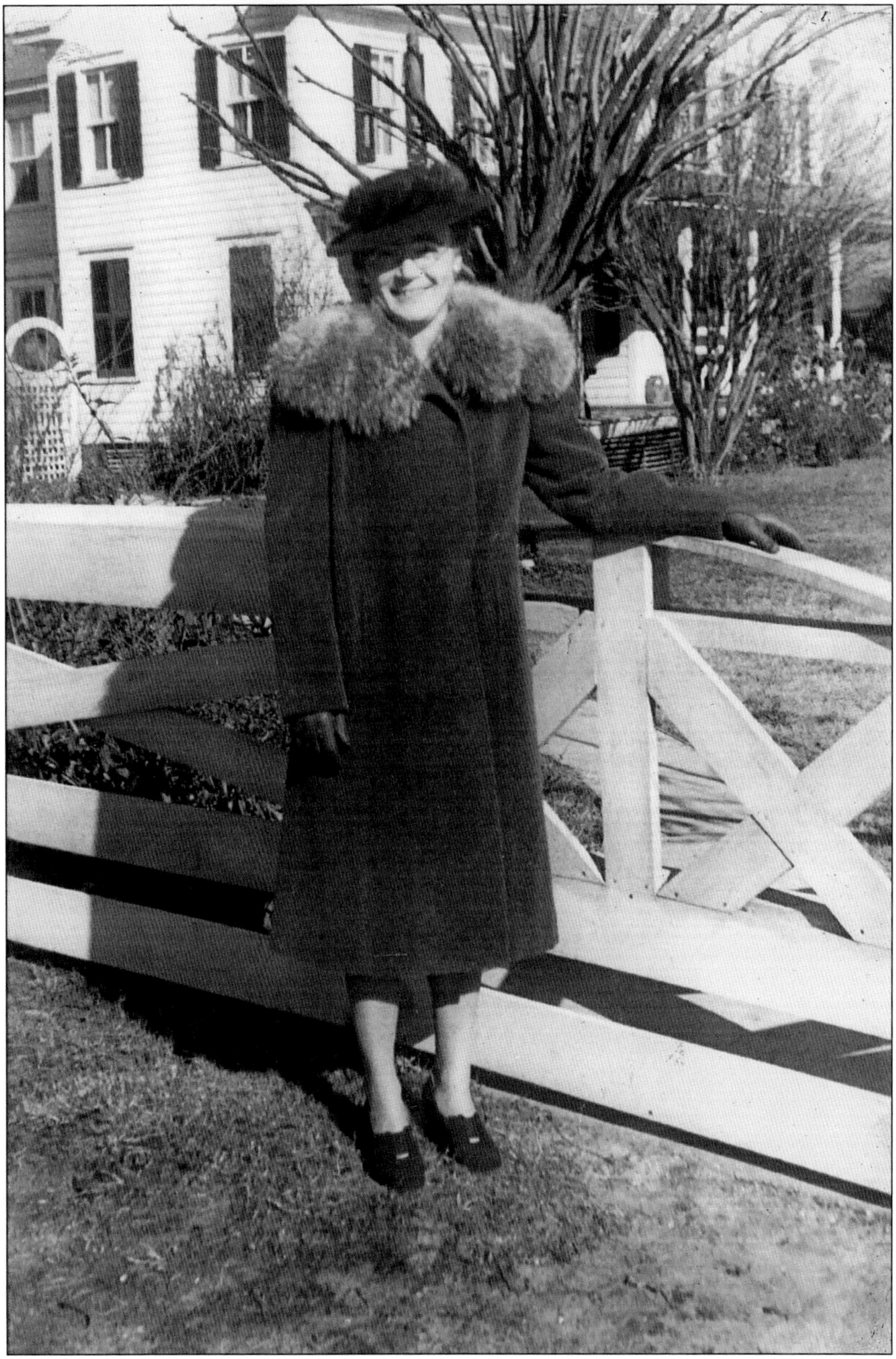

Winnie Marie Wood Walston, mother of Jean Walston, is pictured above.

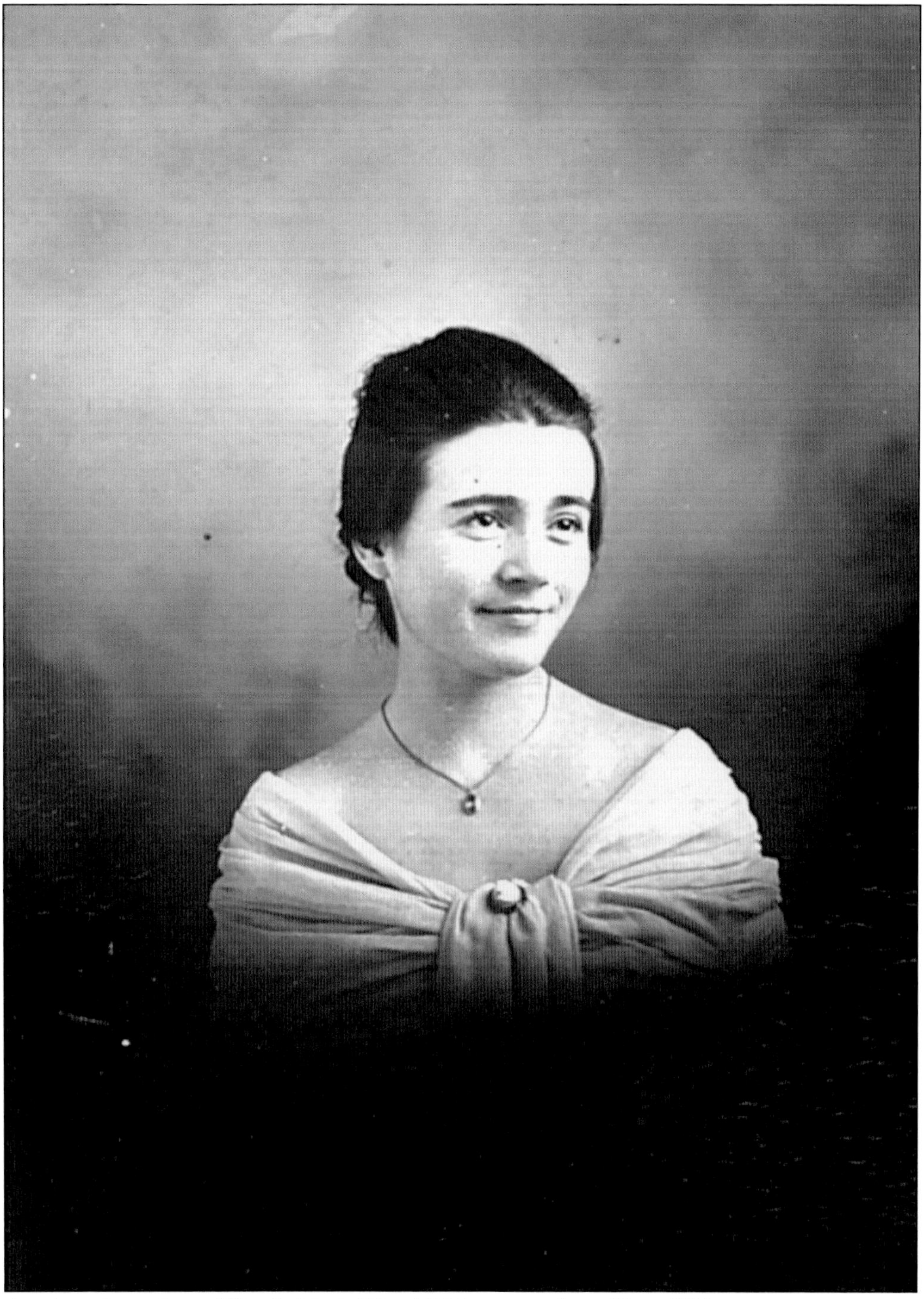

Another photo shows Winnie Marie Wood Walston, mother of Jean Walston.

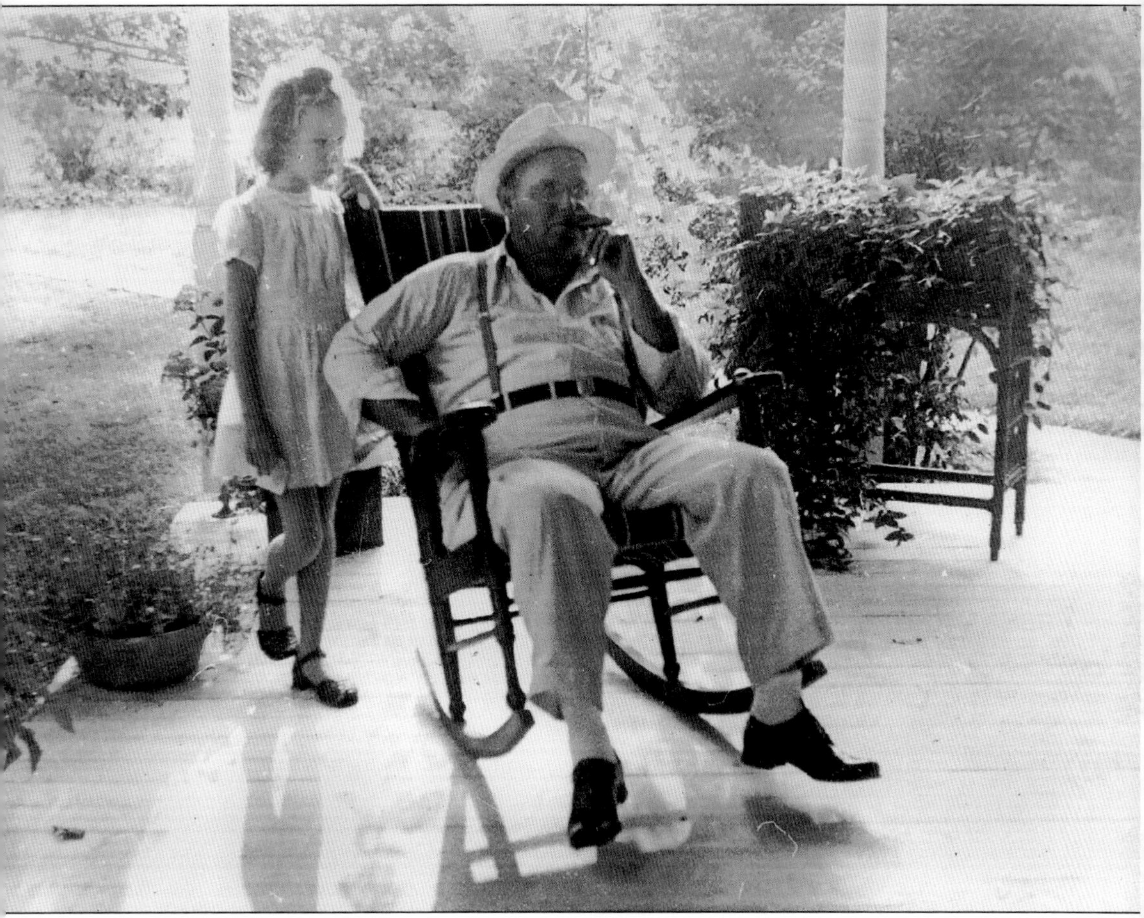

This picture taken on September 19, 1942, shows Bettye Lou Wood Murphy, age eight, along with Paul Walston.

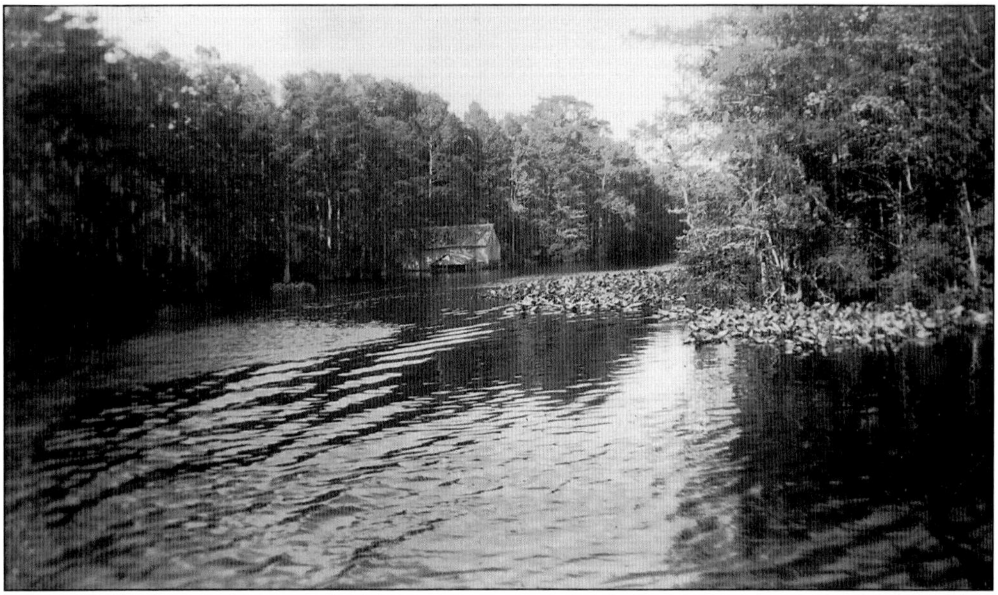

Both of the photos show Newbegun Creek and were taken in May of 1940.

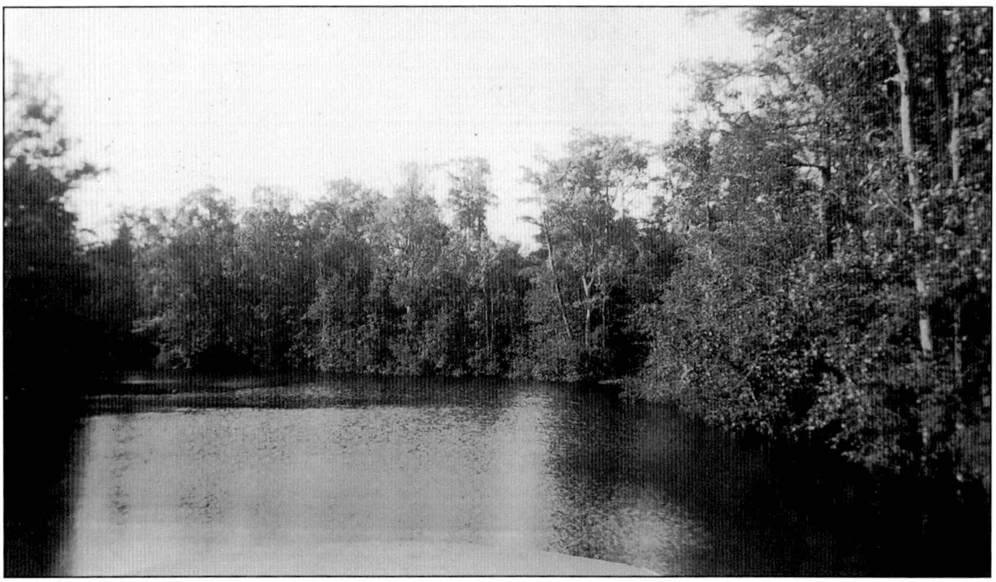

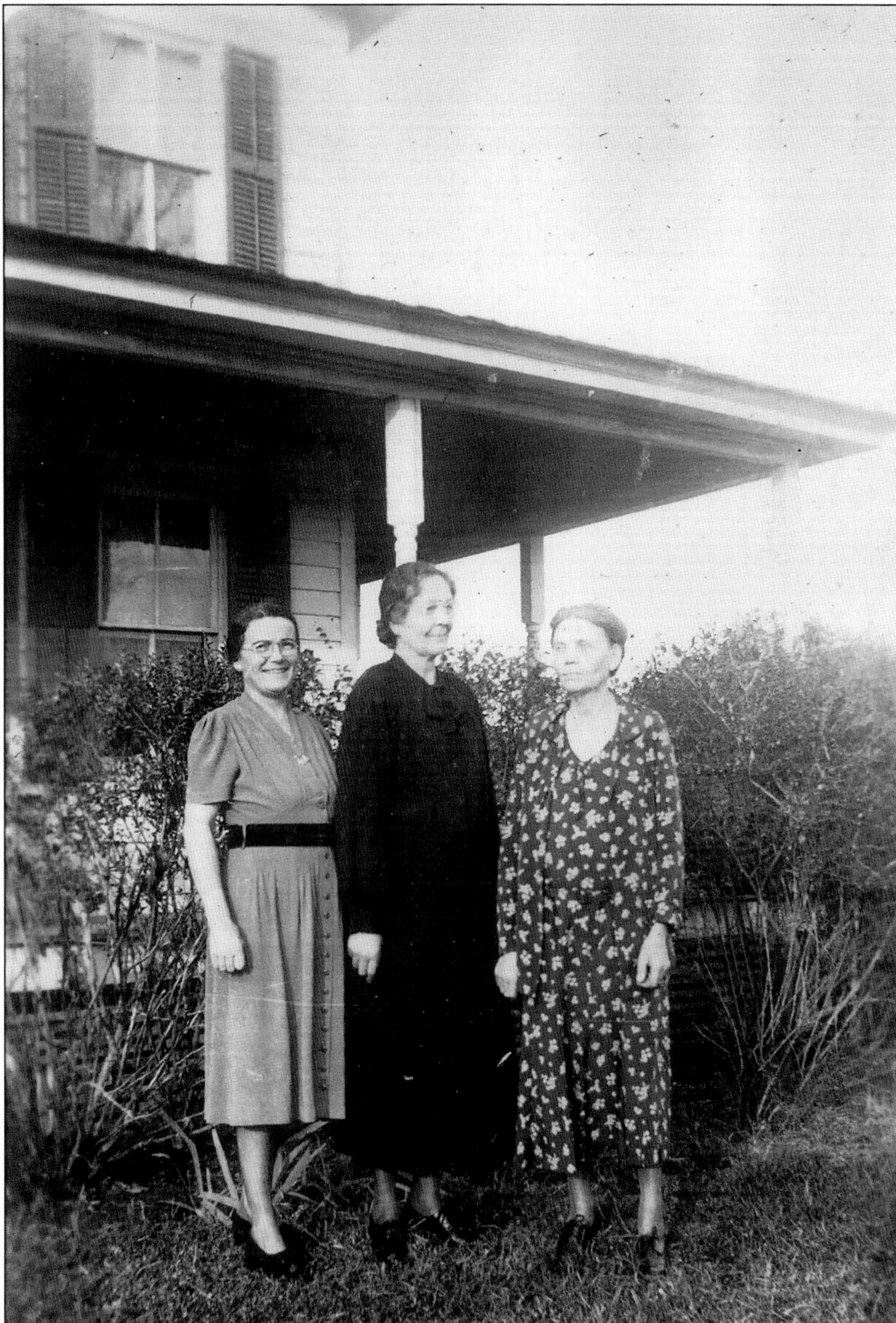

Shown from left to right are Winnie Wood Walston, Alice Keats, and Betty Keats as they celebrate Christmas of 1938.

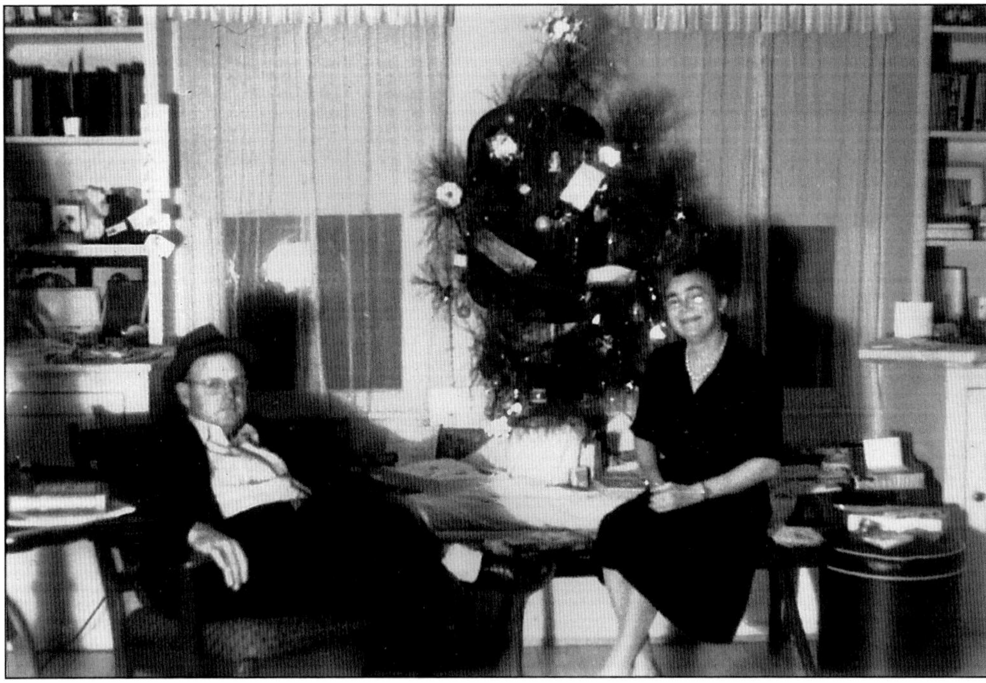

Paul Walston and Winnie Wood Walston are seen in their living room in this December 29, 1946 photo during the Christmas holidays.

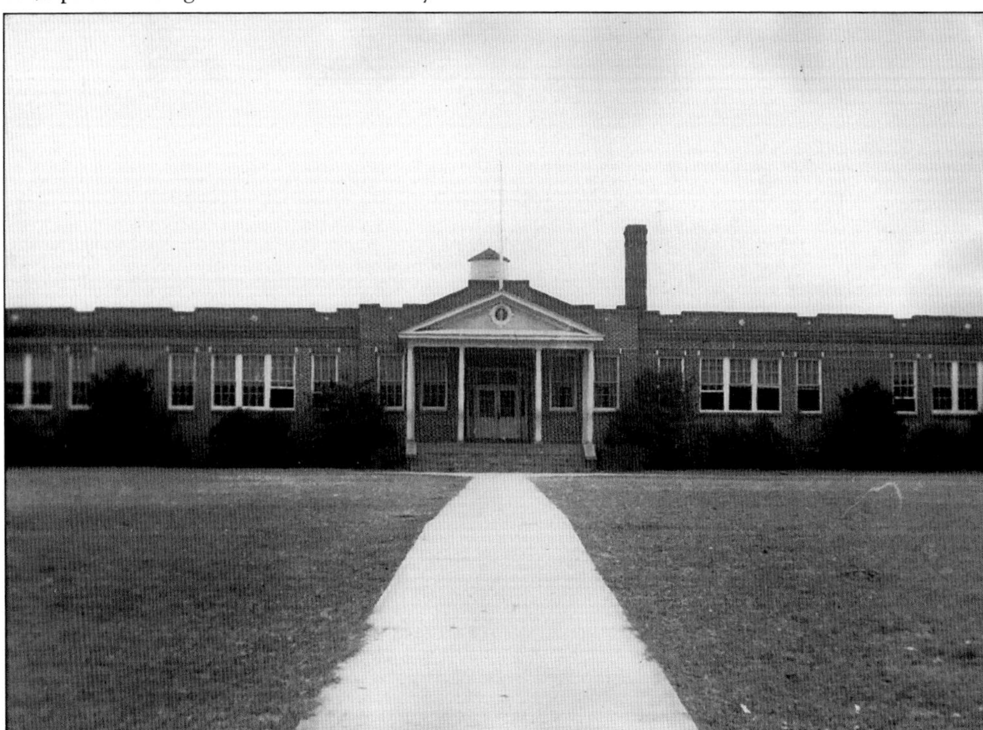

Central High School is shown here during the 1938–1939 school year. It is now demolished and stood where Central Elementary School now stands.

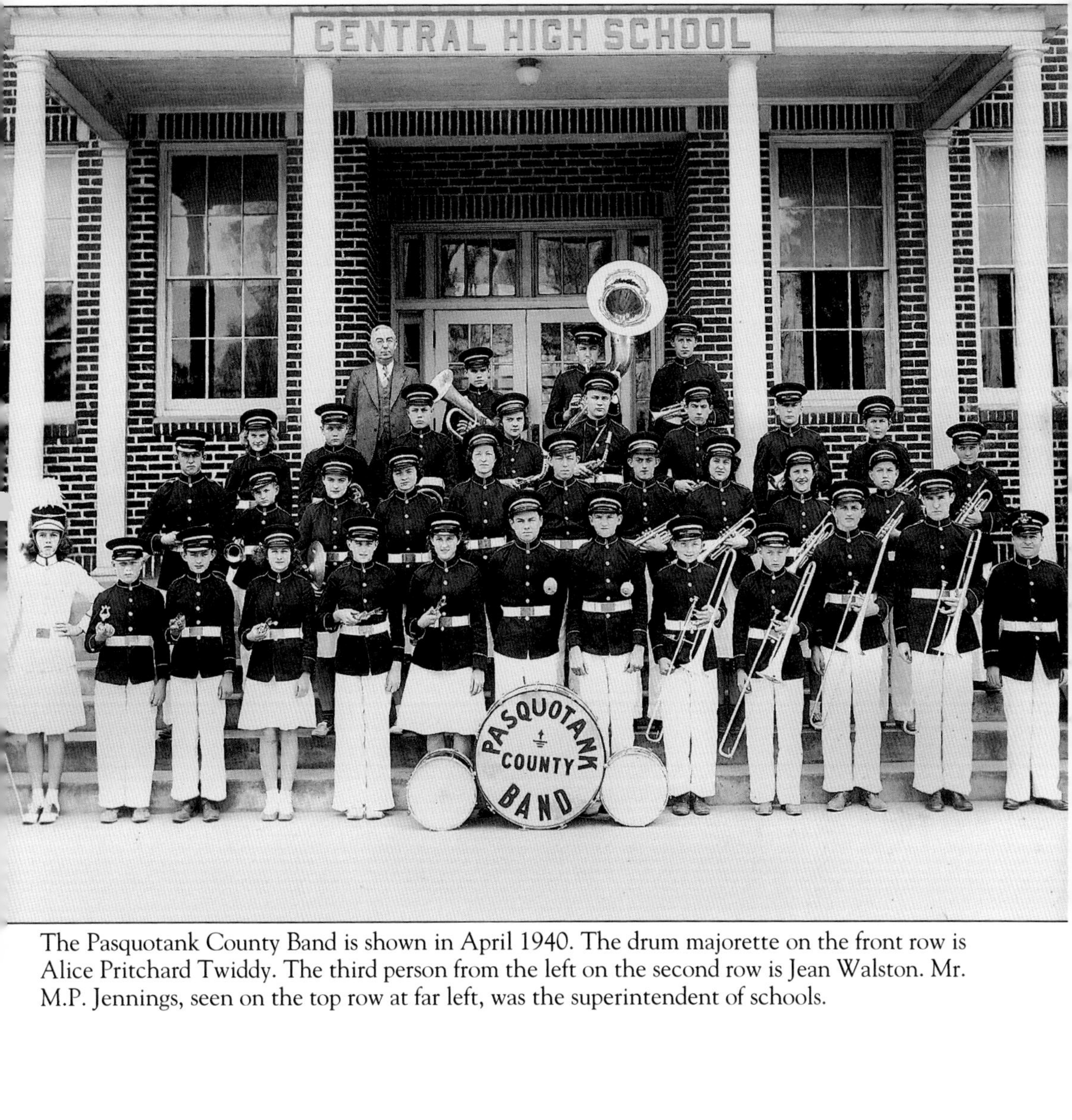

The Pasquotank County Band is shown in April 1940. The drum majorette on the front row is Alice Pritchard Twiddy. The third person from the left on the second row is Jean Walston. Mr. M.P. Jennings, seen on the top row at far left, was the superintendent of schools.

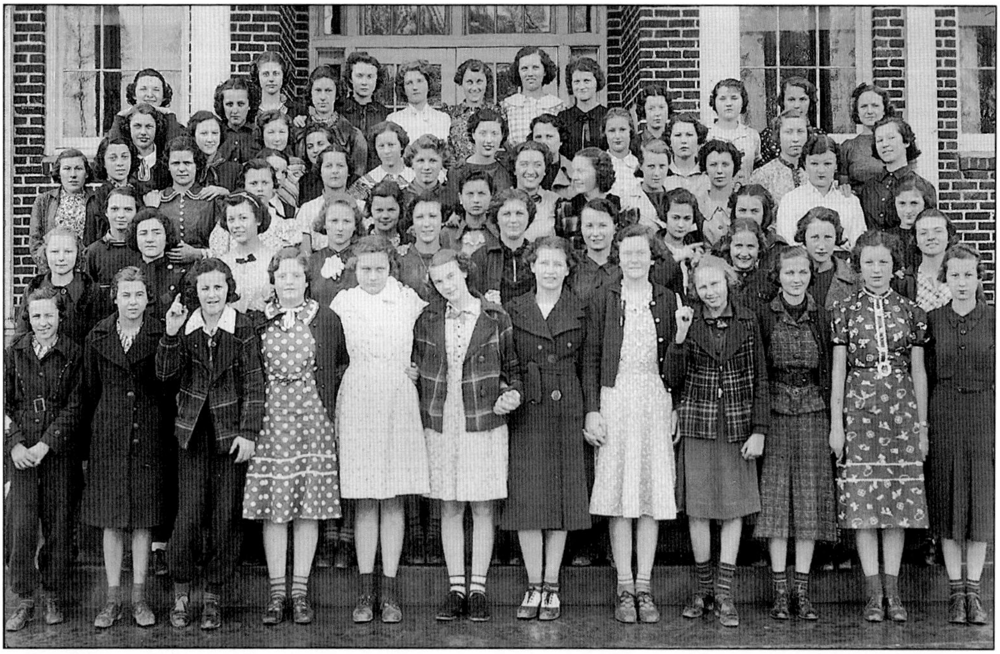

The 1937–1938 Home Economics Department of Central High School is shown in this photo.

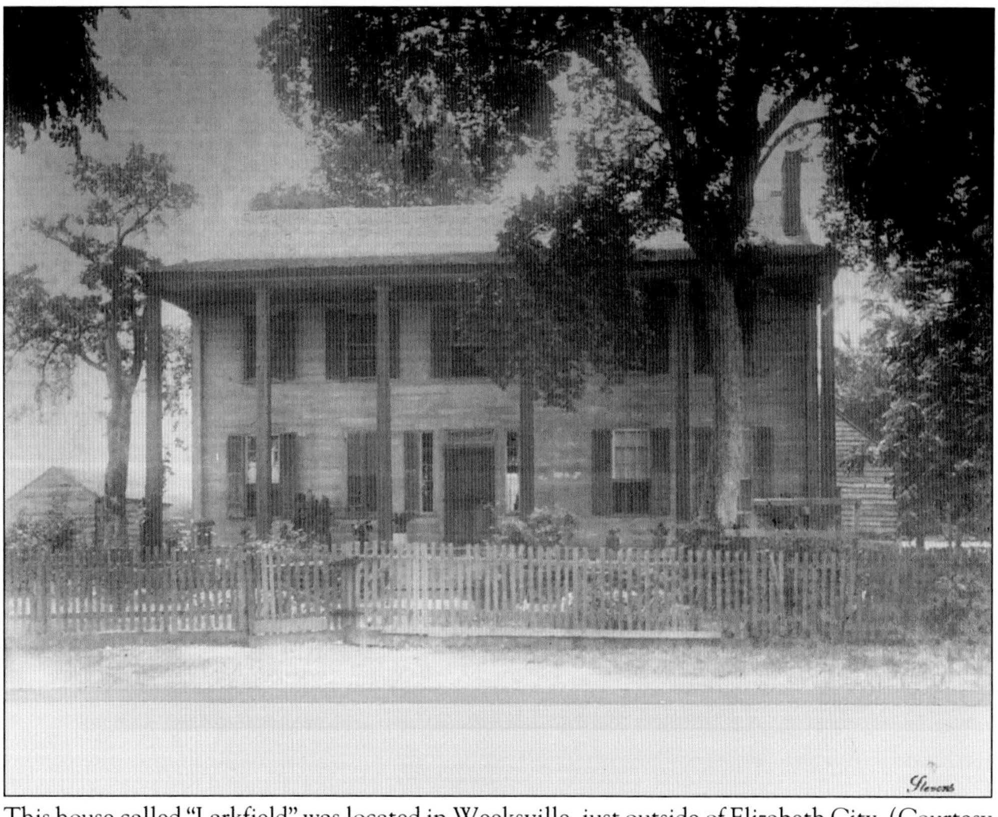

This house called "Larkfield" was located in Weeksville, just outside of Elizabeth City. (Courtesy of Museum of the Albemarle.)

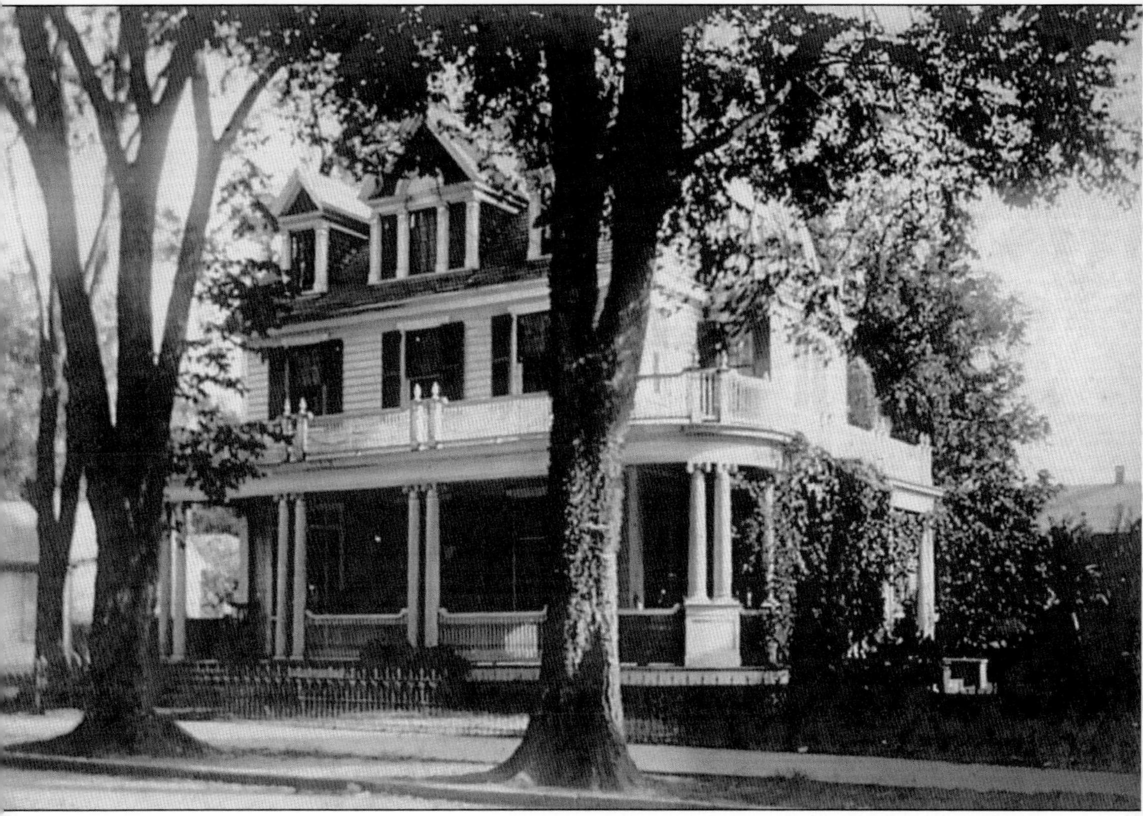

Dr. Blades's house stood on the corner of Main and Elliott Streets. It is now the site of a parking lot.

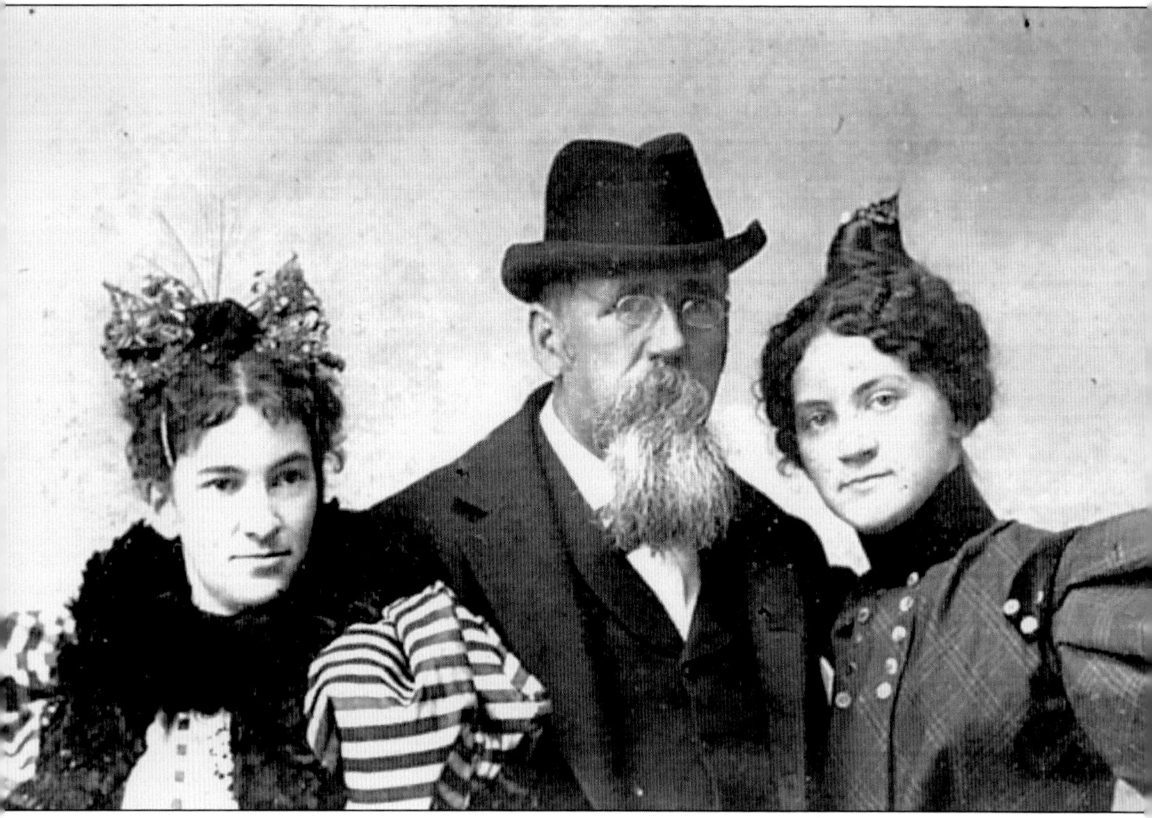

John Engle is shown here with two of his daughters, Kate Engle and Jo Engle.

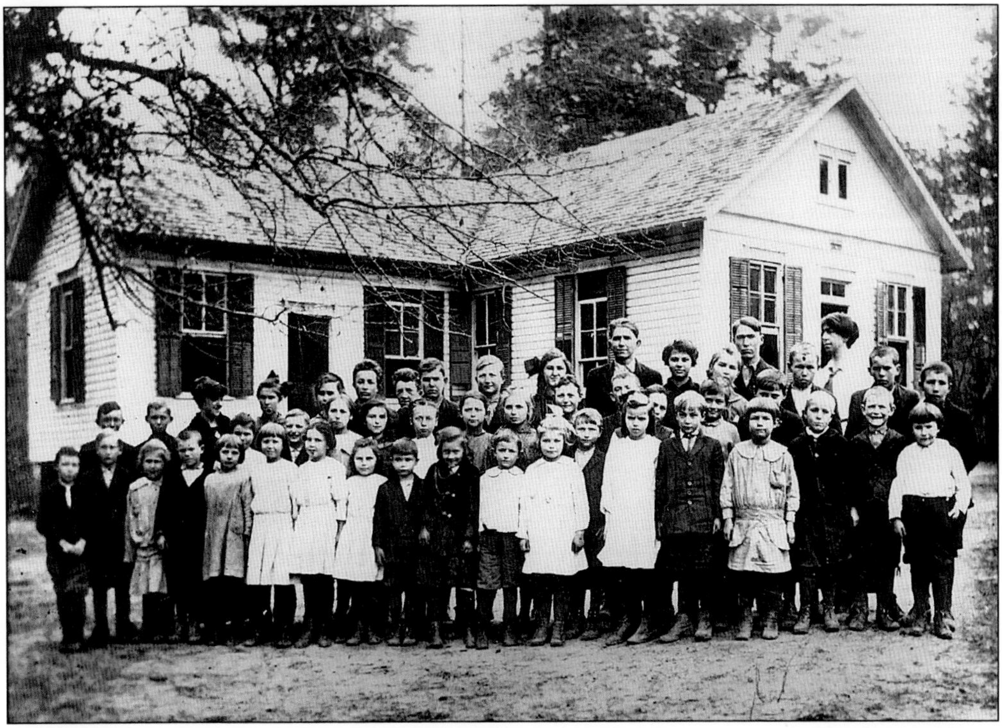

This picture of Corinth School was taken in 1911. (Courtesy of Museum of the Albemarle)

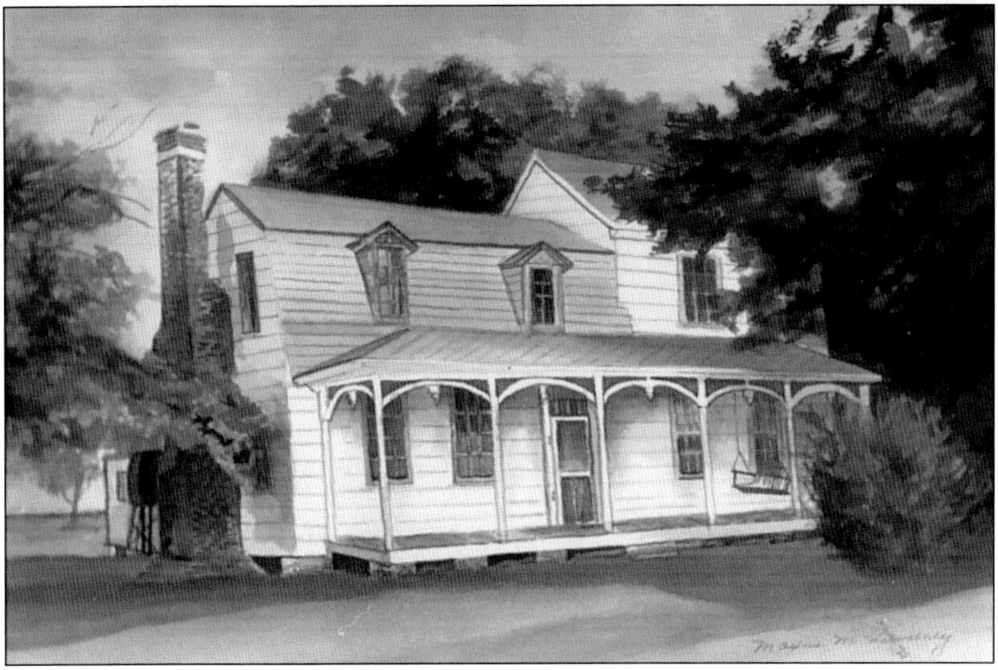

The Pendleton-Morris-Barclift house was built in Nixonton around 1790. This was the time that Nixonton was the chief port and the county's seat of government. Members of the Pendleton family occupied the home until 1868. The Pendleton Foundation is in the process of restoring the home to its original state. (Painting by Maxine Sweeney.)

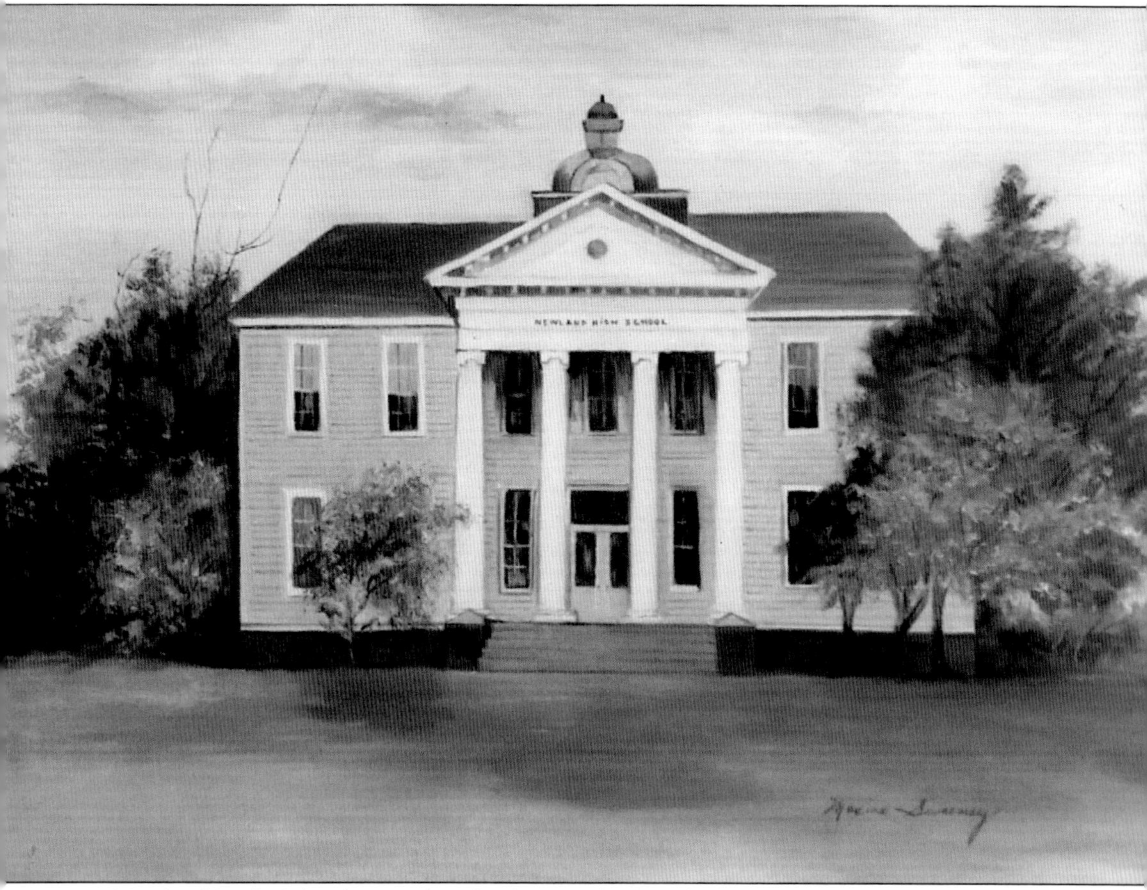

Newland High School opened as the first rural, white high school in the county in 1918. The school was an impressive Neo-Classical Revival structure. The school has undergone drastic alterations during the years. (Painting by Maxine Sweeney.)

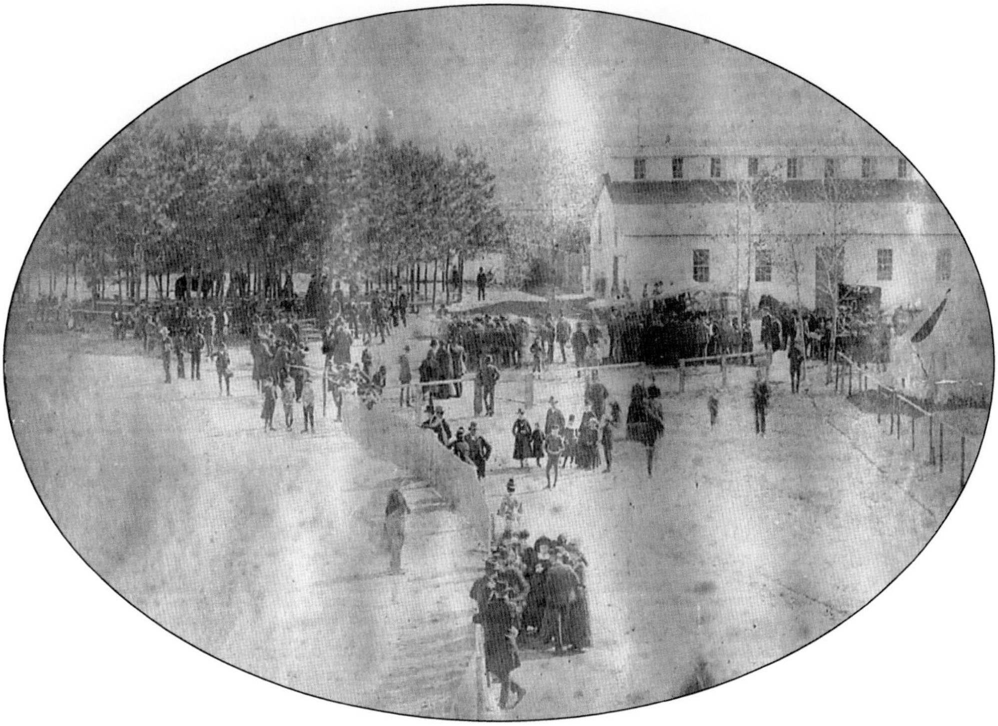

Shown here are pictures of the old Elizabeth City Fairgrounds located out Halstead Boulevard. A portion of Elizabeth City State University now occupies this property.

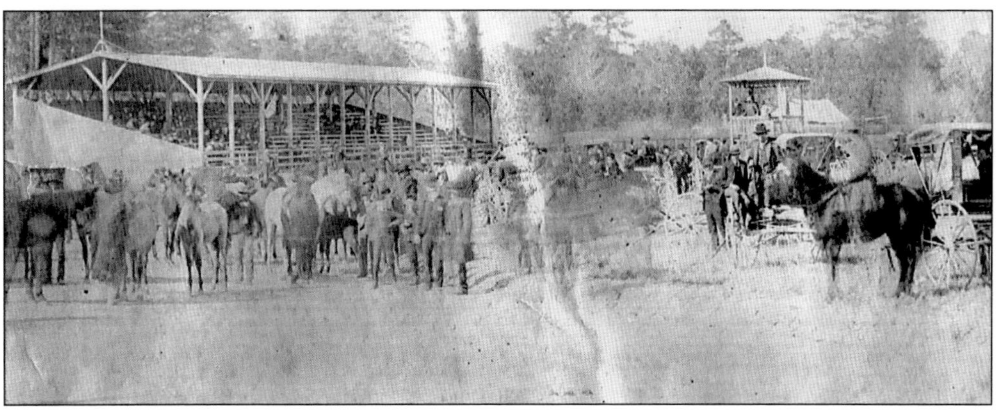

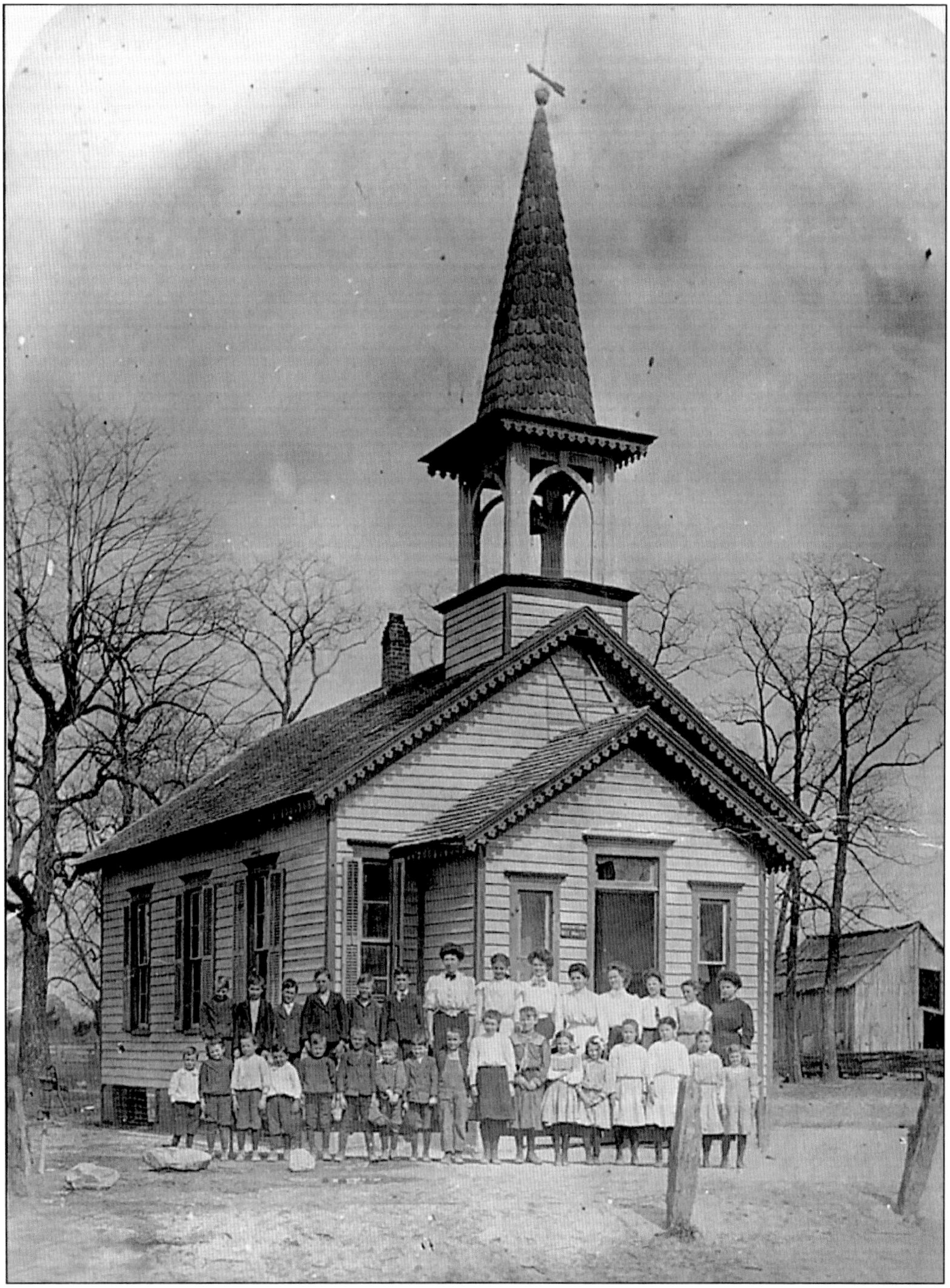

Students pose in front of the Nixonton Public School around 1909. (Courtesy of Museum of the Albemarle)

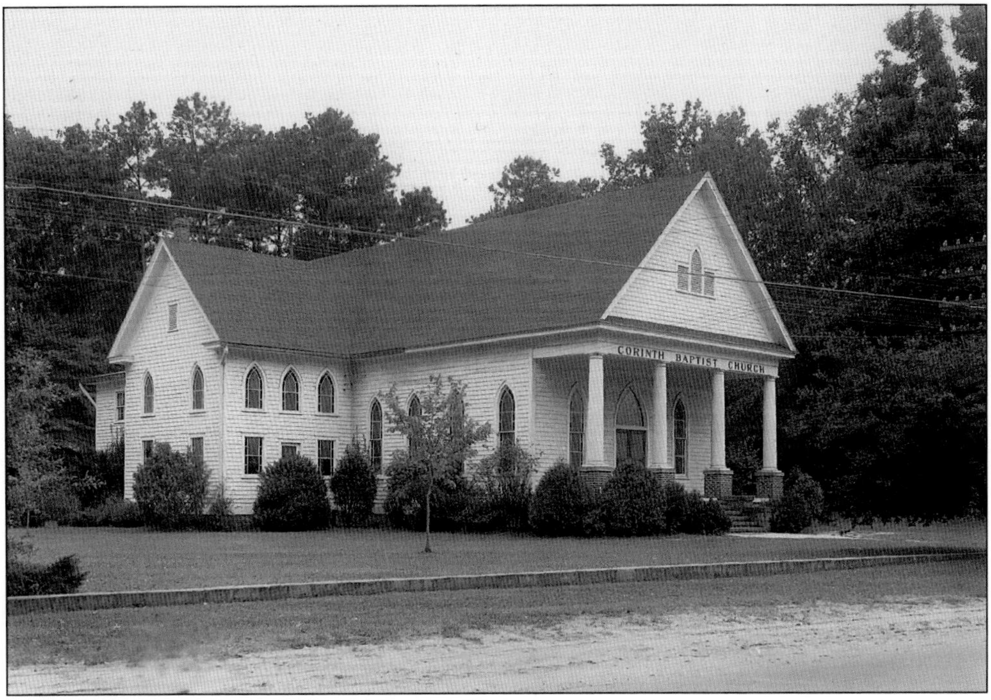

Corinth Baptist Church is shown here as it looked in 1951. It was once heated with wooden stoves; the church has since been remodeled. (Courtesy of Museum of the Albemarle.)

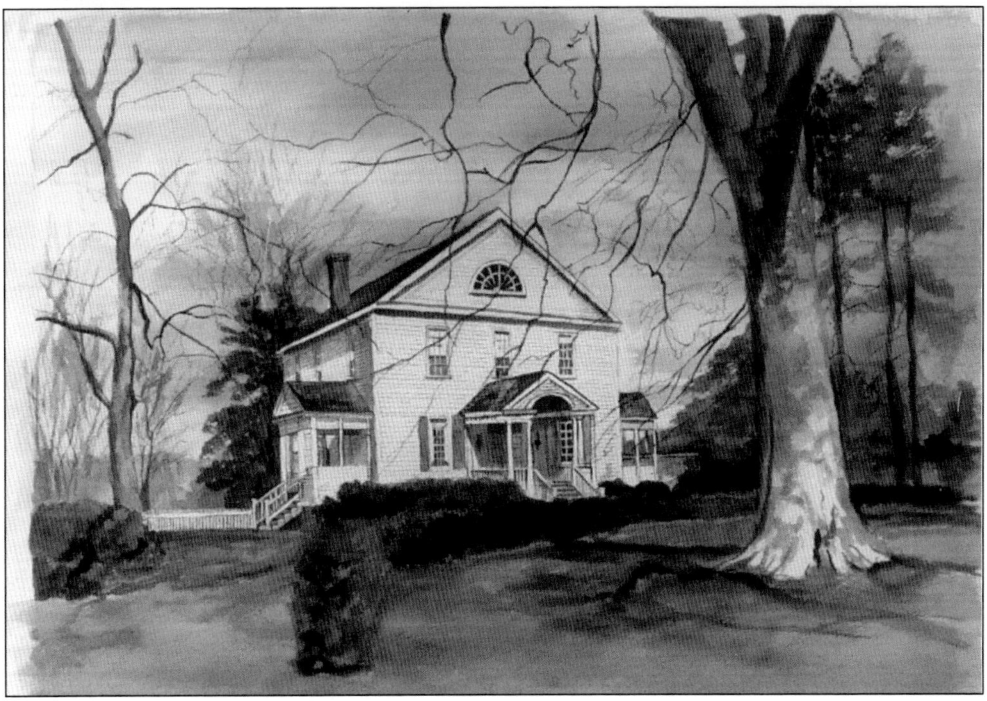
The Hinton-Morgan house located north of Elizabeth City, near Morgans Corner, was erected in 1826 for Mr. William Smith Hinton and his wife, Mary "Polly" Hinton. This home is among the best of the transverse-hall plan houses in North Carolina. (Painting by Maxine Sweeney.)

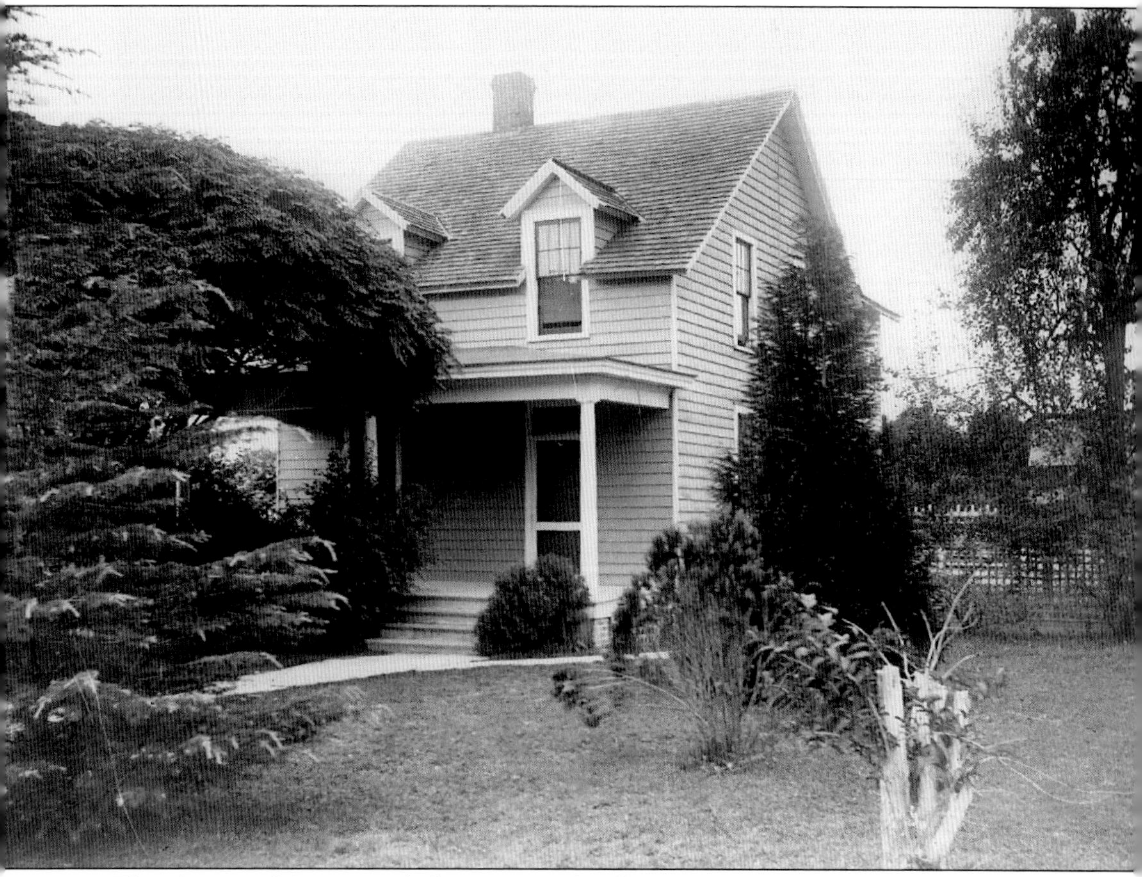

This photo is of George Pool's home in Weeksville. (Courtesy of Museum of the Albemarle.)

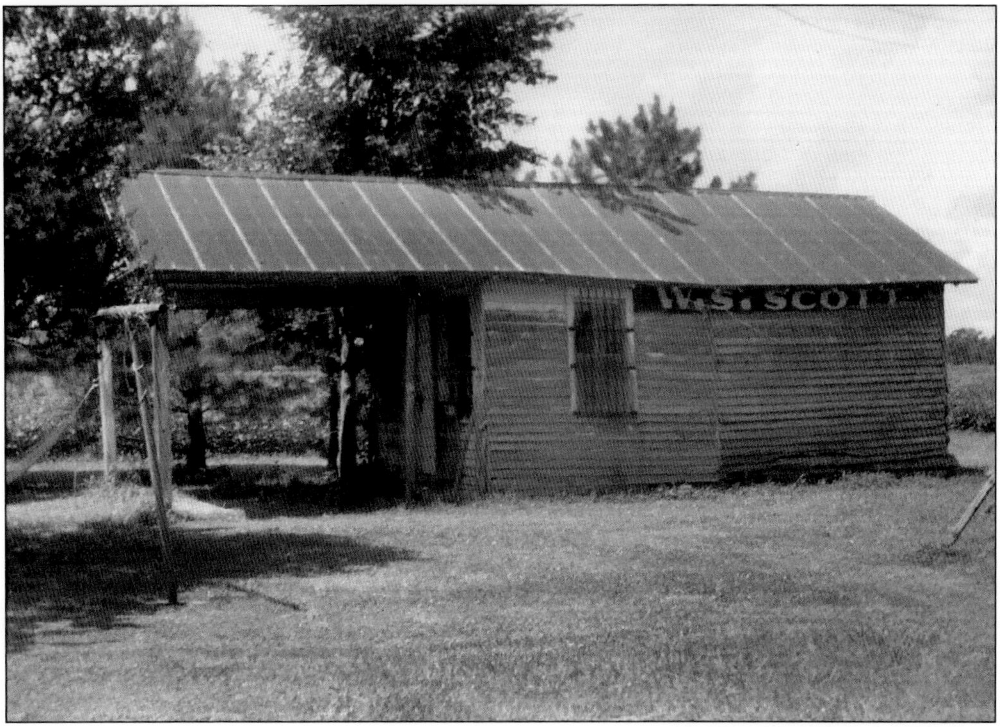

Paul Harris Sr. rented this old Texaco Gas Station and County Store to W.S. Scott, *c.* 1906.

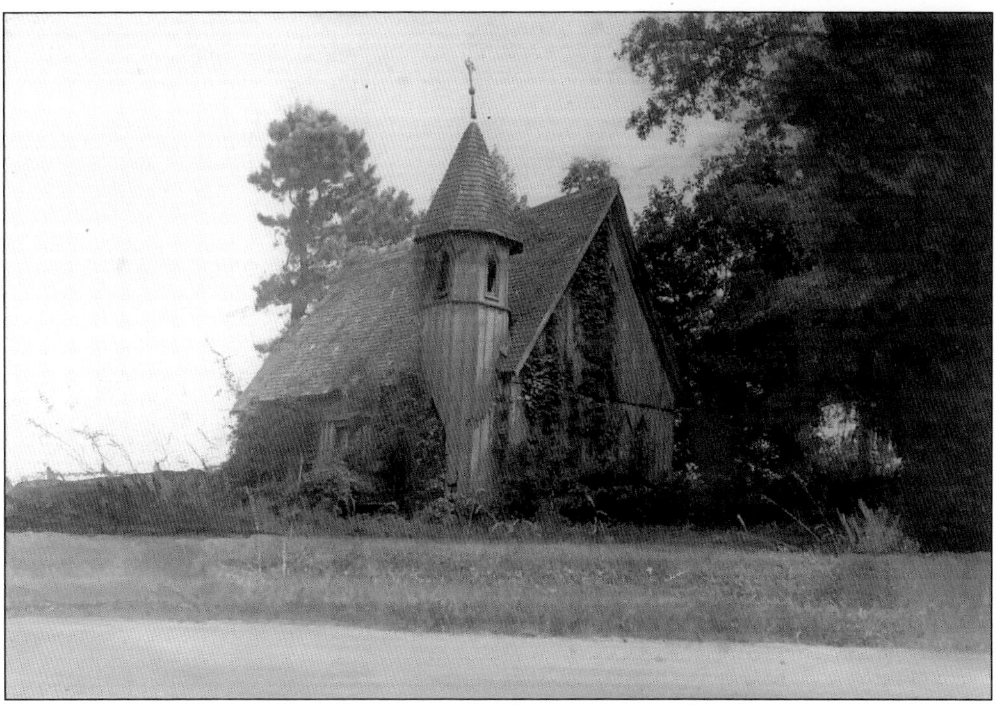

Saint John's Episcopal Church (1880) was located in the Weeksville area of Pasquotank County. The church was deconsecrated in 1929 and is now demolished.

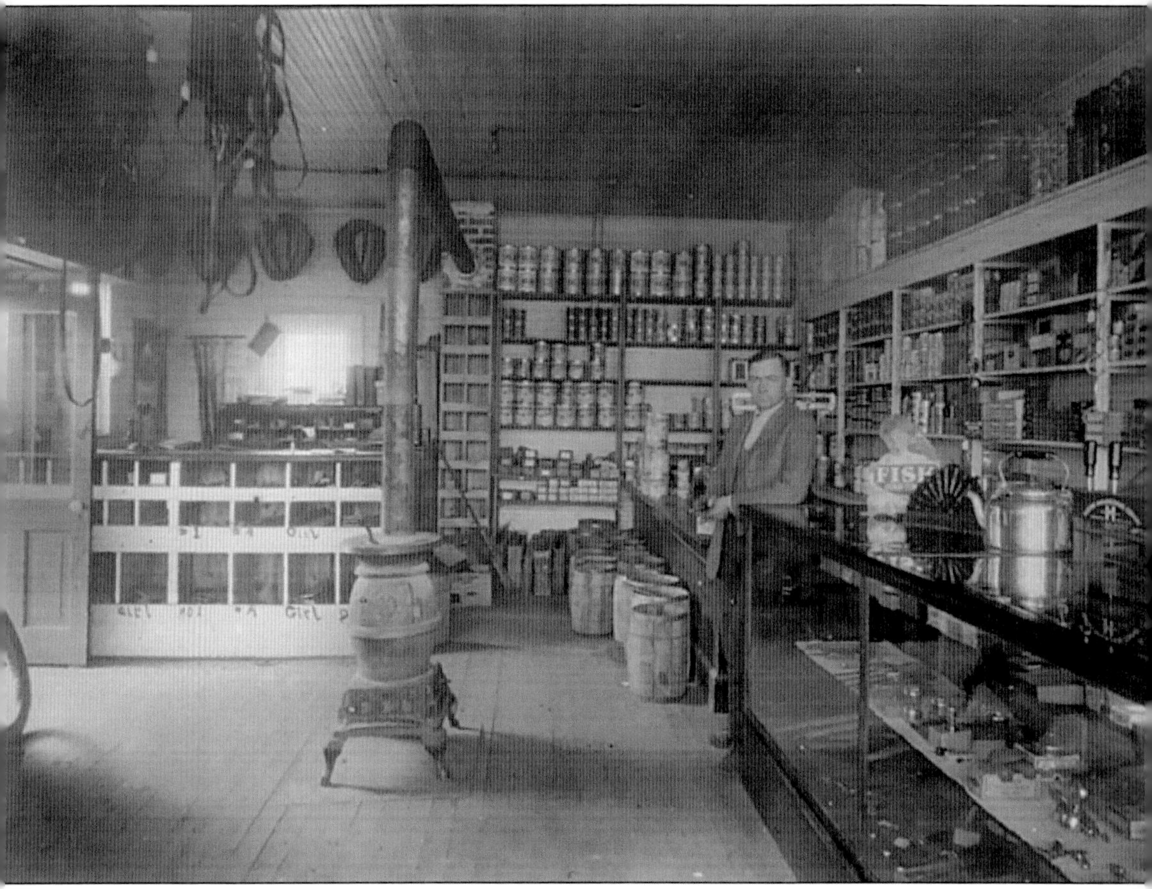

The C.V. Perry Store was located on the west end of Main Street. (Courtesy of Museum of the Albemarle.)